Also by Neville Teller

Audio Drama: 10 Plays for Radio and Podcast

Neville Teller was born in London, read Modern History at Oxford University, and then had a varied career in advertising, marketing, general management, publishing, the Civil Service and a national cancer charity. At the same time he was consistently writing for BBC radio as dramatist and abridger. He has more than 50 BBC radio dramatizations to his credit. Latterly, as guest playwright for an American independent radio production company, Shoestring Radio Theatre, his work is being heard by radio and on-line across the United States. In the Queen's Birthday Honours in 2006 he was awarded an MBE "for services to broadcasting and to drama".

AUDIO DRAMA
2

10 MORE PLAYS FOR
RADIO AND PODCAST

Neville Teller

Matador
Unit E2 Airfield Business Park,
Harrison Road, Market Harborough,
Leicestershire. LE16 7UL
Tel: 0116 2792299
Email: books@troubador.co.uk
Web: www.troubador.co.uk/matador
Twitter: @matadorbooks

ISBN 978 1803136 806

British Library Cataloguing in Publication Data.
A catalogue record for this book is available from the British Library.

Typeset in 11pt Adobe Jenson Pro by Troubador Publishing Ltd, Leicester, UK

Matador is an imprint of Troubador Publishing Ltd

*For Sheila
and the family*

CONTENTS

FOREWORD

Before Shakespeare launches on his account of Henry V's adventures in France, he has his Chorus address the throng of groundlings waiting in anticipation for the play to begin.

"Piece out our imperfections with your thoughts...", he begs of them.
"Think, when we talk of horses, that you see them
Printing their proud hooves in the receiving earth..."

Aware of the restrictions that a stage, scenery and props impose in recounting great events in dramatic terms, Shakespeare knew how much depended on the words he conjured up and on the actors who mouthed them. He was also anticipating what audio drama would be able to help an audience achieve four hundred years later. The radio medium would allow its listening audience overcome the restriction of perceiving only what was set before it — a restriction inevitably imposed in theatre, film and TV drama. With nothing to see, the radio listener would nevertheless "see" horses, hundreds of them, whinnying and stamping.

The unique quality of audio drama — the term being increasingly used in recognition of the ways, in addition to radio, now available to disseminate it — is that it builds a private and exclusive picture in the mind of each separate member of its audience. It becomes a personal experience, individual and different, for each person listening.

Audio drama gives the widest possible scope to the imagination of both writer and listener. In a radio play you can have inanimate objects converse, you can have people speak and also communicate their innermost thoughts; in an instant you can be whisked from earth to Mars, from the top of mount Everest to the deepest coal mine. And the images that listeners experience are the most vivid of all – images in their own mind.

Audio drama allows writers almost limitless freedom of expression, and perhaps that is why it has attracted the most brilliant writers and poets, often at the beginning of their careers – among them Louis MacNeice, Henry Reed, John Betjeman and Laurie Lee. Major works have been created for radio, including Samuel Becket's "All That Fall", Harold Pinter's "A Slight Ache" and Robert Bolt's "A Man for All Seasons", while the list of writers who made their dramatic debut on BBC radio is long and glittering, and includes Joe Orton, Tom Stoppard, John Mortimer, Brendan Behan, Angela Carter and Susan Hill.

Somebody once wrote to the papers about how disappointed they had been at a stage performance of Dylan Thomas's "Under Milk Wood". I responded, pointing out that the piece was originally written for radio, and represents the high-water mark of the now-defunct BBC Radio Features department, which raised the art of radio to its greatest height.

The producer who brought "Under Milk Wood" to listeners was Douglas Cleverdon, and he later wrote that he had persuaded Thomas to drop his original idea of a plot in favour of exploiting the versatility of the radio medium. It is precisely because "Under Milk Wood" is constructed as a collage of voices, moves rapidly in time and space, and alternates speech and unspoken thoughts, that it makes brilliant radio and indifferent theatre.

Writers who want to try their hand at audio drama might be inhibited by the thought of coming to grips with an unfamiliar medium. Despite the plethora of advice available on-line, some of it contradictory and much of it not particularly helpful, outside suggestions cannot really assist the creative process. A writer's inner vision, or flash of inspiration, is unpredictable. What might help is advice on bringing an imaginative concept to life in audio terms – advice which I hope the audio dramatisations in this volume exemplify.

Surprisingly, there is no universally agreed format for audio drama scripts. Search "audio drama" on Google, and dozens of suggested templates are thrown up, while the sample scripts on the BBC's Writer's Room website appear in a host of different presentations.

There are one or two basic requirements, though. An audio drama script needs to be set out in three distinct areas of the page. The extreme left is reserved for the characters' names, best printed in bold capitals; next, nicely indented, comes the dialogue; beyond that, further indented, come the technical directions. As you will see from these scripts, my practice is to print them in bold capitals, and enclose them within brackets. Other templates – to my mind rather unattractive – show them in underlined capitals.

Normal practice is to set line spacing at one-and-a-half, and it is essential to number your pages. It might be impossible for a producer who lets an unnumbered script fall to the floor ever to reassemble it. There is no real need in the early stages of writing an audio drama to divide the play into separate scenes, or to number the speeches. These steps follow when the script is being prepared for production.

The sound palette available to the audio dramatist consists essentially of four elements: the spoken word, music, sound effects and technical devices.

Dialogue can, of course, make or break a drama, and an audio dramatist in particular needs an understanding of how to make characters, but also the piece as a whole, live through what is said. Narration is an important element in many audio dramas, and its tone, place and purpose within the piece needs to be carefully adjudged, especially if the narrator is also a character within the play. Some basic instructions to actors should be included, in lower case italics and in brackets, in the dialogue section. A scene set at a tea-table could include "eating, drinking," by the character's name. If a character is moving towards or away from the listener while speaking, the dialogue script should specify "advancing" or "retreating".

Judicious use of music, even just a snatch, can establish mood and period in an instant. It can also be used to punctuate a drama, or to emphasise an especially dramatic point. The writer needs to indicate in the technical directions where music should appear, and perhaps the type of piece in mind, but once a script has been accepted for production, it is the producer who will normally have the final say.

Sound effects should be indicated in the script within the technical directions – for example, if you need a door to be opened. A word of advice: if you direct that a door is opened, you must also remember that often – not always – it will need to be closed, or the sound picture conveyed to the listener is of a permanently open door. It will niggle some of your audience when they should be concentrating on other things. If a telephone is lifted and a conversation held, you will normally need to specify that the receiver is replaced. Doors, telephone receivers, crockery and cutlery if characters are talking over a tea-table, are "spot effects" – that is, sound effects produced in the studio and recorded with the dialogue.

Technical directions include a range of effects that can enhance the sound picture. For example, if you place characters inside a church, or within a cavern, the voices will need to be provided with an echo by the studio manager, via his magical console. Your script will need to specify both the location, and the need for an echo. When two characters are on the telephone, one will be with the listener, the other's voice will need to be electronically altered. Indicate which one. This the studio manager will do, on your instruction as to which character's voice needs to be "on distort".

The most basic of all audio drama techniques, perhaps, is the fade – that is, fading the volume as a scene ends, sometimes when a character is speaking, sometimes on a sound effect or music. It implies a change of venue or the passage of time. "Fade" or "Fade out" would be the technical direction. Depending on the effect required, the listener could be carried into a new scene gently ("Fade in"), or brought straight in ("Full up").

A look through this volume, or a search on-line, will provide an aspiring audio dramatist with radio drama scripts, and the techniques of writing for a listening audience will become apparent.

Back in 2019 I published *Audio Drama: 10 Plays for Radio and Podcast* – a collection of ten of my own radio dramatisations which had been broadcast either by the BBC or across the United States. The book was intended primarily for lovers of radio drama and for audio drama podcast producers looking for material on which to exercise their technical skills. The volume was well received, and during the coronavirus pandemic that hit the world in 2020, podcast producers in various countries used those scripts to mount virtual audio productions of their own.

It is in light of that book's favourable reception that I feel encouraged to offer the audio-appreciative community this second volume of 10 audio dramatisation scripts. All these radio dramatisations have been produced and broadcast across the USA and into Canada by Shoestring Radio Theatre, an independent radio production company founded in 1988 by producer Monica Sullivan, and based in San Francisco. Once again, I make them available with no strings attached. The works on which they are based are literary classics, and are in the public domain. The copyright in the audio dramatisations rests with me, and I am content to provide them to audio or podcast producers to use as they see fit.

To both readers and producers of audio drama I say: "Enjoy."

LADY AUDLEY'S SECRET

A PLAY FOR RADIO
BY NEVILLE TELLER

BASED ON THE NOVEL BY
MARY ELIZABETH BRADDON

Running Time: 90'

FIRST BROADCAST ACROSS THE USA ON 28 JULY 2016
IN A PRODUCTION BY SHOESTRING
RADIO THEATRE, SAN FRANCISCO
DIRECTED BY STEVE RUBENSTEIN

CHARACTERS

NARRATOR

LADY AUDLEY   *Age 25. Sweet and charming on the surface; hard, cunning and manipulative just below.*

SIR MICHAEL   *Mid-50s. Upright, honourable gentleman. Head over heels in love with Lady A.*

PHOEBE   *About 27. Country girl – a bit rough in manner, but loyal to Lady A. In fear of Luke.*

LUKE   *30. Coarse loutish fellow. No finer feelings.*

GEORGE TALBOYS *30s. Young Englishman from gentry stock – hunting, shooting, fishing family.*

ROBERT AUDLEY *30s. Well educated lawyer – a scion of the Audley family. Old English county stock.*

BARMAN

RECEPTIONIST

MANAGER

LANDLADY

CAPTAIN MALDON *50s. Cunning and rather drunken old rogue. A willing participant in Lady A's schemes, for the money*

BOY

ALICIA AUDLEY *Mid-20s – Sir Michael's daughter. Dislikes Lady A, who has usurped her as female head of Sir M's household*

LANDLORD 1

BUTLER

CLERK

COACHMAN

MRS PERKINS *Middle aged, motherly type. Housekeeper in Robert's legal chambers*

HARCOURT TALBOYS *60. Disagreeable, opinionated type. Little time for others' views. Self-assured.*

DAWSON *50s. Calm professional type. Surgeon. Courteous.*

MAID

GROCER

DRESSMAKER

MRS VINCENT   *Elderly school-mistress type. Slow. Precise.*

LANDLORD 2

MRS BARKAMB   *Middle-aged country woman. Lower middle class.*

BAILIFF

MOSGROVE   *40s. Eminent London psychiatrist. Cool, calm, professional.*

MONSIEUR VAL   *Mid-40s. French accent. Owns and is medical chief of a private nursing home for the insane. Authoritarian. The man in charge*

(MUSIC. DOWN FOR)

NARRATOR: I must warn you that the history I'm about to relate is full of wickedness. It is a tale of evil, deception and death. But redeeming features are also woven into the story – love and compassion, honesty and friendship. So bear with me as the events unfold, and you will not be disappointed.

(OPENING ANNOUNCEMENT. UP MUSIC. DOWN FOR, AND LOSE)

NARRATOR: It was in the middle years of Queen Victoria's reign that Sir Michael Audley of Audley Court, in the good old English county of Essex, married for a second time. Sir Michael was fifty-five years old. He had been a widower for seventeen years when he heard about the governess recently acquired by his neighbour, Mr Dawson the surgeon, to instruct his two daughters. Lucy Graham had come from London, in answer to an advertisement in The Times newspaper, and it was not long before news of her beauty, her grace and her kindliness became the talk of the district.

(FADE IN UNDER FOLLOWING CHOPIN'S ETUDE NO 3 IN E MAJOR)

Everyone who met her fell under her spell, and her charming temperament was enhanced by her many accomplishments. She taught her girls to play Etudes by Chopin, to paint in watercolor and in oils, to complete intricate samplers in needlework. Every Sunday she proceeded to church three times, and the vicar, seeing her soft blue eyes, framed by a cloud of flaxen curls, uplifted to his face as he preached his simple sermon, declared that Lucy Graham was the sweetest girl that ever lived. Perhaps it was the sight of her in church that caused Sir Michael Audley to feel a strong desire to be better acquainted with Mr Dawson's governess.

(FADE PIANO)

He had only to hint his wish to the worthy doctor, for a little party to be got up, to which the vicar and his wife, and Sir Michael and his daughter, Miss Alicia Audley, were invited. That one evening sealed Sir Michael's fate. He could not resist the tender fascination of those melting blue eyes, that wealth of flaxen curls, the low music of that gentle voice. Less than a month later, sitting opposite Lucy Graham in the surgeon's sitting-room, to which he had returned several times in the previous weeks, he offered her his hand in marriage.

(INTERIOR. FADE IN)

LADY A: Oh, Sir Michael, you ask too much of me. Who am I? A mere governess. Think what my life has been – poverty, trials, humiliations. I cannot be blind to the advantages of marrying you – and nor will others be. I will be the object of so much scorn…

SIR MICHAEL: Lucy, Lucy. Tell me honestly. Do you dislike me?

LADY A: Dislike you? Oh, no. No.

SIR MICHAEL: Is there someone else you love?

LADY A: I love no one else.

SIR MICHAEL: Then, Lucy, I see no reason why we shouldn't make a very happy couple. As for the world's opinion, there is not a single person who will not envy me my beautiful, charming, much-loved young wife. Is it a bargain, Lucy?

LADY A: It is … Michael.

NARRATOR: And so, to the delight of all who knew her and had been charmed by her beauty and good nature, Lucy Graham the governess was transformed into Lady Audley. Adored by her new husband, she was provided with an unlimited allowance to spend on whatever took her fancy in the way of clothes or jewels. Sir Michael even commissioned a well-known society painter to portray her in some of her finery, so that he could forever be reminded of the beauty of the young wife he had won. The only person in the whole district who was less than enamoured of the new Lady Audley was Sir Michael's daughter Alicia. She had cared for him since the death of her mother, and was now replaced as hostess of Audley Court by a stepmother very nearly her own age.

The new Lady Audley was, of course, in need of a personal maid. While still governess to Mr Dawson, the surgeon, Lucy had become very friendly with the girl employed as nursemaid to the family. Phoebe Marks came of simple country stock, but she was very sensible and had something of the carriage of a gentlewoman. Lucy asked her to come to Audley Court as her maid, and the Dawsons found themselves with not one, but two domestic vacancies.

As for Lady Audley, she found in Phoebe not only a maid but a confidante. Phoebe became privy to her innermost secrets. Phoebe, though, did not confide everything to her mistress – especially not that she was regularly meeting a young local in a secluded part of the grounds.

(OPEN AIR. BIRDS)

PHOEBE: (*distant, calling, approaching*) Luke! Luke, where are you?

LUKE: Right here, my girl. And getting a bit tired of waiting. I was just about to come up to the house to ask if you was in.

PHOEBE: Oh, don't ever do no such thing, Luke. It'd be more than my job's worth, if you was to turn up on the doorstep. I knew you was here. I can see the well from my bedroom window. I knew you was sitting on it, waiting.

LUKE: Well, you certainly took your time coming down.

PHOEBE: You glad to see me, Luke?

LUKE: Course I am. I really missed you when you was away abroad with me-lady on her honeymoon.

PHOEBE: Goodness what a great thing it was for Miss Lucy Graham-that-was to travel with her maid, staying at all those grand hotels – and a husband that thinks there ain't one spot on all the earth good enough for her to put her foot on.

LUKE: Aye, it's a fine thing, Phoebe, to have lots of money. Think about that when we're married. We'll need every penny you manage to save from your wages.

PHOEBE: What was she in Mr Dawson's house, only three months ago? Nothing but a servant, just like me. And now she gives me more as her lady's maid than the two of us earned together back then. Why, I've seen her come out of the parlour with her hands full of sovereigns and silver that the master's just given her…

LUKE: Never you mind her, Phoebe my girl, you just think of us. What would you say to running a public house, once we're wed? There's a good deal of money to be earned in a public house.

PHOEBE: …and you should just see the inside of the house, specially me lady's rooms – all pictures and gilding and great mirrors that stretch from the ceiling to the floor.

LUKE: She's a lucky one, right enough. Is she at home tonight?

PHOEBE: No, she's gone out with Sir Michael to a dinner party. They won't be back till after eleven.

LUKE: In that case, why not show me all this finery?

PHOEBE: Why not? Get off that well, Luke, afore you fall in. Come on, we'll get into the house by the side door. But we must be as quiet as mice. Mrs Barton the housekeeper mustn't find us, or I'm out of a job, and that'll be goodbye to your public house. Come on.

(FADE OUT. FADE IN INTERIOR)

PHOEBE: This is the entrance to my lady's apartments. Just look at all those dresses flung about on the sofa. Those are the ones she tried on this evening, before deciding what to wear. I've got all these things to put away before my lady comes home, Luke. You might as well sit down while I do it.

(MOVEMENT, SWISH OF MATERIAL UNDER FOLLOWING)

Gorgeous, aren't they, these gowns. Just look at that material. Oh, I wish I could show you the jewels, Luke.

LUKE: Well, do.

PHOEBE: I can't. She always keeps the keys herself. That's the case on the dressing table there.

LUKE: What, that great thing? That's big enough to hold every garment I own.

PHOEBE: And it's as full as it can be of diamonds, rubies, pearls and emeralds. What a pity I can't show them to you. Why goodness gracious me! Look at this! My lady has left her keys in the pocket of the dress she was wearing this afternoon. I can show you the jewellery after all. Come over here, Luke.

(KEY TURNS IN LOCK)

LUKE: Oh my good Lord, just look at them sparklers. I never seen anything like it in my life. Why, just one of them diamond things would set us up for life. This one, for instance.

PHOEBE: Put that down this instant, Luke. Don't even think such things. She knows every one of the jewels in this box. If even one goes missing, there's no-one could have taken it but me. And that's me out of my position.

LUKE: I suppose so.

PHOEBE: So hand over that bracelet. There. Back you go.

(LID CLOSES. KEY TURNS)

LUKE: What's this funny knob on the lid?

PHOEBE: Don't know. Give it a twist.

LUKE: Look here!

PHOEBE: Well I never. A secret drawer. I never seen that before. What's this inside? Oh, my word. Look at this, Luke. A baby's shoe, all wrapped up. And see here. A lock of hair. Obviously from some baby's head. Well, well. She's a sly one. Now, Luke, you'll bear witness where I found this.

LUKE: Phoebe, you're not going to take those things away.

PHOEBE: Oh, I'll keep them safe, Luke, never you fear. I'd much rather have these things than that diamond bracelet that took your fancy. Much rather. Yes, Luke, you'll have that public house you're after. I think I can promise you that.

(FADE OUT. FADE IN BUSY VICTORIAN LONDON STREET – HORSE-DRAWN VEHICLES, CROWDS. DOWN FOR AND HOLD UNDER)

GEORGE: *(calls)* Robert! Robert Audley!

ROBERT: Hullo! Good grief – it can't be! Is it you, George?

GEORGE: George Talboys in person! How are you Robert?

ROBERT: As well as I'm ever likely to be. But you're not looking too chipper, George. Where on earth have you been? What have you been doing with yourself?

GEORGE: Look, Brown's Coffee Shop is just over the road. Let's go there, and I'll tell you.

(FADE OUT. FADE IN CHATTER, CROCKERY)

GEORGE: I landed in Portsmouth this very morning, and took the first train to London.

ROBERT: Landed? Where from?

GEORGE: Australia.

ROBERT: Good grief!

GEORGE: I've been away three and a half years, and I'm desperate to find my wife and let her know I'm back – and that we're wealthy. I can see her now, just as I left her, asleep with our baby in her arms, and with nothing but a few blotted lines to tell her why her faithful husband had deserted her.

ROBERT: Deserted her? You didn't!

GEORGE: It broke my heart, but I had to do it. Let me explain. Perhaps you remember that in that last school-term at Eton, when you decided you were going to become a lawyer, I was set on joining the army. My father agreed to support me, and I signed up in a cavalry regiment. We were stationed in a seaport town when I met my darling. She lived with her rogue of a father – a drunken old hypocrite, retired from the army on half pay, and willing to sell his daughter to the highest bidder. That happened to be me – a young man in regular employment with a handsome allowance from his father. But as soon as my father got word that I intended to marry the penniless daughter of a tipsy old soldier, he was furious. He threatened to cut off my allowance on the day that we wed, and he did so. I couldn't stay in the regiment without an income, so I had to resign my commission. We were forced to lodge with my darling's father, and my small savings were slowly eaten away. By the time our baby son was born I had spent months seeking employment, but without success. Now abject poverty stared us in the face, and one day my little love broke down.

LADY A: (crying) Look at us George. Poor as church-mice. We go nowhere, we see no-one, and every day I have to ask father for the pennies to buy us food. If we're not careful, the baby will starve to death, and then where would we be? You ought not to have married me, George, if you could give me nothing but poverty and misery – indeed you should not. (tears)

GEORGE: Feeling precisely the same, I flung myself out of the house and wandered the streets. Finally I found myself at the sea shore. I wandered down the rickety pier, and sat at the end smoking and thinking bitter thoughts.

After a while two men also came down the pier, speaking of the Australian gold-diggings, and the fortunes that some were making out there. One of them was going to sail out there in a day or two, and he was trying to persuade his companion to come with him. Soon I joined in the conversation, and it was not long before I was convinced that going out to Australia was the best thing I could do. My wife would be safe under her father's roof, and if I went and made my fortune, I could return in a year or two to a rosy future.

I went back to the house, to find the old man drinking brandy downstairs, and my wife asleep in the bedroom, with our baby son by her side. I knelt by the bedside and prayed for them both. Then I divided the remainder of our money – something over forty pounds – into two equal portions. I left one for her, and put the other in my pocket.

I crept down the stairs, to find the old man nodding over his paper. "Where you going?" he said. "Into the street for a smoke," I replied. I left the house, and three days later I was at sea, bound for Melbourne.

ROBERT: And out in Australia, things went well?

GEORGE: Not till I had despaired of success. Not till poverty and I had become old companions. I saw myself one day in a broken bit of looking-glass, and I was frightened by the gaunt, half-starved creature who stared back at me. But I toiled on through it all, through disappointment and despair, fever and starvation – and finally I conquered. One dreary morning, just three months ago, in drizzling rain and up to my neck in clay and mire, a monster nugget turned up under my spade. Monster! You never saw so much gold in one chunk. In a second I'd become the richest man in Australia. I fell down on the wet clay, with that great lump of gold pressed to my heart, and I cried like a child. I travelled post-haste to Sydney, turned my gold into a fortune, and took passage to England.

ROBERT: Did you never write to your wife while you were away?

GEORGE: Not until my luck turned. Then I wrote and said I'd be in England almost as soon as my letter. I gave the address of Seymour's coffee house in Westminster where she could write and tell me where to find her – though she is scarcely likely to have left her father's house. Seymour's coffee shop – that's my next port of call. I expect to find a letter from her awaiting me.

ROBERT: Then let's be off. I'll come with you.

(FADE OUT. FADE IN SAME BACKGROUND)

GEORGE: (*over chatter*) Nothing? Are you sure?

BARMAN: Certain, sir. Nothing for Talboys.

ROBERT: Don't despair, George. There are a thousand reasons why she might not have written yet. Come on, have a brandy and soda. Two, please, barman.

BARMAN: Right away, sir.

ROBERT: Cheer up, George. Sit yourself down. Here, have a look at today's "Times".

(RUSTLE OF NEWSPAPER)

NARRATOR: I cannot tell you how long George Talboys sat staring blankly at one paragraph among the list of deaths, before his dazed brain took in its full meaning. But finally, with a face changed from bronze to a sickly gray, he pushed the newspaper over to Robert Audley.

GEORGE: Look. Look there.

ROBERT: (*reads*) "On August 24, at Ventnor, Isle of Wight. Helen Talboys, aged 22." Oh, George – how truly terrible.

GEORGE: The Isle of Wight? What on earth was my darling doing there? And what's happened to the baby – our son?

ROBERT: There's only one thing for it, George. We have to go to the Isle of Wight – to Ventnor.

(FADE OUT. FADE IN. HOTEL LOBBY)

RECEPTIONIST: Can I help you, sir?

ROBERT: Yes – we're wondering whether a Mr ... What's your father-in-law's name. George?

GEORGE: Maldon. Captain Maldon.

ROBERT: Whether a Captain Maldon is staying here?

RECEPTIONIST: Not in this hotel, sir.

ROBERT: It's very important we find him.

RECEPTIONIST: I'll ask our manager. He knows everything that goes on in Ventnor. *(retreating)* I won't be a moment.

GEORGE: The old man was certainly a rogue, but he'd never have sent his daughter here to die alone. If she came here, then he's here too.

MANAGER: *(approaching)* Are you the gentlemen enquiring about Captain Maldon?

ROBERT: Indeed we are.

MANAGER: Captain Maldon arrived in Ventnor about a month ago with his daughter and small grandson. I'm very sorry to tell you that his daughter died. They buried her last week.

GEORGE: Oh God! It's true then.

ROBERT: Bear up, George. You don't happen to know where Captain Maldon is living?

MANAGER: Yes. He's lodging at number 4, Lansdown Cottages. Right by the sea.

(FADE OUT. FADE IN SMALL SITTING ROOM)

LANDLADY: Oh, they'll be back in about half-an-hour. They won't be late for their tea. Poor little boy. They came to Ventnor only ten days before the young woman died. When they arrived she was in the last stages of decline, poor thing, and day by day I watched her sink lower and lower. Can I ask – are either of you gentlemen related to her?

ROBERT: This is Mr Talboys, ma'am. He's the lady's husband.

GEORGE: What you tell me cuts me to the very heart. Did she speak of me? Did she speak of me – at – at the last?

LANDLADY: No, no, she went off quiet as a lamb. She said very little from the first, but on the last day she knew nobody, not even her little boy. If you'd like to see where they've laid her, Mr Talboys, my lad will show you the way to the churchyard. It's just round the corner.

NARRATOR: So George Talboys, his friend Robert Audley, and the landlady's son walked to the quiet spot, and stood by the mound of earth that marked the newly dug grave. After a while George asked to be directed to a stone mason. One had his premises hard by the church, and sitting down amid the litter of the man's yard, George Talboys wrote this brief inscription for the headstone of his wife's grave: "Sacred to the memory of Helen, beloved wife of George Talboys, who departed this life on August 24th 1867, aged 22 years."

(FADE IN. SITTING ROOM)

MALDON: …and this is little Georgie.

GEORGE: Hello Georgie. I'm your father, come across the sea to find you. Will you love me?

BOY: Don't know you. I love Grandpa. He gives me sugar plums.

MALDON: Georgie's very fond of his grandfather. Aren't you, my lad?

GEORGE: Then he'd better stay with you, Captain Maldon. I'll make you an allowance for his keep and education, and put a good sum in trust to accumulate till he's of age. My friend here will be trustee, and I'll appoint him guardian to the boy, if he will accept the charge.

ROBERT: Of course I will, if you wish it, George. But why not take charge of the boy yourself?

GEORGE: Because, Robert, I'll be sailing in the very next vessel that leaves for Australia. All this has finished me, as far as leading a civilized life is concerned. I'll be better off in the backwoods. All I want is to put half the world between me and my poor darling's grave.

NARRATOR: But Fate had willed a different course for George Talboys. When he had settled all his legal matters, he bade his friend farewell and took the train to Liverpool – only to find that a ship had only just sailed for Australia, and that there would not be another for a month. All he could do was to return to London and throw himself on Robert Audley's hospitality.

ROBERT: My dear chap, I'm only too delighted to put you up. These rooms of mine are quite spacious enough for two. You're more than welcome to stay with me for as long as you wish.

GEORGE: Just until the next sailing to Australia, Robert.

NARRATOR: But a day or two before he was due to travel again to Liverpool, Robert Audley came in one day, full of a new scheme.

ROBERT: A wonderful opportunity, George. A chance like this comes once in a lifetime. A barrister friend of mine – Joshua Selcombe, a sterling fellow, George

– he has to go to St Petersburg on business for six months, and he wants me to go with him. I said I would – on condition that you came too. He was delighted. He said the three of us would have a rare time together in Russia. What do you say, George? Will you come?

GEORGE: Russia… Australia … what does it matter? Just so long as I'm out of England.

(CROSSFADE)

ROBERT: My dear Alicia – I feel I should write and let you know that I am about to depart these shores for a short while. I leave in a few days for a six month stay in Russia – St Petersburg to be exact. Would you please be kind enough to inform my uncle, Sir Michael, of my impending absence. I hasten to reassure you that I shall not be alone. The trip is being organized by a fellow barrister, Mr Joshua Slocombe, and we shall be accompanied by an old school-friend from Eton, George Talboys. Mr Talboys is a recent widower, and I am hopeful that the trip will do something to restore his spirits. I hope to revisit Audley Court shortly after my return to England next spring. I send you my love, and to my uncle my deepest respects and regard. Robert Audley.

(CROSSFADE)

ALICIA: My dear Robert – How cruel of you to run away to that horrid St Petersburg before the hunting season! Lady Audley tells me to request you to secure her a set of sables. You are not to consider the price, but to be sure they are the handsomest that can be obtained. Papa is perfectly absurd about his new wife – but she and I cannot get on at all. Not that she is disagreeable to me – she makes herself agreeable to everyone – but she is so irretrievably childish and silly,

What sort of person is this Mr Talboys? If he is very agreeable, you may bring him here to Audley Court as soon as you are back from your travels.

Your affectionate cousin, Alicia Audley.

NARRATOR:	In due time Robert and his friend returned to London from their Russian excursion, and about a week later, following an exchange of letters between the Audley cousins, they set out for the Essex village of Audley. They reached the only hostelry, the Sun Inn, in time to order a good dinner.

(GRANDFATHER CLOCK STRIKES FIVE)

ROBERT:	(*over striking clock*) Five o'clock, George. Get your hat. They don't dine at Audley Court until seven. We'll have plenty of time to stroll down and see everyone before they start to dress. Ah landlord, will you pour the last of the Beaujolais before we leave.
LAND 1:	Certainly, gentlemen.

25

(CLINK OF GLASS. POURING)

Excuse me, Mr Audley – did I hear you speak of walking to Audley Court?

ROBERT: You did, indeed. We plan to visit my uncle and his family this evening.

LAND 1: You'll be wasting your time, sir, I'm afraid. Sir Michael, Lady Audley and Miss Alicia have all gone to the races up at Chorley, and they won't be back tlll nigh on eight o'clock. But they must pass by here to go home.

ROBERT: Then we'll stroll down to the village, and be back here in good time. What do you say, George?

GEORGE: By all means.

NARRATOR: So the two young men wandered through the village, explored the old church, and reconnoitred the streams in which they proposed fishing the next day. At around half past seven they made their way back to the inn, and seating themselves at the open window, looked out at the peaceful prospect.

It was dusk when the landlord spied an open carriage, drawn by four horses, approaching, and ran out to stop the coachman. It drew up before the old swinging inn sign.

ROBERT: There's my uncle. I'll run down and speak to him.

NARRATOR:	George, sheltered by the window curtains, looked out at the little party. Alicia sat with her back to the horses, and he could see, even in the dusk, that she was a handsome brunette. But Lady Audley was seated at the side of the carriage furthest from the inn, and he could see nothing of the fair-haired paragon of whom he had heard so much.

(OPEN AIR. HORSES WHINNYING, HOOVES ON GRAVEL)

SIR MICHAEL:	*(calling)* Why, Robert. This is a surprise.
ROBERT:	I'm not here to intrude on you at the Court, uncle. George and I have come down for a few day's fishing. We're staying at the inn.
SIR MICHAEL:	George? George who?
ROBERT:	George Talboys.
ALICIA:	Oh, he's come, has he? I'm so glad. I'm dying to see this handsome young widower.
ROBERT:	Then I'll run indoors and fetch him.
SIR MICHAEL:	Not tonight, Bob. I can see that my wife is worn out after our long day at the races. Bring your friend to dinner tomorrow.
ROBERT:	Thank you, uncle. We accept with pleasure. Goodnight Lady Audley. Alicia.

(MAN CALLS "GIDDY-UP". CARRIAGE AND HORSES SET OFF. MIX TO MUSIC. FADE A LITTLE, BUT HOLD BENEATH FOLLOWING)

LADY A: Phoebe, I want you to do me a favour.

PHOEBE: Of course, my lady.

LADY A: You shall not go unrewarded – I'll give you a five pound note...

PHOEBE: Oh, my lady...

LADY A: ...but I must ask you to keep your own counsel , and tell no-one.

PHOEBE: I'm very good at keeping my mouth shut, my lady.

LADY A: I know you are, Phoebe. That's why I know I can trust you to perform this little service.

PHOEBE: What would you have me do?

LADY A: Just this. It's very simple. I want you to take the first train to London tomorrow morning and... *[once in town, you are to go to...]*

(CROSSFADE TO MUSIC. UP MUSIC. HOLD A LITTLE. FADE BENEATH FOLLOWING AND LOSE. FADE IN CROCKERY, CUTLERY)

SIR MICHAEL: I fear the day at the races quite wore you out, my love. I trust you slept well.

LADY A:	Very well, Michael. I feel quite restored.
SIR MICHAEL:	You certainly look as lovely as ever.
BUTLER:	(*approaching*) Excuse me, my lady.
LADY A:	Yes? What is it?
BUTLER:	A telegram has just arrived for you.
LADY A:	A telegram? Goodness gracious me. Whatever can be the matter?

(TEARING ENVELOPE, PAPER)

SIR MICHAEL:	Nothing serious, I do hope, my love.
LADY A:	Oh dear. It's from Mrs Vincent – you know, the schoolmistress I lived with before I went to the Dawsons as governess. She's very ill, and implores me to go and see her before it's too late. Poor soul. I must go to her, Michael.
SIR MICHAEL:	Of course you must. She was kind to you when you needed help. She has a claim on your generosity. Get ready quickly, Lucy. We'll be in time for the express to London.
LADY A:	You'll come with me?
SIR MICHAEL:	Of course, my darling. Did you think I'd let you go alone?

(FADE OUT. FULL UP. INTERIOR AUDLEY COURT)

ALICIA: I'm afraid Lady A has been summoned up to town, my father has gone with her, and so our dinner party is postponed.

GEORGE: Till when, Alicia?

ALICIA: Who knows? Till they return.

ROBERT: Well, I'm not inclined to hang around waiting. My lodgings at Fig Court are not all that comfortable, but they're better than this.

GEORGE: To be honest, I'll be glad to get back. I haven't seen little Georgie for nearly a month. As soon as I'm in town, I'll take a trip down to Southampton for a visit.

ROBERT: We'll catch the early train tomorrow morning.

ALICIA: Tired of Audley already, Robert? I suppose you're yearning for the glittering society of London.

ROBERT: You have a very strange conception of our life in town, Alicia. All I'm yearning for is a decent tobacconist. I feel as though I've been smoking dried cabbage.

ALICIA: And so, Mr Talboys, you will lose the chance of meeting the prettiest woman in Essex.

ROBERT: The prettiest woman in Essex would have a poor chance of getting much admiration out of my friend, Mr George Talboys. His heart is in Southampton, where he has a little urchin who loves sugar plums.

ALICIA: Well, my step-mother seemed very anxious in her letter to know how long you were staying in Essex, and whether there was any chance of her being back in time to meet you. Look here, cousin Robert…

(PAPER)

"Be sure you answer my question about Mr Audley and his friend."

ROBERT: Yes, indeed. And what pretty handwriting she has. As beautiful as she is.

ALICIA: Give me my note, Robert. I want to catch the last post with my reply.

ROBERT: Well, now that we're actually here in Audley Court, I'd like to show my friend around. Would you spare a few minutes to act as our guide?

ALICIA: By all means. Come through here.

(MOVEMENT. SLIGHT ECHO)

This is the great hall.

GEORGE: My goodness, the size of those portraits.

ROBERT: Ancestors, my dear George. Some very worthy — like those clerics. And some very warlike.

GEORGE: Your family's certainly got a military background.

ALICIA: All the way back to William the Conqueror, Mr Talboys. *(calls)* Oh, Phoebe. Phoebe!

PHOEBE: *(remote, advancing)* Yes, Miss Alicia. Gentlemen.

ALICIA: I am showing Mr Robert and his friend around Audley Court. After we've seen the drawing room, I'd like to show them Lady Audley's rooms. Are they in good order, Phoebe?

PHOEBE: They certainly are, Miss Alicia.

ALICIA: Phoebe, would you do something for me? Lady Audley wishes to know if she will have the chance of meeting these gentlemen before they leave Essex. Would you please send her a note to say that they are unfortunately leaving by the first train tomorrow morning.

PHOEBE: Of course, Miss Alicia. *(retreating)* I'll write straight away.

ALICIA: *(calling)* Make sure you catch the last post.

PHOEBE: *(remote)* I will, Miss.

ALICIA: And now, I must show you our drawing room, before taking you upstairs.

(FADE OUT. FADE IN. DOORS OPENING)

ALICIA: And this … is my lady's suite of rooms.

ROBERT: Magnificent. Do you not think so, George?

GEORGE: So many mirrors. Luxury beyond belief.

ALICIA: My father can deny her nothing. Everything her heart desires he lavishes on her. Oh, come through to the little sitting room. Here's another of my father's extravagances. He wanted his beautiful wife preserved forever, just as she is today. He commissioned a portrait. It's very nearly finished.

ROBERT: This I must see. And so must you, George. Since you can't meet the beautiful Lady Audley in person, at least you can feast your eyes on her portrait.

ALICIA: Here, let me remove the dust sheet.

(CLOTH)

NARRATOR: The figure revealed was indeed that of Lady Audley, all her beauty perfectly portrayed, but the vivid canvas seemed almost on fire. The face glowed with a lurid brightness, and the deep blue eyes shone with a strange light. The crimson dress hung about her in folds that looked like flames.

The fair head emerged out of the lurid mass of colour as if out of a raging furnace.

ROBERT: My word, what a striking composition. It quite takes one aback. It's as if the artist had looked deep into her soul, and found something horrifying there. Do you know, I'm not at all sure I like it. What do you say George? George! It's no good, Alicia, he's struck dumb by her beauty!

ALICIA: Mr Talboys! What's the matter? Are you all right?

GEORGE: Robert, I don't think we should go back to town tomorrow. I'd like to stay on and meet Lady Audley.

ROBERT: You *are* taken with her, old boy. I knew you would be. Very well, we'll spend a few more days at Audley.

(FADE OUT. FULL UP)

LADY A: They did what, Phoebe? You allowed them into my rooms! How dare you!

PHOEBE: I couldn't prevent them, my lady. Miss Alicia insisted on showing them around the house.

LADY A: But my portrait. It's not yet completed. How could you let them see that?

PHOEBE: I wasn't with them, my lady. Miss Alicia had told me to write and tell you that the gentlemen were leaving this morning.

LADY A: But they haven't left. They're still in Audley – and Sir Michael has invited them to dinner tonight. I'm in no fit state to receive guests. We spent all yesterday searching London for my old friend, all in vain.

PHOEBE: I'm sure you did, my lady.

LADY A: *(sharp)* Phoebe! I'm quite worn out. I shall spend the morning in bed.

PHOEBE: Very well, my lady.

LADY A: After lunch I may go out into the grounds with a blanket, and lie down by the stream. A doze in the afternoon may restore my spirits.

PHOEBE: A very good idea, my lady.

(FADE OUT. FADE IN EXTERIOR. BELL RINGING FROM WITHIN HOUSE. FRONT DOOR OPENS)

BUTLER: Yes, sir?

GEORGE: My card. My name is Talboys. I am dining with Sir Michael and Lady Audley this evening, but I would like to speak with them now, if that is possible.

BUTLER: I am sorry, sir, but Sir Michael is out. My lady is in the grounds, but I don't know exactly where. Miss Alicia is in the house.

GEORGE: No, it's Lady Audley I wish to see. I will find her.

BUTLER: Very good, sir.

(FADE OUT ON FRONT DOOR CLOSING. FULL UP)

ALICIA: Do you know, Lady Audley, that Mr Talboys has been asking for Sir Michael and you? Filbert told me that he called earlier this afternoon and left his card.

LADY A: I wonder what he wanted? I thought he was coming to dinner this evening with Robert.

ALICIA: So they are. In fact, they should be arriving at any moment.

(REMOTE BELL RINGING)

No sooner said, than done. This must be them.

(DOOR OPENS)

BUTLER: Mr Robert Audley.

(DOOR CLOSES)

ALICIA: Robert! How nice to see you.

LADY A: Mr Audley.

ROBERT: (*remote approaching*) Good evening, ladies.

Uncle. Is George Talboys here?

SIR MICHAEL: Hullo Robert. Why – have you lost him?

ALICIA: He called here at about two o'clock. Filbert told me. He wanted to speak to Lady Audley, or to you, father. But neither of you were in the house.

ROBERT: This is very puzzling. The last I saw of him was at lunch. Afterwards we went our separate ways. I took my fishing rod and tackle out to the local stream. I expected to see him when I returned to the inn to dress for dinner. But he wasn't there, and he never arrived, so I thought he must have made his way here to the Court ahead of me.

LADY A: Well, as you see he's not here. He may yet arrive in time for dinner. But I'm pleased you're here, for I can thank you very much for the Russian sables. They are superb.

ROBERT: My pleasure, Lady Audley.

SIR MICHAEL: She looks quite splendid, draped in sable.

ROBERT: I can imagine. But I must say I'm rather uneasy about my friend.

LADY A: Uneasy? Why on earth?

ROBERT: I'll tell you why, Lady Audley. George had a bitter blow a year ago, when he learned that his wife had died. He has never got over it. He has become very quiet, but he talks very strangely on occasion. I sometimes think that one day this grief will get the better of him, and he will do something rash.

LADY A: Dear me! I did not think that men were capable of such deep and lasting affections.

ROBERT: George certainly is. I firmly believe that his wife's death broke his heart, especially since they had not seen or heard from each other since the day he left for Australia. And now this disappearance – I cannot help worrying about him.

SIR MICHAEL: I am certain that he will let you know what has happened soon enough. He may have been called back to town suddenly…

ROBERT: …but no note!

SIR MICHAEL: …or he may have gone for a hike and got delayed somewhere. There may be a dozen good reasons for his non-appearance. Now, Lucy, my dear, I wonder if you would delight us with a little music on the piano before we go in to dinner.

LADY A: If you wish it, Michael.

(MOVEMENT)

(*retreating*) Chopin's "Tristesse" Etude I know is a favourite of yours. Will you turn the pages, Alicia?

ALICIA:	Of course.
ROBERT:	Why, you've hurt your arm, Lady Audley.
LADY A:	Oh, it's nothing. I bruise at the slightest touch.
SIR MICHAEL:	What is it, Lucy? How did it happen?
LADY A:	Please don't trouble yourself about something so trivial. I simply wound a ribbon too tightly around my arm a few days ago. This bruise is the result.
SIR MICHAEL:	Hold the candle, Robert. Let me look at it. My poor darling.
LADY A:	I can certainly play nothing, if you hold my arm so, Michael.
SIR MICHAEL:	I'm sorry my dear. Do please begin.
	(CHOPIN'S ETUDE NO 3 IN E MAJOR. HOLD A LITTLE. FADE OUT. FULL UP)
MALDON:	Well, this is something of a surprise. Mr Audley, is it not? And what brings you to Southampton, Mr Audley?
ROBERT:	I'm here in the hopes of finding your son-in-law, Captain Maldon.
MALDON:	Well, you've missed him by a couple of hours.

ROBERT: What? You mean he's been here? When?

MALDON: Late last night. But he stayed for less than an hour.

ROBERT: Good heavens. Why on earth is the man putting me through such worry? What does it all mean?

MALDON: So you don't know what he intends doing?

ROBERT: What do you mean, captain?

MALDON: Why he's off to Australia. He sails tonight from Liverpool. He came here in the middle of the night to have a last look at little Georgie before leaving England, perhaps for good he said. He kissed the boy without waking him, and left for Liverpool by the mail train at just after two o'clock.

ROBERT: I just don't understand it. What possible reason could he have for leaving England like this, without a word to me?

MALDON: Perhaps he'll write to you from Liverpool?

ROBERT: He should, Captain Maldon. We've been good friends ever since our schooldays. It isn't kind of George Talboys to treat me like this. It isn't like him.

NARRATOR: The more he thought about it, the more Robert Audley became convinced that there was some hidden mystery surrounding his friend's strange behaviour. What if his impoverished old father-in-law had tried to get his hands on the money left in trust for little Georgie? What if the old man had decoyed George down to Southampton and made away with him, inventing the story of his return to Australia?

He decided that he would himself travel to Liverpool and see if he could trace his friend on to a ship bound for Australia. Once there, he quickly established that only one emigrant ship had sailed in the past three days – the *Victoria Regina* – bound for Melbourne. He made straight for the shipping office.

(OFFICE BACKGROUND – CHATTER)

CLERK: No, sir, no-one of that name on the passenger list.

ROBERT: Did any of the passengers make a booking at the very last moment?

CLERK: Well, now you mention it, sir, we did have a very late booking.

ROBERT: Can you remember who that was?

CLERK: Indeed, I can. He came in yesterday afternoon, at about three o'clock.

ROBERT: And what name did he give?

CLERK: I have it here, sir. Mr Thomas Brown.

ROBERT: Can you describe him?

CLERK: I'm afraid not, sir. We were very busy at the time. I did not take much notice of him.

NARRATOR: There was nothing more that Robert Audley could do. He took the train to London, and was back in his chambers by about six o'clock that evening. There his housekeeper, Mrs Perkins, brought him his dinner and a bottle of wine from a nearby tavern. The evening was raw and chilly, and Mrs Perkins had lit a good coal fire. After his meal, Robert sat staring into the blaze.

ROBERT: *(close)* No, George Talboys never sailed for Australia. If he's alive, he is still in England. If he's dead, then his body is hidden somewhere in England. The question is where? And why did he disappear like that?

NARRATOR: He sat for hours, thinking. Then, very late, he stood up, went over to his desk took out a sheet of paper and dipped his pen in the ink.

ROBERT: Journal of facts connected with the disappearance of George Talboys.

One: On our return from Russia, we go to Essex. I see Lady Audley, but she refuses to be introduced to George because she is too fatigued by her day at the races.

Two: Sir Michael invites George and me to dinner for the following evening.

Three: But the next morning my lady receives a telegram summoning her to London. The dinner is postponed.

Four: My cousin Alicia shows me a letter from my lady asking to know when George and I propose leaving Essex.

Five: We call at Audley Court. During our visit, Alicia instructs the maid, Phoebe, to write to my lady saying George and I intend leaving Essex early the next morning.

Six: In my lady's rooms we see her unfinished portrait. George is much affected by it.

Seven: Next day, he says he wants to meet Lady Audley, and postpones our return to town. After lunch I go fishing, and he takes himself to Audley Court. Neither Sir Michael nor Lady Audley are available.

Eight: He does not return to the inn, nor does he come to dinner at the Court that evening.

Nine: According to Captain Maldon he made his way to Southampton in the middle of the night, saw his little boy, and declared his intention of returning to Australia by ship from Liverpool.

Ten: There is no trace of him in Liverpool.

(FADE UP MUSIC BENEATH THE FOLLOWING)

It's as dark as midnight from first to last. The key to the riddle must lie either in Southampton or in Essex. I'll start my search in Audley Court. I return to Essex in the morning.

(UP MUSIC. DOWN FOR)

NARRATOR: We left Robert Audley deeply worried about the fate of his friend, George Talboys, who had mysteriously vanished. So concerned was he, that he decided to write down every detail of the events leading up to George's disappearance – a catalogue which seems to involve the lovely Lady Audley in some way. But how?

(UP MUSIC. DOWN AND FADE BENEATH FOLLOWING)

LADY A: Well, Phoebe, now that Luke has been appointed under-groom here at the Court, you'll be seeing even more of him. But you're surely not in love with him, are you? He's such an awkward, ugly creature.

PHOEBE: I don't think I can love him, my lady. But we're cousins – we've been together since we were children – and I promised, when I was just fifteen, that I would be his wife. I daren't break that promise now. I must marry him.

LADY A: You'll do nothing of the kind.

PHOEBE: I'd be in fear of my life if I didn't.

LADY A: You silly girl. You think he'd murder you if you broke your word? If he's capable of murder, then he's just as likely to kill you after you're married. In any case, I can't do without you, Phoebe. No, we'll give him a few pounds and send him about his business.

PHOEBE: My lady, I beg you, don't try to thwart me in this. Don't ask me to thwart him. I tell you I must marry him. You don't know what he is. It'll be the ruin of me and the ruin of others if I don't marry him.

LADY A: Oh, very well, Phoebe. There must be some secret at the bottom of this.

PHOEBE: There is, my lady.

LADY A: I shall be very sorry to lose you, but I look on you as my friend, so I shall not stand in your way. Tell me, what does Luke mean to do for a living when you are married?

PHOEBE: He would like to buy a public house.

LADY A: Then a public house he shall have – and the sooner he drinks himself to death, the better. Sir Michael dines at a bachelor party this evening, and Alicia is away with her friends. You can bring your cousin into the drawing room after dinner, and I'll tell him what I mean to do for him.

(FADE OUT. FADE IN)

LADY A: …and I understand that you would like to own a public house, Luke, after you are married. So, in addition to the wedding feast, I propose to give you fifty pounds, no less, to purchase one.

PHOEBE: Oh, my lady. Well, Luke, tell my lady how thankful you are.

LUKE: But I'm not so over-and-above thankful. Fifty pound ain't much to start a pub. You'll make it a hundred, my lady.

LADY A: I shall do nothing of the kind. I wonder at your impertinence in asking.

LUKE: Oh yes you will, though. You'll make it a hundred, my lady.

PHOEBE: Oh, my Lord.

LADY A: Phoebe Marks! You have told … this man?

PHOEBE: Forgive me. Oh, forgive me, my lady. He forced it from me – or I'd never, never have told. Never!

NARRATOR: So one morning, late in November, with the yellow fog low upon the meadows, Phoebe Marks and her cousin Luke, were wed in Audley village church. When the bride signed the marriage register she had no need to change her name, for Luke was also a Marks – and now the landlord of the Castle Inn, Mount Stanning, a lonely little village, a few miles from Audley. My lady had provided the seventy-five pounds necessary for the purchase of the good-will and fixtures, together with twenty-five to cover the stock of ales and spirits. A new maid was brought from London to attend on my lady – a showy damsel who complained bitterly about how dull it was at Audley Court. She was soon to learn how wrong she was.

(FADE IN. DRAWING ROOM)

LADY A: That friend of yours, Mr George... George...

ROBERT: Talboys?

LADY A: To be sure, Robert. Mr George Talboys. Have you seen him lately?

ROBERT: I have not seen him for three months – not since the 7th of September, the day we parted company after lunch. I went off fishing. He, although he did not tell me so, came here to Audley Court to see either you or Sir Michael, but neither of you were in the house. I never saw him again.

LADY A: But you sought him.

ROBERT: I certainly did. I travelled down to Southampton, where his little boy is living with his father-in-law, a Captain Maldon, who told me that George had visited him and the boy the previous night, and had said that he intended to travel back to Australia on the next available ship out of Liverpool. So I hastened to Liverpool. There I discovered that only one ship had left for Australia in the past few days, and that no George Talboys was listed among the passengers.

LADY A: And what do you infer from all this?

ROBERT: Two virtual certainties – that George Talboys never went to Liverpool, and that he never went to Southampton either.

LADY A: But you traced him there. His father-in-law had seen him.

ROBERT: Lady Audley, I have reason to doubt Captain Maldon's integrity. In short, I do not believe the story he told me.

(FADE OUT. FADE IN. BEDROOM)

LADY A: Michael, my darling. how long is that nephew of yours going to stay here?

SIR MICHAEL: As long as he likes, my pet. I have no son as yet, and he stands in the place of one. I love his company. I have told him he can regard Audley Court as his home…

LADY A: What a typically kind and generous gesture.

SIR MICHAEL: … but not, of course, if his lazy habits, or his smoking, or his dogs, or anything about him is displeasing to you.

LADY A: It isn't that. Mr Robert Audley is a very agreeable young man, and very honourable. But you know, Michael, I'm rather a young aunt for such a nephew, and…

SIR MICHAEL: And what, my love?

LADY A: Well, Alicia is rather jealous of any attention Mr Audley pays me, and – and I think it would be better for her happiness if your nephew were to bring his visit to a close.

SIR MICHAEL: He shall go tomorrow morning, Lucy. I'm a blind, neglectful fool not to have thought of this before. My lovely little darling, it was scarcely just to Robert to expose him, poor lad, to your fascinations. He shall go first thing tomorrow.

NARRATOR: And indeed he did, without a word of complaint, asserting with passion that he would never, by word or deed, bring the slightest hint of dishonour on his beloved uncle's head. He left Audley Court, but he did not take the evening train for London. Instead he walked to the little village of Mount Stanning and, once there, made his way to the inn. There he asked Phoebe Marks if she could provide him with a set of rooms – which she was very pleased to do, for he was the first, and indeed the only, paying guest the inn had known.

PHOEBE: (*whisper*) Want a shilling, little Billy? Well you know Audley Court? Run there and say you've a message for my lady from Phoebe Marks. Say it's a message, mind, not a note. Ask to see my lady, and make sure you place this letter in her own hands. No one else's. Then the shilling's yours. All right? Well run along, then. Make haste.

(FADE OUT. FADE IN. CROCKERY)

PHOEBE: I trust you enjoyed your breakfast, Mr Audley.

ROBERT: Very much, Mrs Marks. You are a good cook.

PHOEBE: Thank you, sir. I'm interrupting you because you have a visitor.

ROBERT: A visitor? For me?

PHOEBE: Indeed sir, She's just outside. Shall I show her in?

ROBERT: Please.

PHOEBE: *(remote)* Lady Audley.

(DOOR SHUTS BENEATH FOLLOWING)

LADY A: *(remote, advancing)* What a morning, Robert. The horses were positively blinded by the snow.

ROBERT: Lady Audley. I wonder you ventured out on a morning like this.

LADY A: I came over because I wanted to see you very particularly.

ROBERT: Indeed?

LADY A: Yes, Robert. I felt you had not been well treated – that, in short, an apology was due.

ROBERT: I do not wish for any apology.

LADY A: But you are entitled to one. We were very glad to have you at Audley, but my dear, silly husband must take it into his head that it is dangerous for his poor little wife's peace of mind to have a nephew in his twenties as a member of the family. So our pleasant little circle is broken up.

ROBERT: Lady Audley, heaven forbid that either you or I should ever bring grief or dishonour on my dear uncle's generous heart.

LADY A: You talk in riddles, Mr Audley. But tell me, what on earth induced you to come up to this dismal inn?

ROBERT: Curiosity.

LADY A: Curiosity?

ROBERT: Yes, I was interested in the owner – Luke Marks. I had a word with him last night. A dangerous man, my lady. A man in whose power I should not like to be.

LADY A: Mr Audley, I cannot conceive what you mean. But you clearly dislike me. What have I done to you?

ROBERT: I had a friend, Lady Audley, whom I loved dearly. Since I have lost him, I find my feelings towards other people are strangely embittered.

LADY A: You mean the Mr Talboys who went to Australia?

ROBERT: I mean the Mr Talboys who I was told set out for Liverpool in order to sail to Australia.

LADY A: And you do not believe that he went?

ROBERT: I do not.

LADY A: But why not?

ROBERT: A week after he disappeared I posted an advertisement in the main Australian papers, asking him, or anyone who had met him, to contact me. There are only a few days left in which I might reasonably expect to receive an answer.

LADY A: And if you do not?

ROBERT: I shall then feel justified in concluding that my friend is dead, and I shall examine the belongings he left at my chambers.

LADY A: And what are they? Coats, boots, pipes?

ROBERT: Letters. Letters from his friends, his old schoolfellows. his father, his brother officers.

LADY A: Yes.

ROBERT: Letters, too, from his wife.

LADY A: Indeed. Have you ever seen any of the letters written by the late Mrs Talboys?

ROBERT: Never. I dare say she wrote in the usual womanly scrawl. There are very few who write so charming and uncommon a hand as yours, Lady Audley.

LADY A: So you know my handwriting?

ROBERT: Very well indeed.

NARRATOR: She stayed for only a few minutes after this exchange. Robert Audley escorted her to her carriage, and watched it as it drove off – not towards Audley, but in the direction of Brentwood. Some hour and a half later, as Robert stood at the door of the inn, watching the snow falling on the whitened fields opposite, he saw the carriage drove back, empty this time.

(OPEN AIR)

ROBERT: *(calls)* Have you taken Lady Audley back to the Court?

COACHMAN: *(calls)* No, sir. I've just come from Brentwood station. My lady started for London by the 12.40 train.

(OFF BACKGROUND)

NARRATOR:	Robert packed his portmanteau, paid his bill, and made his own way to the station, where he caught the 3 o'clock express to town.
	(FADE IN BENEATH FOLLOWING VICTORIAN RAILWAY STATION – CROWDS, STEAM ENGINES)
	His train pulled into London Bridge station at exactly 4.15, and he was making his way across the concourse towards the exit, when he very nearly collided with a lady who was hurrying towards another platform.
ROBERT:	Excuse me, madam. I do apologise. Why, Lady Audley!
LADY A:	Robert? You in London already?
ROBERT:	Well, the Castle Inn is a dismal place.
LADY A:	Indeed it is.
ROBERT:	Let me see you to your train.
LADY A:	That's very kind of you. It leaves in three minutes. Platform 3, I believe. Ah yes, here we are.
	(CARRIAGE DOOR OPENS)
ROBERT:	An empty first class carriage. This will suit you very well.

LADY A: Thank you, Robert. You'll think me very foolish to travel on such a day – and without my dear darling's knowledge too – but I went up to town to settle a terrific milliner's bill, which I did not want my best of husbands to see. For, indulgent as he is, he might think me extravagant, and I cannot bear him to suffer, even in his thoughts.

ROBERT: Heaven forbid that you ever should, Lady Audley.

(WHISTLE. CARRIAGE DOOR SLAMMED SHUT. STEAM TRAIN BEGINS TO CHUG AWAY)

LADY A: (*calls*) Amen to that, Robert.

(UP TRAIN. HOLD A LITTLE. FADE. FULL UP)

MRS PERKINS: Welcome back, Mr Audley. Welcome back, indeed. Chambers has been very dull without you.

ROBERT: Well, thank you, Mrs Perkins. I've missed your cheerful face as well. Has anything happened in my absence?

MRS PERKINS: Not a thing, sir.

ROBERT: And today – no-one has asked for a key to my rooms?

MRS PERKINS: Good heavens, no sir. Only the locksmith that you ordered.

ROBERT: What locksmith? I ordered no locksmith.

MRS PERKINS: But he had your instructions, sir. He came by here at three o'clock this afternoon. He asked for the key to your rooms because you had said the locks all needed repairing. I asked him how he had received his orders, and he showed me a letter that you had written from the country. So I let him in, and he got to work immediately. I left him proceed with his work, and told him to return the main key when he had finished. It only took him about half an hour.

ROBERT: I wager it took him much less than that, Mrs Perkins, to complete the task he was paid to do.

MRS PERKINS: Why, sir, what on earth do you mean?

ROBERT: You recall my friend, Mr Talboys?

MRS PERKINS: Indeed I do sir. Whatever happened to the gentleman?

ROBERT: If only I knew, Mrs Perkins. If only I knew. But this is his portmanteau. I have not touched it since he disappeared, but I keep the key in this drawer.

(DRAWER PULLED)

Here it is. I'm going to open his trunk.

MRS PERKINS: Do you think you should, sir?

ROBERT: Indeed I do, Mrs Perkins.

(KEY IN LOCK. LID FLUNG OPEN. FADE IN MUSIC BENEATH FOLLOWING)

And yes, here are all his papers. He showed them to me before he locked the portmanteau. Now let me see... No... No... It's as I thought. The bundle of letters from his wife are no longer here.

MRS PERKINS: Mr Audley!

ROBERT: Precisely. And that was the locksmith's mission – to access this trunk and purloin that particular package. Mrs Perkins , we have both been the victims of an audacious plot.

(UP MUSIC. HOLD A LITTLE. FADE BENEATH FOLLOWING, BUT HOLD UNDER)

ROBERT: (*close*) Why do I go on with this, when I know that it is leading me, step by step, day by day, to a conclusion that I must avoid? Must I go on to what I know will be a bitter end? Or can I sit here tonight, and say that I have done my duty by my missing friend? Can I with a clear conscience say that I have searched for him, but have searched in vain? Can I justify dropping the chain of evidence I have been slowly putting together? Or must I go on adding link to link until the circle is complete? I think and believe that George Talboys is dead. Must I go on and discover how and where he died? Will I be doing his memory an injustice if I don't continue to the end? Oh, but how greatly I fear what the effect of that final discovery will be. What am I to do? What am I to do?

(UP MUSIC. HOLD A LITTLE. DOWN FOR)

Justice to the dead first. Mercy to the living afterwards.

(UP MUSIC. FADE OUT. FULL UP)

NARRATOR: The very next day Robert Audley travelled to Southampton, where he located and inspected the boarding school with the best reputation in the district. He then repaired to Captain Maldon's house, where he found little Georgie Talboys only too eager to go to school, though somewhat sad at leaving his grandfather. That evening Robert took the little boy to the safety of the well-appointed educational establishment, and left feeling he had done his duty by his dead friend. His next port of call was George Talboys's father – the father who had disowned his son for marrying Helen Maldon.

HARCOURT: My son did me an unpardonable wrong by marrying the daughter of a drunken pauper. From that hour I no longer had a son. I told you as much in my reply to your recent letter, Mr Audley.

ROBERT: I have reason to believe that you indeed have no son, Mr Talboys. I have bitter cause to believe that he is dead – that he died last September. He disappeared on that day, and I have found no trace of him since. Subsequent events lead me to believe that he may have been murdered.

HARCOURT: Utter nonsense. A very clever trick, no doubt – but not clever enough to deceive me. He has simply removed himself in order to alarm me, and ultimately to obtain my forgiveness. I do not know, sir, whether you are party to this deceit, but if you are, you may inform him that he might as well spare himself the trouble. However long he chooses to absent himself, I will not forgive him. So he might as well return without delay. Good day to you, Mr Audley.

(MUSIC. DOWN AND HOLD UNDER)

ALICIA: Dear Cousin Robert – I write to inform you that Papa is very ill. This winter has been very severe here at Audley, and poor dear Papa took cold two weeks ago. He could not shake the infection off, and has been in his bed for the last eight days, sometimes with a fever. Do come and see him. He has spoken about you several times, and I know he will be glad to have you with him. Come at once.

(UP MUSIC AND FADE OUT. FULL UP)

SIR MICHAEL: (*weak*) Ah, Robert. My dear, dear boy. How glad I am to see you.

ROBERT:	And I to see you. But not in this state, uncle. What have you done to yourself?
SIR MICHAEL:	A mere nothing. It will pass – and even faster, now that you are here. I am in very good hands – am I not, Mr Dawson?
DAWSON:	I like to think so, Sir Michael. Yes, Mr Audley, I think I can say that he is on the mend. A few more days of bed rest, and I hope to see him well on the way to a complete recovery.
ROBERT:	That is very good news. Mr Dawson, I am especially pleased to find you in attendance on my uncle, for I have something very particular to ask you. Perhaps we could talk as I could see you out?
DAWSON:	By all means. Good evening, Sir Michael. I shall call again tomorrow.

(FADE OUT. FADE IN)

	And what is it you wish to know, Mr Audley? If you are at all alarmed about your uncle, I can set your mind at rest.
ROBERT:	It is not about my uncle. I wish to ask you two or three questions about another person – the person who once lived with your family as Miss Lucy Graham, the person who is now Lady Audley.

DAWSON: Mr Audley! You can scarcely expect me to answer questions about your uncle's wife without Sir Michael's express permission. I always respected the lady as Miss Graham, and I esteem her doubly as Lady Audley – not on account of her altered status, but because she is the wife of one of the noblest men I know.

ROBERT: You cannot respect my uncle, or his honour, more sincerely than I do, Mr Dawson. But I have the very best of reasons for asking you certain questions. After all, it was at your house that he met the present Lady Audley.

DAWSON: That is certainly the case.

ROBERT: She called herself an orphan, I believe, without a relative or friend in the world. That was all I could ever learn of her antecedents.

DAWSON: Why would you wish to know more?

ROBERT: For a very terrible reason. Mr Dawson, for some months I have been struggling with suspicions and doubts that refuse to be set aside. I may be wrong – and heaven grant that I am – but the chain of circumstantial evidence grows stronger, not weaker, with every fact that I uncover. Everything I have learned leads me to believe that the woman who bears my uncle's name is unworthy to be his wife. I must either confirm my fears or set my doubts at rest. Pray heaven it is the latter. To help me, I need to know all there is to know about Lady Audley's circumstances before she married my uncle.

DAWSON: I'm totally bewildered by what you tell me, Mr Audley – and not a little alarmed. I admire and respect Lady Audley more than I can say, but I suppose to withhold the little information about her that I do possess would be nothing more than obstinacy. When she married your uncle Lucy Graham had lived in our household for some thirteen months. She came to us from a school in Brompton, south London, run by a Mrs Vincent. It was Mrs Vincent's strong recommendation that led me to employ Miss Graham without enquiring further into her antecedents.

ROBERT: Did you actually meet this Mrs Vincent?

DAWSON: No. When Miss Graham responded to my advertisement, she referred me to the lady. I ascertained from the educational directory that Mrs Vincent did indeed own the school named, and I wrote to her for a reference.

ROBERT: Can you recall the address you wrote to?

DAWSON: Indeed. It was Crescent Villas, Brompton. Number 9, I believe.

ROBERT: Ah, yes. I've heard that address before. This Mrs Vincent telegraphed to Lady Audley last September saying she was very ill, perhaps dying, and asked her to visit. My uncle accompanied

Lady Audley to town, but when they came to Crescent Villas they found that Mrs Vincent had moved, and they could not discover where she was living. It was a fruitless journey.

DAWSON: Is this one of the circumstantial links in your chain?

ROBERT: Perhaps. Well, thank you Mr Dawson. You take me back two-and-a-half years in the history of Lady Audley's life, but I still have a blank of three years to fill before I can exonerate her from my horrible suspicions. Good evening to you.

DAWSON: And to you, Mr Audley.

(FADE OUT. FADE IN. CROCKERY)

LADY A: Your tea, Robert.

ROBERT: Thank you.

LADY A: You are not seriously alarmed about your uncle, are you?

ROBERT: No. Thank heaven, I don't think there's the slightest cause for anxiety.

LADY A: Only you were alone with Mr Dawson for such a long time just now. I was quite alarmed at the length of your conversation. Were you talking of Sir Michael all the time?

ROBERT: No, not all the time.

LADY A: Why, what could you find to say to Mr Dawson, or he to say to you? You are almost strangers to each other.

ROBERT: Suppose Mr Dawson wished to consult me about some legal matter.

LADY A: Was that it?

ROBERT: If it were, it would be very unprofessional of me to say, my lady.

(EDGE OUT. FULL UP)

NARRATOR: Robert took the train from Audley the next morning, and reached London Bridge station a little after nine. He called a cab, and drove straight to Brompton. After some difficulty, the cabman located Crescent Villas, not that Robert expected to find Mrs Vincent in residence, but he hoped that he might discover where she had removed to.

(FADE IN)

MAID: The mistress says she doesn't want to be bothered about Mrs Vincent any more. She said that Mrs Vincent used to live here, but she left about fifteen months ago with a quarter's rent unpaid, and she has no idea where she went.

(CROSSFADE)

GROCER: I don't know where Mrs Vincent is, but I wish I did. She owes me more than twelve pounds in unpaid grocery bills, and that's a sight more than I can afford to lose, I can tell you

(CROSSFADE)

DRESSMAKER: Yes, I've been making clothes for Mrs Vincent for upwards of six years. I think of her as a friend. She left this neighborhood owing me money, but she had dreadful difficulties. I'm the only person hereabouts she entrusted with her various changes of address, and she does give me small sums on account from time to time. I'm so sorry for her.

ROBERT: I wish her no harm, I assure you. I am merely seeking a little information that I know she can provide.

DRESSMAKER: Well then, sir, she's presently living at Acacia Cottage, Peckham Grove. Number six. I took a dress to her there yesterday.

ROBERT: Thank you very much. I am much obliged to you. And you may rely upon it, Mrs Vincent will not suffer any inconvenience through me.

(FADE OUT. FULL UP)

MRS VINCENT: I'm afraid I can be of little help to you, Mr Audley. I know nothing of Miss Graham's history since she left my establishment. I believe she obtained a situation in the family of a surgeon in Essex, after I had recommended her to him. I have never heard from her since.

ROBERT: But you have written to her?

MRS VINCENT: Never.

ROBERT: You did not send a telegram to Miss Graham last September saying you were seriously ill, and asking her to visit you?

MRS VINCENT: Most certainly not. I have never been seriously ill in my life.

ROBERT: I hope you will not object if I ask one or two questions about Miss Graham. For example, when exactly did she come to your school?

MRS VINCENT: I think she took up her post in August 1854, just before the start of the new school year.

ROBERT: And where did she come from?

MRS VINCENT: I am not exactly sure. I believe it was from some seaside resort.

ROBERT: But did you not have some references?

MRS VINCENT: Mr Audley, we came to a business arrangement. Miss Graham waived the question of salary, and I waived the question of references. She told me that she had quarrelled with her papa, and wanted

66

to find a home far away from him and everyone she had known. I agreed to provide her with bed, board and lodging in exchange for her acting as teacher in my establishment. She was clearly well educated, and perfectly capable of undertaking that role. And she did so extremely well. She made a very favorable impression on the parents and relatives of my pupils.

ROBERT: I have only one last thing to ask, Mrs Vincent. Did Miss Graham leave anything behind? Books, knick-knacks – any kind of property?

MRS VINCENT: The only thing she left behind was an old hat box. I use it to store spare papers. It's right here. Would you like to see it?

ROBERT: I would indeed. Thank you very much.

NARRATOR: Robert knelt down to examine the scraps of railway labels and addresses which were pasted here and there on the box. It had evidently travelled considerably. The only direction which had not been either defaced or torn away was the last, which bore the name of Miss Graham, passenger to London. Looking very closely at this label, Robert discovered that it had been pasted over another. He peeled it off very carefully to reveal the label beneath. Then, using the utmost caution, he managed to remove this lower label from the box. He placed it between two blank pages of his pocket book.

ROBERT: Mrs Vincent, I need intrude on you no longer. I am extremely grateful to you. I wish you good morning.

(BURST OF MUSIC. DOWN FOR AND HOLD UNDER FOLLOWING)

ROBERT: (*close*) In my pocket book now is the connecting link between Lucy Graham and the woman who is now Lady Audley. Lucy Graham entered Mrs Vincent's establishment in August 1854, but Mrs Vincent knows nothing at all of Lucy Graham's life from the day of her birth until the day she entered her employment. To discover the full truth, I must start at the other end. I must discover what happened to Helen Talboys from the moment George left for Australia until the day of the funeral in Ventnor churchyard. And I start with the seaport town in which George told me he had first met Captain Maldon and his daughter – Wildernsea, up in the north-east corner of England.

(MUSIC, MIX TO SHRIEK OF STEAM ENGINE POUNDING. MIX TO WHEELS RATTLING AWAY ON RAILROAD LINE. FADE BENEATH FOLLOWING)

LAND2:   But you should see Wildernsea in the summer, sir. We're usually booked solid from June to October. At this time of the year...

ROBERT:	It means I have the best suite of rooms in the hotel, and at a very good price.
LAND2:	My pleasure, sir.
ROBERT:	Tell me, how long have you owned this place?
LAND2:	Six years, sir. My wife and I came here in November 1852. We moved in as the builders moved out. I'd been in business in Hull, but my wife and I wanted a different kind of life. So I sold up, and we purchased this brand new hotel.
ROBERT:	I wonder if you remember a retired naval officer at that time – the name was Maldon.
LAND2:	Captain Maldon? I certainly do, sir. One of our best customers. He spent virtually every evening in our bar. His daughter married a young officer that was stationed here with his regiment – we provided their wedding breakfast. They went off to the continent for a time, then came back here. But the gentleman ran away to Australia, and left the lady a week or two after her baby was born. You can imagine the sensation that created here in Wildernsea. That poor young woman, Mrs... Mrs... I forget the name...
ROBERT:	Talboys?
LAND2:	That's it sir. Talboys. Mrs Talboys was greatly pitied by everyone. She was such a pretty lass, and had such winning ways.

ROBERT: Can you tell me how long Captain Maldon and his daughter remain in Wildernsea after Mr Talboys left them?

LAND2: Now, I'm not too sure about that, sir. But Mrs Barkamb could certainly tell you. She owns the house in which Captain Maldon and his daughter lived – 17 North Cottages.

ROBERT: Thank you, landlord. I shall make a point of visiting Mrs Barkamb tomorrow.

(FADE OUT. FULL UP)

ROBERT: Mrs Barkamb, I seek a very simple piece of information, and the proprietor of the Victoria Hotel tells me that you are the most likely person to know it.

MRS BARKAMB: Indeed, Mr Audley. I will, of course, assist you, if I am able. What is it you wish to know?

ROBERT: The exact date of Mrs Talboys's departure from Wildernsea.

MRS BARKAMB: I see. Can I help you, I wonder? Mrs Talboys left rather abruptly, you know.

ROBERT: No, I was not aware of that.

MRS BARKAMB: Oh yes. Poor little woman. She tried to support herself after her husband deserted her by giving music lessons – she was a very good pianist, you know. She was doing quite well, but I suppose her father took the little money she had to spend in the bar of the hotel and public houses. However that was, they had a very serious misunderstanding one night, and the next morning Mrs Talboys simply walked out, leaving her baby with a wet-nurse whom she employed to breast-feed him.

ROBERT: But you don't know the date.

MRS BARKAMB: I do not. But wait! I do remember that Captain Maldon wrote to me that very day – he always came to me with his troubles. If I could find that letter, it might be dated.

ROBERT: It might, indeed.

MRS BARKAMB: I keep all my correspondence in that escritoire by the window. *(retreating)* If you could give me … a minute … or two … to go through these pigeon holes…

(PAPERS)

Oh dear, such an accumulation of papers. Wait a minute, though. Here we are. *(advancing)* Captain Maldon's very letter. And it encloses a note to him from Mrs Talboys. Here you are, Mr Audley. And it is indeed dated. See. "North Cottages, August the 16th, 1854."

(SLIGHT ECHO ON BOTH MALDON AND LADY A)

MALDON: My generous friend, I am in the depths of despair. My daughter has left me! You may imagine my feelings. We had a few words last night on the subject of money – often the cause of friction between us – and this morning I found she had left. Helen left me the enclosed note on the kitchen table.

LADY A: I am weary of my life here, and wish to find a new one. I go out into the world to seek another home, and a happier future, severing all my links to a hateful past. Forgive me if I have been difficult. You should forgive me, for you know the reasons. You know the secret which is the key to my life. Helen.

(MUSIC. DOWN FOR FOLLOWING AND FADE QUICKLY BENEATH. AUDLEY COURT DRAWING ROOM)

LADY A: So you have come back to us, Robert, you truant. And now that you have returned, we shall keep you prisoner – shall we not, Alicia?

ALICIA: I will have nothing to do with the movements of so erratic an individual. Since Robert Audley has decided to act like some ghost-haunted hero, I have given up trying to understand him.

LADY A: So pray where have you been wandering during the last day or two, Robert?

ROBERT: I will make no secret of where I have been, Lady Audley. I have been in Yorkshire, at the small seaside resort where my poor friend George Talboys lived at the time of his marriage.

LADY A: Excuse me, I must dress for dinner. Your uncle and I are going to a dinner party this evening. Pray excuse me.

ROBERT: Lady Audley, I must ask you to spare me half an hour. I returned to Essex especially to speak with you.

LADY A: What about? What can you possibly want to talk to me about?

ROBERT: I will tell you when we are alone. If you will excuse me, cousin Alicia, I should like to walk with Lady Audley for a little in the grounds.

ALICIA: Mysterious as ever. Very well, Robert. I shall leave you to your enigmatic conversation. (*retreating*) Enjoy your walk.

(REMOTE DOOR OPENS AND CLOSES. FADE IN. OUTDOORS. BIRDS. FOOTSTEPS ON GRAVEL. FADE THEM UNDER FOLLOWING. FADE IN)

ROBERT: The Lime Walk, I think, Lady Audley. I want to talk to you without fear of interruption. That is the safest place, I think.

LADY A: If that is what you wish.

ROBERT: You are trembling, Lady Audley.

LADY A: I am shivering. It is very cold. Can we not postpone this until tomorrow?

ROBERT: Gather your shawl around you, Lady Audley. I am afraid there is no postponing this conversation. I must speak with you.

LADY A: Very well.

ROBERT: Of course, you might have escaped this ordeal. I have given you fair warning. But you have chosen to obstruct me and block me. You have not been successful.

LADY A: I have not the faintest idea what you are referring to. And you are making me ill, Robert. I suffer dreadfully from my nerves. I am worth a fortune to poor Mr Dawson. He is always sending me all kinds of abominable mixtures, but he can't cure me.

ROBERT: Do you remember what Macbeth asks his physician, my lady: "Canst thou not minister to a mind diseased"? Mr Dawson may be much cleverer, but I doubt if even he can do that.

LADY A: Who said that my mind was diseased?

ROBERT: I say so, my lady. You tell me that you suffer from nerves, and that all the medicines your doctor prescribes have no effect. I am no physician, but shall I tell you why you are nervous in this house?

LADY A: If you can.

ROBERT: Because for you this house is haunted.

LADY A: Haunted? Who by?

ROBERT: The ghost of George Talboys.

LADY A: George Talboys! George Talboys! Why do you keep tormenting me about this George Talboys, who's decided to keep out of your way for a few months? Are you going mad, Mr Audley? Have you selected me as a victim of your monomania? What is George Talboys to me?

ROBERT: He was a stranger to you then?

LADY A: Of course he was a stranger. What else should he be?

ROBERT: Shall I tell you the story of my friend's disappearance, as I read it?

LADY A: No. I wish to know nothing of your friend. If he is dead, then I am sorry for him. If he is alive, I have no wish to see or hear of him. Now, if you don't mind, will you let me go inside and talk to my husband. Or do you intend to keep me here till I catch my death of cold?

ROBERT: I wish to detain you until you have heard what I have to say, Lady Audley. I will detain you no longer than that. When you have heard me, you may do as you please.

LADY A: Very well, then. Say what you have to say. I promise to listen very carefully. But please be speedy about it.

ROBERT: When my friend, George Talboys, returned to England, the thought uppermost in his mind was the thought of his wife.

LADY A: Whom he had deserted. At least I remember your telling me something to that effect when you first told me your friend's story.

ROBERT: It was his wife in his heart and his mind. All his hopes were pinned on making her happy, and lavishing on her the fortune he had gained through his own efforts in the gold-fields of Australia. I saw him within a few hours of his landing in England, and I can bear witness to the love and anticipation with which he awaited his reunion with his wife. I can also bear witness to the devastation and anguish inflicted on him when he read the announcement of his wife's death in the Times newspaper. Lady Audley, I now believe that that announcement was a black and bitter lie.

LADY A: Indeed. And what reason could anyone have had for announcing the death of Mrs Talboys, if Mrs Talboys were still alive?

ROBERT: The lady herself might have had a reason.

LADY A: What reason?

ROBERT: Well, suppose she had used George's absence to win a richer husband? Suppose she had married again, bigamously, and decided to use the false announcement to throw poor George off the scent?

LADY A: Your suppositions are ridiculous, Mr Audley. Do you have any reasonable grounds for them?

ROBERT: I have examined the back numbers of the Times newspaper, which I know is required reading in Sir Michael's house. On July the 2nd, 1857, a brief paragraph appeared to the effect that a Mr George Talboys, who had realized a fortune in nuggets on the Australian gold-fields, was travelling to London in the clipper *Argus*. A small piece of evidence, Lady Audley, but pointing strongly to the fact that news of Mr Talboys's forthcoming arrival would have been known to anyone interested. Do you follow me?

LADY A: Not very clearly. What has this to do with the death of Mrs Talboys?

ROBERT: This, my lady. I believe that the news of Mr Talboys's imminent arrival gave rise to a conspiracy – a conspiracy carried out by Helen Talboys and her father, Captain Maldon. I believe that the announcement in The Times of Helen Talboys's death was false.

LADY A: A conspiracy?

ROBERT: Yes. An artful and wicked woman, already married, had married bigamously and secured a splendid position, with not a care for the misery she might inflict on the honest heart of the man she betrayed.

LADY A: You said the announcement of Helen Talboys's death was false. But you went to Ventnor with your friend, Mr Talboys, to see his wife's grave. Who was it who died at Ventor, if it was not Mrs Talboys?

ROBERT: Ah, Lady Audley, I intend to have the answer to that question very, very soon. I have put together the chain of evidence, link by link. I need only a little more information until it is complete. Do you think I shall fail to discover those missing links? No Lady Audley, I shall not fail. I shall discover the history of the woman buried in Ventnor churchyard, and I shall uncover the conspiracy, unless...

LADY A: Unless? Unless what?

ROBERT: Unless the woman I wish to save from degradation and punishment accepts the mercy I offer her while there is still time.

LADY A: Any woman who succumbed to that would be foolish indeed. You are suffering from delusions, Mr Audley. What could be more ridiculous than this idea you have taken into your head? Your friend, Mr George Talboys, chooses to leave the country without giving you due notice. You yourself told me that he had become a different man after his wife's death. What more likely than that he tired of the monotony of life in England and ran back to the gold fields in which he had made his fortune? But this simple explanation does not satisfy you, and you build up some absurd theory of a conspiracy – a conspiracy that has no existence except in your overheated brain. Helen Talboys is dead. The Times announcement declares it. Her own father tells you so. By what right, Mr Audley, do you come to torment me about George Talboys or to assert that his wife is still alive?

ROBERT: By the right of circumstantial evidence. I have in my possession a letter written by Helen Talboys. The handwriting is identical to yours.

LADY A: And to a thousand other ladies, I have no doubt. Handwriting, indeed.

ROBERT: But what did Helen Talboys say in her letter, addressed to her father? That she was weary of her old life and wished to cast it aside and start a new one. What do people do when they begin a new existence? They change their names. Helen Talboys left Wildernsea on the 16th of August 1854 and disappeared. She emerged on the 17th of August as Lucy Graham, the friendless girl prepared to take on a teaching job for no remuneration, provided no one enquired into her past life.

LADY A: Mr Audley, you are mad! This Helen Talboys ran away from home on the 16th of August, I happened to take up my post on the 17th. What on earth does that prove?

ROBERT: By itself nothing, my lady. But I have the evidence of two labels, one pasted over the top of the other, which I removed in Mrs Vincent's presence from a hat box belonging to you. The top label bears the name of Lucy Graham; the one underneath that of Helen Talboys. Those labels are irrefutable evidence that you, Lady Audley, and Helen Talboys are one and the same.

LADY A: They are nothing of the sort. If I were in a court of law, I could bring forward witnesses to refute your absurd charge. You claim that Helen Talboys is not dead and buried. I warn you that people who persist in such follies, against all the evidence, are sometimes confined to the lifelong imprisonment of a private lunatic asylum.

ROBERT: So you refuse to accept my warning? You refuse to leave this place and the generous gentleman you have deceived and fooled?

LADY A: I do.

ROBERT: Very well. I have only one more thing to say. My friend, George Talboys, was last seen entering these gardens, he was last heard enquiring for you. He was never seen to leave this place. I believe that he met his death here, in these grounds, and that his body lies here somewhere. Lady Audley, I will not rest until I find the body of my dead friend, even if I have to root up every tree in these gardens. And believe me, I will ensure that the author of this whole conspiracy is brought to justice.

(FADE IN MUSIC BENEATH FOLLOWING)

LADY A: And you can believe me, Mr Audley, when I warn you that you will find me an implacable enemy. Only one of us can emerge victorious from this duel. This is a battle to the death.

(UP MUSIC. DOWN FOR AND FADE BENEATH FOLLOWING)

LADY A: Alicia, my dear, have you ever considered your cousin's character?

ALICIA: Good heavens, no, Lady Audley. Why should I study his character?

LADY A: But have you never thought him eccentric?

ALICIA: Eccentric? Well, yes, I suppose Robert is a little eccentric.

LADY A: His father and mother – were they at all odd?

ALICIA: Well, my aunt was a very reasonable woman, even if she did marry for love. But my Uncle Robert – well, now you come to mention it, I suppose you could call him a trifle eccentric. I believe Robert inherits all his absurdities from his father.

LADY A: I thought as much. Madness is often transmitted from a father to his children. Your cousin is very good-hearted, but he must be watched, Alicia. I do believe he is insane.

ALICIA: Insane? Are you trying to frighten me?

LADY A: Indeed, I am not. I only wish to put you on your guard. He has talked to me this evening in a way that has filled me with absolute terror. I shall speak to Sir Michael about this very seriously tonight.

ALICIA: Papa will never believe you.

LADY A: You are quite mistaken, Alicia. He will believe anything I tell him.

(FADE OUT. FULL UP)

SIR MICHAEL: Lucy, you must tell me what has distressed you. Come, my love. Tell me what it is.

LADY A: *(choking back tears)* Oh, Michael, I am so silly. But really he has made my quite hysterical.

SIR MICHAEL: Who? Who has made you hysterical?

LADY A: Your nephew. Mr Robert Audley.

SIR MICHAEL: Robert? Lucy, what do you mean?

LADY A: He asked me to go out into the garden with him. He said he wanted to talk to me. But once out there, he said such horrible things...

SIR MICHAEL: What horrible things, Lucy?

LADY A: Oh, my dear love, how can I tell you? It will distress you so much. My darling, have you ever thought your nephew a little...

SIR MICHAEL: A little what, my darling?

LADY A: A little out of his mind. Madness is sometimes hereditary. Could he have inherited it...?

SIR MICHAEL: Neither from his father nor his mother, my love. What on earth has put this idea into your head?

LADY A: It's the only way I can account for his behaviour. I believe he is suffering from monomania, brought on by the disappearance of his friend, George Talboys. He has dwelt on this one idea until he has lost the power to think of anything else. He declared tonight that George Talboys was murdered, here in Audley Court, and that he will not rest until he has discovered his friend's body.

SIR MICHAEL: Murdered? Here in Audley Court?

LADY A: That is what he believes.

SIR MICHAEL: Are you certain this is what he said? Did you misunderstand him?

LADY A: I don't think I did. Michael, I shall never be able to see Mr Audley again.

SIR MICHAEL: But, my darling, why were you so frightened by his wild talk? It could not affect you.

LADY A: But it does. He seems to connect me in some vague way, which I cannot quite understand, with the disappearance of this Mr Talboys.

SIR MICHAEL: Impossible, Lucy! You must have misunderstood him.

LADY A: I don't think so.

SIR MICHAEL: Then he *must* be insane. I have to think this over and decide what is best to be done.

(FADE OUT. FULL UP)

LADY A: (*very close*) Dare I defy him? Could I frighten him into stopping? No, that would not do it. Would he stop at the thought of what his uncle must suffer if I am disgraced? It hasn't stopped him so far. Will he stop at all, now that he has gone so far? Will anything stop him – but death?

(KNOCK AT DOOR. LADY AUDLEY'S BEDROOM)

LADY A: *(calls)* Come in!

(DOOR OPENS)

Oh, it's you, Phoebe. Come in. Come in and shut the door. It's cold.

(DOOR CLOSES)

PHOEBE: *(remote, advancing)* I hope you don't mind me calling on you, my lady.

LADY A: Of course not. Take off your bonnet and come and sit here near the fire and talk to me. I'm very glad you came. I feel horribly lonely and unhappy.

PHOEBE: I'm sorry to hear that, my lady.

LADY A: Phoebe, I'm being persecuted by a man I never injured. He is pursuing and tormenting me.

PHOEBE: I think I know who you mean, my lady. Is it the gentleman who came to the Castle Inn two months ago, when I warned you…

LADY A: Yes, yes.

PHOEBE: The same gentleman is at our place tonight, my lady.

LADY A: I might have known as much. He has gone there to wring my secrets from your husband. Fool! You've left him alone with Luke. Do you want to destroy me?

PHOEBE: Oh, my lady I didn't come of my own free will. I didn't want to leave the house. I was sent here.

LADY A: Sent here? Who sent you?

PHOEBE: Luke, my lady. You wouldn't believe how hard he can be on me if I go against him.

LADY A: But why have you come?

PHOEBE: For help, my lady. Luke is so extravagant. Nothing I say makes him more steady. If it wasn't for me, we'd have been ruined before this. Now the bailiff is in the house, demanding the Christmas rent. It is three months unpaid. We're to be sold up tomorrow, unless…

LADY A: Unless I pay your rent for you, I suppose.

PHOEBE: Indeed, indeed, I wouldn't have asked, but he made me come.

LADY A: And he will make you come whenever he is in need of money. You have become my pensioners, for as long as I live. Do you know, Phoebe Marks, that my jewel box is half-emptied to meet your claims?

PHOEBE: Oh my lady, you know that I am not the one imposing on you.

LADY A: I know nothing. Hold your tongue, girl, and let me think. Let me think… Robert Audley is with your husband, and there's a bailiff in the house, and your brutal husband is no doubt brutally drunk by now. No, there's no help for it. The money must be paid.

PHOEBE: If you do pay it, I want to tell him that it will be the last he will receive from you if he remains at the Castle Inn.

LADY A: Why?

PHOEBE: Because I want him to leave. He's not fit to be the landlord of a public house. He's scarcely ever sober after dark, and when he's drunk he gets wild and doesn't know what he's doing. We've had two or three narrow escapes already.

LADY A: Narrow escapes? What can you mean?

PHOEBE: We've nearly been burned to death in our beds through his carelessness. The Castle Inn is such a rackety old structure – all tumble-down and rotten rafters – that no company will insure it. Luke knows how dangerous it is, but when he's tipsy he doesn't know what he's doing. Only a week ago he left a candle burning in one of the outhouses, and it fell over into the straw. It was only by chance that I discovered the fire, or else the whole place would have been burnt down.

That was the third time the same sort of thing has happened since we've had the place.

LADY A: Burnt in your beds. It would have been a good thing for me if your precious husband had been burnt in his bed before tonight. I'll give you the money to send the bailiff away. You know as well as I do that I dare not refuse you. Pass me my purse, Phoebe. Over there, by your hand.

PHOEBE: Oh, my lady, I quite forgot – I was given a letter to bring to you. When Mr Audley heard that I was coming down here, he asked me to hand this to you.

LADY A: Give it to me. Quickly.

(ENVELOPE TORN. PAPER)

ROBERT: (*as if reading*) Should Mrs George Talboys have survived her supposed death, as recorded in *The Times* and on the tombstone in Ventnor churchyard, and if she is the lady I have accused of this conspiracy, there would be no great difficulty in identifying her. I am prepared to bring Mrs Barkamb, the owner of North Cottages, Wildernsea, to Audley Court for that very purpose. Robert Audley.

LADY A: (*close, furious*) If he stood before me now, I'd kill him. Yes, I would kill him. For he'll do it. He will do it – unless some calamity befalls him, and silences him for ever. Some calamity...

PHOEBE: My lady – what are you doing?

(CLOTHES RUSTLING)

LADY A: I am going out, Phoebe.

PHOEBE: Not tonight, my lady. Not in this weather. And not at this hour.

LADY A: Yes, I am, Phoebe. I am going to Mount Stanning with you to see this bailiff, and to pay and dismiss him myself.

PHOEBE: But why, my lady?

LADY A: I have set my heart on it. I will go and pay this debt myself. I am going to help a favorite servant. Come along. It's not more than three miles to Mount Stanning. We can do that easily in less than an hour.

(FADE OUT. FULL UP OUTDOORS. NIGHT. WIND BLOWING STRONGLY)

LADY A: (*shouting above wind*) There's a light still in the public bar. Your husband hasn't gone to bed?

PHOEBE: (*shouting above wind*) No, Luke will still be drinking with that bailiff man.

LADY A: (*shouting above wind*) There's no other light on. I suppose Mr Audley is in bed and asleep?

PHOEBE: (*shouting above wind*) I suppose so, my lady.

LADY A:	(*shouting above wind*) You're sure he's staying in the inn tonight?
PHOEBE:	(*shouting above wind*) Oh yes, my lady. I helped the girl get his room ready before I came to you.

(FADE OUT. FADE IN. PUB PARLOUR)

LUKE:	(*drunk*) So you're back, are you? Not before time. Our Mr Bailiff here has been keeping me company.
BAILIFF:	How de do, ma'am.
PHOEBE:	Never fear, Luke, our debt will be paid. I've brought her ladyship with me. She's going to settle this business for us.
LUKE:	Lady Audley is here?
LADY A:	(*remote, advancing*) I certainly am, Luke Marks. I have come to pay this man, and send him about his business.
LUKE:	You might have given the money to Phoebe. We don't want no fine ladies up here, pokin' their precious noses into everything.
PHOEBE:	Luke! When her ladyship has been so kind.
LUKE:	Damn her kindness. She won't get no snivelling gratitude from me. Whatever she does, it's because she obliged to do it. What I know...

LADY A: Stop! I didn't come up here in the dead of night to lIsten to your insolence. You – bailiff – how much is this debt?

BAILIFF: Nine pound, your ladyship.

(COINS ON TABLE)

LADY A: There. Please provide me with a receipt.

BAILIFF: Certainly, my lady. At once.

(PEN SCRATCHING ON PAPER)

LADY A: Thank you. You may go.

BAILIFF: *(retreating)* Of course. At once. Goodnight, my lady.

LUKE: *(retreating)* You have the back bedroom. I'll light your way upstairs.

(DOOR CLOSES)

LADY A: Phoebe, I think I'm going to faint. Where can I get some cold water?

PHOEBE: I'll run and get you a glass.

LADY A: No, no. I'll get it myself. I must dip my head in a basin of water, if I want to stop myself fainting. Tell me, what room is Mr Audley sleeping in?

PHOEBE: It was number three I got ready, my lady – the front room – the room next to ours.

LADY A: Will your husband be in your room?

PHOEBE: Certainly not, my lady. His bed is in the attic, when he's in that state. He'll be fast asleep by now.

LADY A: In that case give me a candle. I'll go into your room and get some water for my head. *(retreating)* Stay where you are.

(DOOR OPENS AND CLOSES. FADE IN)

LADY A: It is terribly late, Phoebe. You will see me back to Audley Court, won't you?

PHOEBE: Of course, my lady. But where's the candle? Have you left it upstairs?

LADY A: It blew out as I was coming out of your room. I put it back on your dresser. Now do come along. It's past two o'clock.

PHOEBE: I'll just get my coat, my lady. Give me a moment.

(FADE OUT. FADE IN EXTERIOR, NIGHT. WIND BLOWING)

PHOEBE: My lady, my lady. Look. No there! Look there! Beyond the trees. That light in the sky.

LADY A: Yes. I see it. What is it?

PHOEBE: It's a fire – a fire, my lady. It's at Mount Stanning. It's the Castle Inn that's on fire. I know it is. I know it. I knew this would happen one day. There'll be life lost this night. There's Luke too tipsy to help himself. There's Mr Audley asleep... (*suddenly realises*) Oh my God! Say it's not true, my lady. Say it's not true. It's too horrible. Too horrible...

LADY A: What's too horrible?

PHOEBE: The thought that's in my mind. The terrible thought that's in my mind.

(FADE UP MUSIC BENEATH FOLLOWING)

Oh, God forgive me if I'm wrong. Why did you insist on coming up to the inn tonight – you who are so bitter against Mr Audley and Luke, you who knew they were both under that roof? Oh, tell me that I do you a cruel wrong, my lady. Tell me. For as there is a heaven above me, I think you came to the inn tonight on purpose to set fire to it. Tell me that I'm wrong, my lady. Tell me that I'm doing you a wicked wrong.

(UP MUSIC. HOLD A LITTLE. DOWN FOR FOLLOWING AND LOSE. CROCKERY, CUTLERY)

ALICIA: What a morning, father. We can't go riding in the pouring rain.

SIR MICHAEL: No, I'm afraid there's no riding today. I'm sorry to disappoint you both.

LADY A:	It's just as well, my love. I'm really not feeling very well today.
ALICIA:	And there's no chance of any callers to raise our spirits – unless my cousin Robert comes crawling through the wet from Mount Stanning. Knowing him, he's quite likely to.
SIR MICHAEL:	I'm not too sure that Robert should be allowed into Audley Court. He has taken all sorts of absurd ideas into his head, and he has quite alarmed my lady wife – hasn't he, my dear?
LADY A:	It's best not to say too much about it as yet. Alicia knows what I think.
ALICIA:	Yes, my lady thinks Robert is going insane. I am afraid I don't agree. Odd he may be – crazy he is not.

(FRONT DOORBELL JANGLES IN DISTANCE)

	Good gracious me. I do believe we have a visitor, despite the weather.
SIR MICHAEL:	Lucy! Lucy, my darling. What is the matter?
LADY A:	I told you I was unwell. I think I shall faint.
SIR MICHAEL:	Alicia, look to my lady.
ALICIA:	Yes, papa. I have *sal volatile* in my purse. That will revive her.

(KNOCK ON DOOR, DOOR OPENS)

BUTLER: *(remote)* Mr Robert Audley.

ALICIA: Too late. She *has* fainted.

(FADE IN)

ROBERT: I trust you have recovered, Lady Audley.

LADY A: Not fully. But say what you have to say. You asked to speak with me in private, and I have consented, much against my husband's better judgement. But I wish to spare him the sort of unpleasantness you subjected me to yesterday.

ROBERT: Lady Audley, there was a fire last night at the Castle Inn. It was in fact burnt to the ground. Do you know how I escaped meeting my death?

LADY A: Pray enlighten me.

ROBERT: I escaped because, most providentially, I decided not to sleep in the room that had been prepared for me. When I was shown into it, it struck me as damp and chilly, and the fire was smoking abominably. I decided to pass the night in the ground-floor sitting room – a cheerful, warm room with a most comfortable sofa. I was awakened by the servants calling "Fire", and was easily able to escape into the grounds.

LADY A: Providential indeed.

ROBERT: And who was responsible for the destruction of the Castle Inn?

LADY A: You ask me?

ROBERT: I do, for you know precisely who bears the guilt for that wanton act. It is you, Lady Audley. You. It was your murderous hand that kindled those flames. You wanted me dead, and you committed a monstrous act, regardless of the number of other lives that might be lost in the inferno that you created. As it chances, and by the grace of God, no life was lost in last night's fire, though that poor drunken wretch, Luke Marks, was badly burnt and now lies in a precarious state in his mother's cottage.

LADY A: Well, then, there's no harm done – except to a rickety old building long overdue for destruction.

ROBERT: Lady Audley, you are a woman without heart and without conscience. After last night's terrible deed I should not be surprised at any crime, however horrible, you might be found guilty of. I have sworn to bring the murderer of your first husband to justice, and by heaven nothing shall divert me from doing so. Now listen to me. Unless you confess, in the presence of the man you have deceived so long, who you are, and what you have done, I swear to you I will bring here, to Audley Court, the witnesses who will testify as to your identity and bring upon you the just and awful punishment for your crimes.

LADY A:	All right, all right. You win, Robert Audley. Bring Sir Michael. Bring him, and I will confess anything – everything. What do I care? But your victory – it's hollow. All you have done is to triumph over a lunatic. Oh yes, I murdered your friend, but I'm insane. Bring Sir Michael, bring him quickly. Let him be told the secret of my life.

(FADE IN)

SIR MICHAEL:	*(remote, approaching)* But what's this all about, Robert? My wife told me how you frightened her with tales of murder here in Audley Court. I was very surprised when she agreed to speak with you privately.
ROBERT:	Sir Michael, Lady Audley has something to confess to you. What she has to say will cause you the most bitter grief. But, sir, you must hear it, if only for the sake of your present honour and your future peace. I pray that God may soften this blow for you.
SIR MICHAEL:	What is this, Lucy? What nonsense is Robert is talking now?
LADY A:	Not nonsense, Michael. I do indeed have things to confess. I'd be sorry for you if I could, for you have been very, very good to me – much better than I deserved. But I can't. I can feel nothing – nothing but my own misery. Other people's feelings mean nothing to me.
SIR MICHAEL:	Lucy!

LADY A: Let me continue. I never knew my mother. I was brought up by a woman who fostered me. I was about ten when my father removed me to an orphanage, and that is when I learned that my real mother was locked up in a lunatic asylum, and would never be released. When I was seventeen, my father retired from the army on half-pay, and took me to the other end of England – to Wildernsea. We lived there in poverty, until one day a wealthy suitor called George Talboys appeared. He was the only son of a rich country gentleman, and an officer in a distinguished regiment stationed nearby. He fell in love with me, and married me three months after my seventeenth birthday. I think I loved him as much as it was in my power to love anybody. Not as much as I have loved you, Michael, because when you married me, you raised me to a position he could never have given me.

SIR MICHAEL: *(devastated)* Lucy – oh, Lucy!

LADY A: Yes, I loved George while the money lasted – but his father had disapproved of our marriage and cut off his allowance. We travelled on the continent in great style for a few months, but when we returned to Wildernsea we were reduced to penury. All the time I was pregnant, George tried to find work, but without success. When our son was born, George became utterly despondent. One day we had a terrible argument, and he ran out of the house. The next morning I woke to find a letter by my bed. George had taken himself off to Australia to seek his fortune. He would return when he was a rich man. I had been deserted, and people pitied me. I hated them for their pity. It was during this time, I think, that I crossed the line from sanity to madness. I became subject to deep bouts of depression. It was during one of these dark periods that I decided to cast off my old life and start a completely new one as a new person.

ROBERT: So you answered Mrs Vincent's advertisement, and presented yourself to her as Lucy Graham. And from her establishment you came here to Mr Dawson's family in Audley.

SIR MICHAEL: But how could you agree to marry me when you were already married?

LADY A: Three years had passed, and I had received no news of my husband, not a word. I told myself that I had a right to believe him dead – or at least that he wanted me to believe him dead. Why should his shadow stand in the way of my future happiness?

ROBERT: And then you saw in the newspaper that George Talboys was on his way back to England.

LADY A: I had believed myself cured of my madness – but fate had determined otherwise. Fate would not allow me to be sane. I knew that George Talboys would turn every stone to discover my whereabouts, unless I could convince him that his wife, Helen, was dead. My father was living in Southampton with my son. The ship carrying George Talboys was due to dock in about three week's when I went to Southampton and told my father everything – how I was now Lady Audley, and that money was no longer a problem. He agreed to help me. He told me that his landlady's daughter, Matilda, a young woman of about my age, was dying of consumption in an upstairs bedroom. The doctor had said she was at death's door, and could not last more than a week or two.

I will not dwell on the details. I bought Matilda's mother. I gave her more money than she had ever seen in her lifetime, and she released her dying daughter into our care. My father travelled to Ventnor, in the Isle of Wight, and took lodgings for his invalid daughter and her little boy. Early the next morning he carried over the dying girl and Georgie, who'd been told – no, bribed – to call her "Mama". She entered the lodging house as Mrs Talboys. When she died a few days later, her death and burial were registered in that name. And it was the news of this death that we announced in The Times. When George Talboys visited Ventnor, he ordered the tombstone which records the death of his wife, Helen.

SIR MICHAEL: I can hear no more. If there is more to be told…

ROBERT: There is, uncle. There is.

SIR MICHAEL: …then I cannot hear it. Robert, I must ask you to take on the task of providing for the safety and comfort of this lady, whom I had thought to be my wife. I want to know nothing more. I cannot say farewell to her.

LADY A: Michael!

SIR MICHAEL: (*retreating*) I can only pray that God may pity her.

NARRATOR: Sir Michael walked slowly from the room. He ordered his valet to pack a portmanteau, and to be ready to accompany his master by the last train that night to London.

(FADE IN. INTERIOR)

ROBERT: Hullo, cousin Alicia. I've been looking for you.

ALICIA: Well, now you've found me. And I'm starving hungry. It's way past dinner time. What has happened down in the kitchen? Go and find papa, will you, and ask him to come to dinner.

ROBERT: Alicia, something *has* happened – something rather serious.

ALICIA: Is papa all right?

ROBERT: He is perfectly well, but he has suffered a great grief.

ALICIA: A grief? Oh, Robert, what has happened?

ROBERT: Alicia, my dear, I can give you no details just at the moment – but may I ask you to be a comfort and a friend to your poor father, who is under a very heavy affliction?

ALICIA: Need you ask? What is it you want me to do?

ROBERT: Your father has told me that he is leaving Audley Court today. He has not told me where he is going – but he must not go alone, must he?

ALICIA: Of course not. But surely Lady Audley...

ROBERT: Lady Audley will not be going with him. He is about to separate himself from her.

ALICIA: I don't quite... You mean for a period?

ROBERT: I mean for ever.

ALICIA: Then this grief you speak of...

ROBERT: Is connected with her. Lady Audley is the cause of your father's sorrow. More I cannot tell you at the moment. Please trust me.

ALICIA: I will. Poor, poor Papa. Of course I'll go with him, to be with him and comfort him – wherever he chooses to go.

(FADE OUT. FULL UP. INTERIOR. KNOCK ON DOOR. DOOR OPENS)

BUTLER: *(remote)* Dr Alwyn Mosgrove.

ROBERT: Dr Mosgrove. How very good of you to come – and at such short notice.

(DOOR CLOSES)

MOSGROVE: *(remote, advancing)* I caught the early train from London. Our mutual friend, Mr Wilmington, said that your telegram indicated that it was a matter of some urgency – indeed danger.

ROBERT: Indeed it is.

MOSGROVE: It is not about your own mental health you wish to consult me?

ROBERT: Oh no. I am about to seek your professional help in a most difficult case. Am I correct in assuming that any revelations made by a patient to a physician are sacred, never to be revealed under any circumstances?

MOSGROVE: Quite correct.

NARRATOR: Robert Audley drew his chair nearer to the doctor's, and began the story which Lady Audley had told the previous night. Dr Mosgrove listened carefully, betraying no surprise as it proceeded to its end.

MOSGROVE: I take it you would wish to prove that the lady is insane, and therefore not responsible for her actions?

ROBERT: You are right, Dr Mosgrove. I would prefer to find that excuse for what she has done to the disgrace of criminal charges and a court of law.

MOSGROVE: Then I fear I shall be of no use to you. I will see the lady, if you wish, but I do not believe that she is mad. She has exhibited nothing but cold, clever self-interested calculation is everything that she has done.

ROBERT: But her mother...

MOSGROVE: Madness is not necessarily transmitted from mother to daughter. No, no, I see no signs of insanity is what you have told me. Nor do I believe that any jury in England would accept such a plea in this case. The best thing you can do with this lady is to send her back to her first husband.

ROBERT: Her first husband has been missing for some time, and I have reason to believe he is dead.

MOSGROVE: Mr Audley, there must be no half-confidences between us. You have not told me everything. What has become of the first husband?

ROBERT: I last saw him on the morning that I went fishing, and that he took himself off to Audley Court. I never saw him again, though I went on a wild-goose chase to Southampton and Liverpool in search of him. I believe that Lady Audley's father was again bribed to tell me that my friend had visited him and said he was leaving for Australia.

I believe he was murdered, and lies buried here in the grounds of Audley Court.

MOSGROVE: Thank you. I will see the lady now, and then I must travel back to London. I will, of course, give you my opinion before I leave.

(FADE OUT. FADE IN)

MOSGROVE: I have talked to the lady. She is not insane, but she certainly has the hereditary taint of lunacy in her blood. She has the cunning of madness with the prudence of intelligence. I will tell you what she is, Mr Audley. She is dangerous. Now you suspect that she somehow contrived to murder your friend, but you have no proof. If you *were* able to prove that the lady murdered your friend, then I should certainly not be able to assist you in removing her from the reach of justice. As matters stand, however, I will write on your behalf to a colleague in Belgium. You have a pocket-book?

ROBERT: Indeed I have. What would you have me write?

MOSGROVE: Simply this: "Monsieur Val, Maison de Santé, Villebrumeuse, Belgium". Monsieur Val is the owner and medical superintendent of an exclusive and highly secure clinic in the town of Villebrumeuese. We have known each other for many years. If you travel to Belgium with the lady, he will have received my communication and will doubtless welcome her into his establishment. She would be well cared for.

ROBERT: Dr Mosgrove, how can I thank you sufficiently.

MOSGROVE: You must understand that from the moment she enters Monsieur Val's clinic, she will be shut away from the world. Her life will be virtually over. Her secrets will remain secret. But whatever crimes she may have committed, she will be able to commit no more.

ROBERT: I understand.

MOSGROVE: I would add only this. In my professional judgement you could do no better service to the world than to commit her to my friend's care. The woman I saw ten minutes ago cannot be trusted to live freely in society. If she could have sprung at my throat and strangled me with her bare hands, she would have done so.

ROBERT: She suspected your purpose. then?

MOSGROVE: She knew it. "You think I am insane like my mother," she said, "and you want to lock me up." Mr Audley, the sooner you can get her to Monsieur Val at Villebrumeuse the better.

(FADE OUT. FADE IN)

ROBERT: Ah, monsieur Val.

VAL: (*remote, advancing*) Good afternoon, Mr Audley. Welcome, madam. to my maison de santé.

LADY A: Maison de santé? Is that what you call it in Belgium? In England, monsieur, we know it as a lunatic asylum, a mad-house.

VAL: But no, my dear lady, I assure you. This is an extremely select and superior establishment. Here you will be housed with every luxury. Your comfort and your health will be our first concern. You will have an attendant entirely devoted to your service

LADY A: And my freedom?

VAL: There are no locks on our doors. You may go where you will within the house and the grounds.

LADY A: So I may wander down to town from time to time and visit the shops?

VAL: That, I regret, will not be possible.

LADY A: You mean that I will never again be permitted to venture outside the walls that surround this place?

VAL: A rule, madam, that applies **to** each and every one of our guests.

ROBERT: (*whispers*) Your name here is Madam Taylor. I did not think you would wish to be known by your real name.

LADY A: Monsieur Val, leave me alone with this man who has brought me here.

VAL: *(retreating)* As you wish, madam. As you wish.

(DOOR OPENS AND SHUTS)

LADY A: Mr Audley, you have brought me to a living grave.

ROBERT: I have done what I considered just to others and merciful to you. After the fire at Castle Inn and the disappearance of George Talboys, you could not be allowed to remain at liberty. For the sake of my dear uncle, I have not placed the matter in the hands of the police, for assuredly you would have been brought to trial. In place of an English jail, or possibly the gallows, I have brought you to a place where you will be treated kindly by people who have no knowledge of you or your crimes. You will live a quiet and peaceful life, my lady. All I can say to you is live here – and repent. Above all, repent.

LADY A: Much good may repentance do. Repentance wlll not bring back the dead. Do you know what I have in my mind, as you stand before me? I have the picture of George Talboys, the last time I saw him. You said that you would uproot every tree in the grounds to find the body of your friend. There is no need to do that. The body of George Talboys lies at the bottom of the old well.

ROBERT: God in heaven! You did murder him!

LADY A: I knew he would come to see me. I met him in the lime walk, prepared to bribe him, cajole him, defy him – do anything rather than give up the wealth and position that I had won. He declared his undying love for me, and said that nothing on this earth would prevent him from reclaiming me as his lawful wife. What he did not know was the taint that lay hidden within me – that it was possible to drive me to madness. We were seated on the side of the well, facing each other. When nothing I said moved him an inch, when he insisted that he would bring people to Audley to prove who I really was, when he had goaded me beyond endurance, I stood up and pushed him over the edge.

GEORGE: (*long loud cry on echo; echo stronger as cry fades*)

LADY A: I saw my first husband tumble into the black mouth of the well. I do not know how deep it is, but it must be dry, because I heard no splash, only a heavy, dull thud. I knelt down and listened. The cry was not repeated, nor was there any sound at all. So that is the last resting place of George Talboys...

ROBERT: I cannot remain here. Let me pass.

LADY A: ...and, of course, I wrote to my father in Southampton, telling him to put you on a false trail. You see how I confess everything to you? I have nothing to fear. The law could pronounce no worse sentence than this – life-long imprisonment in a mad-house. In any case, I know full well that you dare not use it against me – you know it would kill your uncle to see me charged with murder in a court of law.

ROBERT: Out of my way!

(DOOR OPENS AND BANGS SHUT)

SIR MICHAEL: *(reads as from letter)* My dear Robert – You will require money in arranging for the comfort of the person I committed to your care. I need scarcely tell you to spare no expense. But perhaps I should mention, for the first and the last time, that I wish never again to hear that person's name, or to know anything about what you have done for her. I am sure that you will act conscientiously and mercifully...

(CROSSFADE)

ALICIA: *(reads as from letter)* Dear Cousin Robert – Luke Marks, the man you saved from the fire at Castle Inn, lies in a very perilous state in his mother's house, not far from Audley Court. He is not expected to live for many days. His wife, Phoebe, is nursing him, and both of them have expressed a most earnest desire that you see him before he dies. Pray come without delay. Your loving cousin, Alicia.

(FADE OUT. EXTERIOR, NIGHT, KNOCK ON FRONT DOOR. DOOR OPENS)

PHOEBE: Oh, Mr Audley, sir. You've come.

ROBERT: I hope I'm not too late, Mrs Marks?

PHOEBE: Happily, sir, not. Luke is sinking fast, but the doctor says he has a day or two yet. Do come in, sir, please.

(DOOR CLOSES)

(*confidentially*) Sir, may I have just a word with you before I take you into Luke?

ROBERT: Of course.

PHOEBE: You know what I told you when I found you safe and well after the night of the fire – what I suspected? What I think still?

ROBERT: I remember.

PHOEBE: I never breathed a word of it to anyone – not even to Luke. He doesn't suspect what I suspect. I beg you not to let a word drop before him.

ROBERT: Yes, yes, I understand. I'll be careful.

PHOEBE: Then, if you'll come along here, sir.

(DOOR OPENS)

(*calls*) Luke, see who has come to call on you.

LUKE: (*weak*) Is that you, Mr Audley?

ROBERT: It surely is, Luke. How do I find you?

LUKE: Not well, sir – but very anxious to speak with you. You, girl, I don't want you. You've got no call to hear what I've got to say. I only want Mr Audley. You get out, Phoebe.

PHOEBE: As you wish, Luke. As you wish.

(DOOR CLOSES)

LUKE: Come closer, sir. Come closer. Now I've never had no call to be grateful to gentle folk. They use us country people like slaves, and toss us aside when they done with us. But when a gentleman goes and puts his own life in danger to save a drunken brute like me – well, the drunken brute is grateful. Sir, may I take your hand to say thank you?

ROBERT: You may, Luke, though I need no thanks. Here it is.

LUKE: There is something else, sir – something else I need to tell you before it's too late.

ROBERT: I am listening.

LUKE: You was uncommon fond of that Mr Talboys, I've heard say, sir.

ROBERT: Indeed I was. But I cannot talk about this with you, Luke. It is too painful.

LUKE: But suppose I can't die with a secret on my mind?

Suppose I've asked to see you on purpose that I might tell it to you?

ROBERT: What secret, Luke? What are you speaking of?

LUKE: Do you see that biscuit tin? There on the shelf? Take it down. Open it. What do you find?

ROBERT: Two pieces of folded paper. Torn from a notebook, I'd say.

LUKE: Unfold them. Read them.

(FADE IN)

GEORGE: *(reads as from letter)* Robert, my dear friend – I write in utter confusion of mind. Something has happened which will drive me from England a broken-hearted man. If your friendship could have done me any good, I would have appealed to it. But nothing can help me. All I can say is God bless you for the past, and teach you to forget me in the future. Your true friend. George Talboys.

(FADE OUT. FULL UP)

LUKE: The other. Read the other.

(FADE IN)

GEORGE: *(reads as from letter)* Helen – May God pity and forgive you for what you have done today, as truly as I do. You shall never hear of me again. To you and to the world I shall be what you wished me to be today. I leave England, never to return. George Talboys.

(FADE OUT. FULL UP)

ROBERT: I don't understand. Luke, where did you obtain these letters? They purport to be written by my friend, but they are not in his hand. These weren't written by George Talboys.

LUKE: Oh indeed they were, Mr Audley. They were written by Mr Talboys, in my presence. They are indeed in his hand – but his left hand. He couldn't use his right, because his arm was broken.

ROBERT: So George is alive! God be praised! Tell me – tell me all. How was my poor friend saved?

LUKE: I was at work up at Atkinson's farm, last September, helping to stack the last of the corn. As the nearest way from the farm to mother's cottage was through the meadows at the back of Audley Court, I used to come that way. Well, that evening of the seventh, Audley church clock was striking nine, and it was well-nigh dark, when I was passing the well. I was real close to it when I heard a sound that made my blood creep – the groan of a man in pain. At first I was struck all of a heap, but when I heard it again, I began searching in the bushes. After a bit, I found a man hidden under a lot of laurels. It was your friend, Mr Talboys, in a terrible state, and with a broken arm.

ROBERT: Dear God.

LUKE: He told me he'd been sitting on the side of the well, had over-balanced and fallen in. The well was all silted up, and he'd fallen some fifteen feet onto mud and leaves, which had broken his fall.

ROBERT: But how did he get out?

LUKE: There's iron stanchions set into the wall. When he'd come to himself, he used his left hand and clambered up. Well, I helped him to his feet, and together we made our way to this cottage. My mother took care of him, got him cleaned up, washed his clothes, and put him to bed. Next day I took him to the surgeon in Brentwood, and his arm was set in splints and put into a sling. That was when he asked the surgeon for a couple of envelopes, for he had something to write. He tore two pages from his notebook, and wrote the letters you have there in your hand. Then he asks me to come along with him to the railway station, and I sees him off on the train to London. There, I've told you everything. Now my conscience is clear. Now I can die in peace.

               (FADE OUT. FULL UP)

NARRATOR: That evening Robert wrote a long letter, addressed to Madame Taylor, care of Monsieur Val, Villebrumeuse, in which he told the wretched woman the story the dying man had told him. He thought that it might be some comfort for her to know that her husband did not perish by her wicked hand.

(EXTERIOR. KNOCKING ON FRONT DOOR. DOOR OPENS)

MRS PERKINS: Bless my soul! If it isn't Mr Audley!

ROBERT: Indeed it is, Mrs Perkins. And how have chambers been in my absence?

(DOOR CLOSES)

MRS PERKINS: Very quiet, sir. Mind you there's lots of letters waiting in your rooms. And there's more than letters. There's a gentleman who's called several times. He's waited tonight because I said you'd written o say you wanted the rooms aired.

ROBERT: A gentleman, you say. Well, let's see.

(DOOR OPENS)

George, by all that's wonderful!

GEORGE: *(remote)* Robert, my dear, dear friend! You've been away for such a long time.

ROBERT: On private matters, George, which concern you deeply.

(FADE MUSIC BENEATH FOLLOWING, PRESET TO END WITH A FLOURISH AFTER CLOSING ANNOUNCEMENT)

ROBERT: Come, my boy. Let us settle down by this roaring fire, and I'll tell you everything. Mrs Perkins, can we call on you for a good dinner and a bottle of wine?

MRS PERKINS: You certainly can, sir. I'll bring the wine straight away, and you'll have your dinner within the hour.

ROBERT: Yes, George, we have a great deal to discuss. Sit yourself down, my friend. How good it is to see you there, for I thought you dead. Everything led me to believe you dead, and not only dead, but murdered...*[but do you know, first of all I went searching for you...]*

(UP MUSIC. DOWN FOR CLOSING ANNOUNCEMENT. UP MUSIC TO END)

THE FATAL CYPHER

BY JACQUES FUTRELLE

DRAMATISED FOR RADIO
BY NEVILLE TELLER

Running time: 30'

FIRST BROADCAST ACROSS THE USA
ON 24 OCTOBER 2018
IN A PRODUCTION BY SHOESTRING
RADIO THEATRE, SAN FRANCISCO
DIRECTED BY KATHERINE DOMINICI

CHARACTERS IN
ORDER OF APPEARANCE

RANSOME Mid-40s A doctor. Professional friendly manner.

VAN DUSEN Mid-50s, A super intelligence. Described as "wizened" but with "an enormous head". Impatient and rather dismissive of people who can't keep up with him. You can almost hear that brain working.

FIELDING Mid-40s. Professional man.

MARTHA Early 60s. Typical African-American servant of the 1900s. Feisty. She's probably the only one who can manage Van Dusen – or dares to.

WARDEN Late-40s. Prison governor. Pretty much a disciplinarian, but a reasonable man. A friend of Ransome, so he deals more gently with him.

SCOTT 50s. A jailor with years of experience, who's seen it all. Born and bred in New England.

ELEANOR HATCH Mid-30s. A hard-boiled woman journalist who's fought her way up in a man's world. There weren't all that number around in 1900, but those who'd made it were good! Resourceful, in control of the situation – and always out for a story.

ELIZABETH: But what does it all mean, Professor?

VAN DUSEN: They may call me the Thinking Machine, Miss Devan, but that doesn't mean I can come up with an immediate answer to every problem.

ELIZABETH: I'm sorry, Professor Van Dusen.

VAN DUSEN: No, no, Miss Devan. I don't imply that the problem is insoluble – or indeed that I shan't be able to solve it in due course. But before we have another look at this letter, perhaps you'd tell me exactly how it came into your possession.

ELIZABETH: It was found in the pocket of my adopted father, Pomeroy Stockton, when we discovered his dead body just nine days ago.

VAN DUSEN: Good gracious – you're the adopted daughter of Pomeroy Stockton?

ELIZABETH: You knew him?

VAN DUSEN: I knew of him. A most unusual man. He was an inventor of sorts, wasn't he? I believe he was working to discover the secret of hardened copper.

ELIZABETH: That's right, professor. He went on an archaeological tour of Egypt in 1902, and discovered that the secret of hardened copper – which had been known to the ancient Egyptians – had been lost. He came back absolutely determined to rediscover it. That's what he'd been working on for the past four years.

VAN DUSEN: And you say you found his dead body?

ELIZABETH: Together with Parker, our butler. I telephoned Mr Stockton's son, John, at once. Mr Stockton was a widower. John was his only child.

VAN DUSEN: And you?

ELIZABETH: My parents were great friends of the Stocktons. I was only five when they were both killed in a yachting accident. Mr and Mrs Stockton adopted me.

VAN DUSEN: And John Stockton – what does he do?

ELIZABETH: He's a junior partner in Dutton and Stockton – the leather manufacturers, you know. He must be quite wealthy. He gives a great deal to charity.

VAN DUSEN: (*thoughtful*) I see. Please continue.

ELIZABETH: Well Father – he was always Father to me – worked most of the time in a small workshop on the ground floor of his house. He'd built it on to the back. There were furnaces, moulds – that sort of thing. And he always worked with the door locked. He wouldn't allow anyone in that room, not even his son. Each time John tried, he was barred from entering, and there was a quarrel. I often heard the two of them arguing. They both had quick tempers, and finally John packed up his belongings, left the house and took lodgings nearby.

VAN DUSEN: I see. And you never entered the workshop?

ELEANOR: Rarely. I acted as father's secretary. I had an office on the first floor.

VAN DUSEN: Please continue, Miss Devan,

ELIZABETH: Well from that time until Monday a week ago John never came to the house, as far as I know. On that Monday, though, at about five in the afternoon, he appeared at the front door. He had a key, but he did knock. Of course he was admitted, but none of the servants saw him leave. That evening Father didn't come out for dinner at 6.30. Mind you, that wasn't unusual for him – he often missed meals when he was immersed in his work.

VAN DUSEN: And next morning?

ELIZABETH: Next morning we found Father dead in his workshop.

VAN DUSEN: What precisely occurred?

(FADE IN)

PARKER: (remote, advancing) I'm afraid there's something wrong. Miss Devan.

ELIZABETH: How do you mean, Parker, "something wrong"?

PARKER: Betty came to see me a few minutes ago, Miss. I understand Mr Stockton's bed wasn't slept in, last night.

ELIZABETH: Well, perhaps he fell asleep in the workshop?

PARKER: That is a possibility, Miss. But there's something else. He didn't come out for dinner last night.

ELIZABETH: He does sometimes get tied up in his work, Let's go and see.

(QUICK FADE OUT. FADE IN. KNOCKING ON DOOR. THEN RATTLING OF DOOR KNOB)

ELIZABETH: Father! Father, are you there? Oh, dear. Of course, it's locked. It always is. Parker, I'm afraid I'll have to ask you to…

PARKER: Yes, yes, Miss. I think I'll have to. Stand away, Miss, if you please. Just a little further.

(WOODEN DOOR SMASHED IN)

ELIZABETH: Father was sitting upright in his chair by one of the furnaces. Smashed on the floor, just by him, was a small bottle of prussic acid. He was dead. I immediately telephoned to his son, John. He came round in just a few minutes. We found this letter in Father's pocket.

VAN DUSEN: Yes, I see. Well, now, let's have another look at it.

ELIZABETH: It reads ... very oddly.

VAN DUSEN: It certainly does. Now let's see:

(PAPER RUSTLES. FADE IN)

OLD STOCKTON: "To those concerned. Tired of it all, I seek the end, and am content. Ambition is now dead; the grave yawns greedily at my feet. And with the labour of my own hands lost, I greet death of my own will, by my own act. To my son I leave all, and you who maligned me, you who discouraged me, you may read this and know I punish you thus. It's for him, my son, to forgive.

I dared in life, and dare dead your everlasting anger. Not alone that you didn't speak, but that you cherished secret, and my ears are locked forever against you. My vault is my resting place. On the brightest and dearest page of life I wrote (7) my love for him. Family ties, binding as the Bible itself, bade me give all to my son. Goodbye, I die. Pomeroy Stockton.

(FADE OUT. FULL UP)

VAN DUSEN: Yes, there are several oddities about that. What do you make of "Not alone that you didn't speak, but that you cherished secret"? What does that mean?

ELIZABETH: Perhaps he missed a word out in his hurry? Perhaps he meant "you cherished secret enmity" – or something like that?

VAN DUSEN: Perhaps. And then there's that peculiar number 7, suddenly inserted in the middle of a sentence. "On the brightest and dearest page of life I wrote (7) my love for him." What is that all about? Tell me, what did John Stockton make of it?

ELIZABETH: He no sooner began to read the letter than he started to tear it up. You can see where.

VAN DUSEN: Oh yes.

ELIZABETH: I persuaded him to give it to me, but he did so only because I promised to destroy it myself after I'd gone through it. The next day he asked if I had. But the more I read it, the more disturbed I became. I just have a feeling that there's something…not quite right about it. I told John I'd burnt the letter, but I'd already decided to bring it to you for your opinion. I think my father may have been forced into writing it.

VAN DUSEN: Really?

ELIZABETH: I do. I've been imagining every kind of ghastly, horrible mystery behind it.

VAN DUSEN: Tell me – was there an autopsy?

ELIZABETH: No. John wanted no fuss and he certainly didn't want the police involved. Father was buried on a death certificate issued by an old friend of John's – a Dr Benton. The possibility of suicide or anything else was buried along with him.

VAN DUSEN: Did Mr Stockton leave a will?

ELIZABETH: Yes. It's to be read in a day or two. It's with his lawyer, a Mr Sloane.

VAN DUSEN: There's another possibility, you know. Perhaps Pomeroy Stockton never saw this letter at all. Perhaps it's a forgery. You did say you found it after John Stockton had arrived.

ELIZABETH: Forgery? Then John...[only pretended to find it in Father's pocket?...]

VAN DUSEN: Whatever it is, forgery or genuine, it's a most extraordinary document – almost poetry. It says things in such a roundabout way.

ELIZABETH: Perhaps there's a cipher in it? A message in code?

VAN DUSEN: Miss Devan, I'm pretty sure you've hit the nail on the head. There *is* a cipher in it.

(FADE IN)

ELEANOR: A cipher, Professor? How exciting. Do let me see.

VAN DUSEN: On one condition, Miss Hatch. Nothing of this must get into your newspaper for the present.

ELEANOR: Professor Van Dusen, I'm a journalist...

VAN DUSEN: I know that only too well, Miss Hatch. All I'm doing at the moment is seeking your help in solving a puzzle. I promise you that if, or when, something newsworthy emerges from our investigation, you will be the first to have the details.

ELEANOR: I suppose I must content myself with that. Now may I see the letter?

VAN DUSEN: Certainly. What do you make of that?

ELEANOR: (*reading, absorbed*) Yes ... very strange ... what an odd way to put things ..."with the labour of my own hands lost I greet death of my own will..." There's a much simpler way of saying that.

VAN DUSEN: The problem is that at some points sense goes out of the window altogether.

ELEANOR: (*reading, absorbed*) Yes...I see what you mean... "not alone that you didn't speak, but that you cherished secret..." What can that mean?

VAN DUSEN: There's something even odder a little way down.

ELEANOR: Yes, I see it. What's that "7" in brackets doing in the middle of the sentence. "On the brightest and dearest page of life I wrote (7) my love for him." It doesn't make sense. There can only be a hidden meaning to it all.

VAN DUSEN: Miss Hatch – Eleanor – I want you to go and interview John Stockton. I need to know how he benefits from his father's will. Also I'm pretty sure there's some personal enmity between him and Miss Devan. Try to find out what that's all about. When you've done that, please go to the Stockton residence in Dorchester and ask Miss Devan to let me see the family Bible. I'm almost sure there is one, and it's probably rather large.

ELEANOR: That's quite a programme, Professor. I'd better get started.

(FADE OUT. FULL UP)

STOCKTON: I've agreed to see you, Miss Hatch, but I had hoped this matter wouldn't come to the attention of the Press. It can only bring disgrace on my poor father's memory.

ELEANOR: If or when I write about this affair, Mr Stockton, I can assure you that I will respect your father and his scientific achievements. Could you tell me how much your father's estate amounted to?

STOCKTON: More than a million. He made most of it through his device for coupling railroad cars. It's now in use across the States.

ELEANOR: How will his property be divided?

STOCKTON: Well, I haven't seen his will, but I understand that the bulk is left to me. Elizabeth Devan, his adopted daughter, will get an annuity and the home in Dorchester.

ELEANOR: Where is this will now?

STOCKTON: I gather it's in the hands of my father's attorney – Mr Sloan. It was to have been read today, but that's been postponed for a few days.

ELEANOR: Excuse me for speaking bluntly, Mr Stockton, but why did you go to great lengths to make it seem your father died naturally, when all the signs point to suicide?

STOCKTON: Obviously to save the family name from disgrace.

ELEANOR: Of course, there's always the possibility of something else.

STOCKTON: Something else? What on earth do you mean, Miss Hatch? What else?

ELEANOR: Miss Devan has produced the letter found on your father, and has said... [she thinks it could point to ...]

STOCKTON: Miss Devan!... Elizabeth!... She promised me she'd destroy that letter. She's crazy. What motive could there possibly be for anyone to kill my father?

ELEANOR: Tell me, Mr Stockton, what's the reason for the ill-feeling between you and Miss Devan?

STOCKTON: We just never got along together, that's all. My father and I had several arguments about her.

ELEANOR: Was one of them on the night before he was found dead?

STOCKTON: Something was said about her.

ELEANOR: When did you leave your father's workshop that night?

STOCKTON: About ten o'clock.

ELEANOR: And you'd been with him since the afternoon?

STOCKTON: That's right.

ELEANOR: No dinner?

STOCKTON: No. We were deep in discussion about a recent invention of my father's that he wanted me to put on the market.

ELEANOR: The fact that he wanted you to take control – could that have pointed to his suicide later that night?

STOCKTON: I suppose so – but I saw no sign of it myself.

ELEANOR: One last question, Mr Stockton. Did your father's house contain a large family Bible?

STOCKTON: Yes, I know it well. I'm sure it's still around somewhere...

(FADE OUT. FULL UP)

ELIZABETH: The Bible? Yes, it was here the other day, but it's disappeared.

ELEANOR: Since your father's death?

ELIZABETH: Yes, the day after.

ELEANOR: Have you any idea who took it, Miss Devan?

ELIZABETH: I know who took it. John – John Stockton.

ELEANOR: Are you sure?

ELIZABETH: Absolutely certain. I saw it in his apartment, where he'd hidden it.

(FADE OUT. FULL UP)

VAN DUSEN: What was she doing in Stockton's apartment?

ELEANOR: I don't know – unless she thinks he had something to do with her father's death, and is investigating on her own account.

VAN DUSEN: Miss Hatch, I'm afraid I must ask you to verify her story. And if that Bible really is in Mr Stockton's rooms, then either bring it to me or tear out page 7 and bring that. One way or another, there are things about that Bible I need to know.

(FADE OUT. FADE IN)

ELEANOR: I made my way into his apartment – I won't bore you with the details...

VAN DUSEN: Very wise. I cannot condone illegal entry.

ELEANOR: ...and I found the Bible.

VAN DUSEN: Indeed? So Miss Devan was right. And page 7?

ELEANOR: Torn out, missing, gone.

VAN DUSEN: Ah. I'm not in the least surprised. Miss Hatch, would you be kind enough to meet me outside the Stockton residence in Dorchester, tonight, at 10 o'clock sharp?

ELEANOR: Of course.

VAN DUSEN: Please don't be late.

(FADE OUT. FULL UP OLD-FASHIONED DOORBELL RINGING INSIDE HOUSE. PAUSE. HEAVY DOOR OPENS)

ELIZABETH: Professor Van Dusen. Miss Hatch. This is a surprise. How can I help you?

VAN DUSEN: I'm sorry for disturbing you, but Miss Hatch and I wondered if we might examine Mr Stockton's workshop.

ELIZABETH: Of course. Please come in.

(DOOR CLOSES. FOOTSTEPS UNDER FOLLOWING. THEY STOP)

Follow me. It's this way. This is the door. It was usually kept locked, but as you can see, it was broken down. Our butler, Parker, had to break in when we could get no reply from Father.

(DOOR OPENS)

Here we are. Come in. Father was found just there, in that chair. The small bottle of prussic acid was lying broken at his feet.

VAN DUSEN: I see. Is this room precisely as it was when the body was found? Has anything been taken from it?

ELIZABETH: Nothing. Except of course for Father's body, and the bits of the acid bottle. No one has been in here since the police left.

VAN DUSEN: I don't see the door key. Where is it?

ELIZABETH: It was never found. The door was locked when we broke in, but the key was missing.

VAN DUSEN: It's not only the key that's missing. I don't see the pen and ink Mr Stockton used to write his note. Can you see them, Miss Devan?

ELIZABETH: I'm afraid not. No. They're certainly not here.

ELEANOR: Mystery on mystery, professor.

VAN DUSEN: Then we shall have to extend our search of the house. You have no objection, I take it, Miss Devan?

ELIZABETH: Of course not. Please search wherever you wish.

VAN DUSEN: Thank you. Then I don't think we need bother you any further. Miss Hatch and I will be able to proceed on our own.

ELIZABETH: In that case, I will leave you to it. *(retreating)* If you need me, I shall be in my room. Good evening.

ELEANOR: Goodbye, Miss Devan.

(EDGE OUT. FADE IN)

ELEANOR: *(whisper)* This must be the door leading down to the cellar.

(DOOR OPENS)

As I thought.

VAN DUSEN: (*whisper*) I don't suppose they run to electricity down there. Do you have a torch with you? No journalist should be without one.

ELEANOR: It's here, in my shoulder bag. Just ... one... second. Ah!

VAN DUSEN: Right you go first and light the way.

(SLIGHT ECHO, GRADUALLY INCREASING DURING THE FOLLOWING. FEET DESCENDING STONE STAIRS)

ELEANOR: These stairs are very steep. Watch your footing, professor.

VAN DUSEN: I'm alright. Ah. Now, Miss Hatch, shine your torch around the walls. Slowly, now. I'm looking for...

ELEANOR: (*urgent, whisper*) There's someone behind us. I heard someone on the stairs.

VAN DUSEN: (*urgent, whisper*) Then put out the torch, Quickly!

(REVOLVER SHOT)

ELEANOR: (*calls*) Professor – are you hurt?

VAN DUSEN: No they missed. But I saw where the shot came from. Hey! You!

(SCUFFLE)

Got you! No, you don't! Miss Hatch – here! Your torch.

ELEANOR: Mr Stockton!

VAN DUSEN: Ah, so you're John Stockton. At last I have the pleasure of making your acquaintance. Though the circumstances could have been more auspicious.

STOCKTON: Miss Hatch? What on earth are you two doing down here? I thought you were a pair of burglars.

VAN DUSEN: Shoot first, and find out later – eh? Is that your philosophy? May I introduce myself? I am professor Augustus Van Dusen.

STOCKTON: You're the famous Thinking Machine?

VAN DUSEN: That is the absurd title I have been accorded by certain organs of the Press. Miss Hatch is one of the guilty parties. Using my much vaunted intelligence, I deduce that you have entered this house without Miss Devan's knowledge.

STOCKTON: You are correct. I came here on a little personal business, and I certainly did not expect to find you down here in the cellar.

ELIZABETH: *(remote, advancing)* What is going on? I heard a shot. John? What are you doing here? What's happened?

VAN DUSEN: Mr Stockton came here tonight to remove the contents from the locked vault in the cellar. He came without your knowledge, and found that we had arrived ahead of him.

ELIZABETH: Murderer! Thief!

VAN DUSEN: Do you know what he wanted from the vault?

ELIZABETH: I can guess. The secret of Father's last invention. Father refused to give it to him, so he killed him. Now he's come back to steal it. How did you get Father to write that letter?

STOCKTON: Elizabeth, for God's sake what are you saying?

ELIZABETH: The truth, at last. You never wanted me to have even a small part of Father's estate. You wanted the lot.

STOCKTON: Elizabeth.

VAN DUSEN: Miss Devan, what do you know about this secret vault?

ELIZABETH: Well nothing, really. I've always thought there must be some sort of safe in the house, because I knew that my father disposed of his most important documents somewhere. The cellar is the obvious place.

VAN DUSEN: Well, let's see what's inside the vault, shall we? Hold the torch, Miss Hatch, if you please.

ELEANOR:	But the door's open, professor.
VAN DUSEN:	So it is. And the cupboard's bare.

(REVOLVER SHOT)

ELIZABETH:	*(screams)* Oh my God! He's killed himself. He's killed himself.
ELEANOR:	Let me see. Out of the way. It's Mr Stockton.
VAN DUSEN:	Dear me. What's happened?
ELEANOR:	It looks as though Mr Stockton shot himself. The revolver's still in his hand.
VAN DUSEN:	Let me see. Oh dear. This doesn't look good. Where were you when it happened, Miss Devan?
ELIZABETH:	Just behind him. Will he die? Is it fatal.
VAN DUSEN:	Hopeless. Let's carry him upstairs. I'll need you both to help me. Now, take care. I'll take his legs. You...[take an arm each, and lift...]

(FADE OUT. FULL UP)

VAN DUSEN:	Miss Devan, please answer me truthfully. Why did you shoot John Stockton?
ELIZABETH:	Me? But I didn't. He shot himself.

VAN DUSEN:	Then how do you account for those powder marks on your right hand?
ELIZABETH:	I – I don't know, Surely you can't imagine that I…
VAN DUSEN:	Miss Hatch, phone at once for an ambulance, and then see if it is possible to get Detective Sergeant Devery here straight away.
ELEANOR:	Yes, of course, professor. But what…*[do you want with the police…?]*
VAN DUSEN:	I intend to give Miss Devan into custody on the charge of shooting this man. Please do as I ask, Eleanor.
ELEANOR:	Yes, of course. *(retreating)* At once, professor. The telephone is in the hall.
ELIZABETH:	You're making a mistake, Professor Van Dusen.
VAN DUSEN:	The only mistake I have made, Miss Devan, is a deliberate one. John Stockton will not die. He's only concussed. The bullet merely grazed his forehead. Look, he's coming round.
ELIZABETH:	Then he won't die.
VAN DUSEN:	You seem disappointed.
ELIZABETH:	Well, shooting himself seemed like a confession of guilt.

STOCKTON: *(groaning)* Oh, my head. What's going on?

VAN DUSEN: Mr Stockton, tell me. Why did she shoot you?

STOCKTON: Shoot me? She didn't. I shot myself.

VAN DUSEN: On purpose?

STOCKTON: I did it myself. *(groans)*

VAN DUSEN: Miss Devan, I beg your pardon. I made a mistake. I hope Miss Hatch hasn't yet telephoned the police. *(retreating)* I must go and stop her at once. Excuse me.

(FADE OUT. FULL UP)

ELEANOR: Thank you for seeing me, Dr Benton. As I told you on the telephone, it's about the death of Mr Pomeroy Stockton. I'm helping my friend, Dr Van Dusen…

BENTON: The Thinking Machine?

ELEANOR: You know about him?

BENTON: Who doesn't? But he usually investigates crime, doesn't he? Mr Stockton certainly committed suicide. I issued the death certificate.

ELEANOR: That's why I'm here, Dr Benton. Would you please describe what happened?

BENTON: John Stockton and I have been friends ever since college days. Immediately after his father was found dead, John phoned me and I left for the house in Dorchester.

(CROSSFADE)

STOCKTON: Al, you've found a trace of prussic acid on his tongue. There's the bottle down there by his chair. My father has committed suicide, but just think of the disgrace if this ever came out. He was a great man, Al – just think of what he's contributed to this nation – and I can't bear to think of his memory being tarnished for all time. Please Al, as a friend, could you give us a death certificate that will allow him a good Christian burial, and help preserve his good name? What do you say?

(CROSSFADE)

BENTON: So I said I'd issue a death certificate specifying natural causes – heart disease, I said. It was wrong ethically, but I did it as an act of friendship, knowing that no harm had been done. Of course, Miss Hatch, now that *you* know, my entire career is at stake.

ELEANOR: Are you absolutely convinced that it was suicide?

BENTON: Without the shadow of a doubt. And then that letter found in Mr Stockton's pocket confirmed it. Miss Devan allowed me to read it.

ELEANOR: Yes, of course, Miss Devan was there. It's rather a strange document.

BENTON: I agree. Possibly written under stress by a man just about to take his own life. Miss Devan thought it might contain a cipher.

ELEANOR: What do you know about Miss Devan?

BENTON: Not much. Even though she's Mr Stockton's adopted daughter, she kept her own name. John told me that he'd once been in love with her, but that they'd broken it off after a time. He never gave me the details. After that, they were never very close. Miss Hatch, I've been completely frank with you, and my professional reputation is in your hands. Will you guarantee to keep what I've told you to yourself?

ELEANOR: Dr Benton, if Pomeroy Stockton indeed committed suicide, I will never publish a word about what you did for your friend. But if his death turns out to be murder, then I'm afraid the truth will have to come out.

BENTON: Murder?

(FULL UP MUSIC. FADE QUICKLY BENEATH FOLLOWING)

VAN DUSEN: (*remote, advancing*) Sorry to have kept you waiting, Miss Hatch. The autopsy took a bit longer than I expected.

ELEANOR: Autopsy? Whose autopsy?

VAN DUSEN: Pomeroy Stockton's, of course.

ELEANOR: I thought he'd been buried.

VAN DUSEN: No, no. I prevented that some time ago. I contacted the Medical Examiner requesting an autopsy. Mr Stockton's body has been in a receiving vault. The Examiner and I performed the autopsy together.

ELEANOR: What did you find?

VAN DUSEN: My dear Miss Hatch – Eleanor – would you allow me to keep that piece of information to myself for a short while? Let me take you through this case step by step. We'll arrive at the results of the autopsy in due course.

ELEANOR: I'm all ears.

VAN DUSEN: Right. Well, these were the questions that needed answering. How did Pomeroy Stockton die? If it wasn't suicide, as it appeared to be, what motive was there for anything else? Then, if there was a motive, who does it lead us to? Finally, what does that letter found in Mr Stockton's pocket actually mean?

ELEANOR: About that letter, professor – does it contain a cipher?

VAN DUSEN: It certainly does. Now here's the letter, Let's spread it out.

(PAPER RUSTLES. FADE IN)

OLD STOCKTON: "To those concerned. Tired of it all, I seek the end, and am content. Ambition is now dead; the grave yawns greedily at my feet. And with the labor of my own hands lost, I greet death of my own will, by my own act. To my son I leave all, and you who maligned me, you who discouraged me, you may read this and know I punish you thus. It's for him, my son, to forgive.

I dared in life, and dare dead your everlasting anger. Not alone that you didn't speak, but that you cherished secret, and my ears are locked forever against you. My vault is my resting place. On the brightest and dearest page of life I wrote (7) my love for him. Family ties, binding as the Bible itself, bade me give all to my son. Goodbye, I die. Pomeroy Stockton.

(FADE OUT. FULL UP)

VAN DUSEN: When I first examined it, what mainly struck me was the general tone of the document. It wasn't what you might call a direct suicide note. It seemed to have another meaning, underneath the words themselves. Then there was the absence of one word – "in" should appear between "cherished" and "secret". This could, of course, have been an oversight while writing under stress – the sort of thing anyone might do. But further on, we find the third indication that it's a cipher we're dealing with – that number 7 in parenthesis.

ELEANOR: Yes, it seems to have no connection whatsoever with what goes before or what follows.

VAN DUSEN: Precisely. And that couldn't have been an accident. So the question loomed: what did it mean? At first I took "7" to be a sort of key to the entire letter. Presuming the whole document was a cipher, I counted seven words up and down from the number. Nothing that made any sense emerged – just a jumble of words. The same happened when I counted letters rather than words.

ELEANOR: But suppose each of the letters was meant to be replaced by another? Isn't that sometimes done in ciphers?

VAN DUSEN: Perfectly correct, Miss Hatch. And of course that idea occurred to me. But my method of working is to exhaust the simplest possibilities first. So what did I do?

ELEANOR: Don't be a tease, Professor. Only you know what you did.

VAN DUSEN: I started with that inexplicable number "7", stuck as it was in the middle of a sentence. And I looked back from it to see if I came upon a word which related to it in some way. And lo and behold, five words back is the word "page". So I counted back another five words, and found "on". Now I had "on page 7." Then I began counting five words *down* from the "7" and came to the word "family". Another five words and we get to "Bible." So now I had "on page 7 family Bible".

ELEANOR: Good gracious. So you broke the code? What does the whole message read?

(PAPER RUSTLES)

VAN DUSEN: I've copied it out. Here you are.

ELEANOR: "I am dead at the hands of my son. You who read, punish him. I dare not speak. Secret locked vault on page 7 family Bible." By heaven, professor, this is astounding.

VAN DUSEN: Now you can see why the word "in" was left out between "cherished" and "secret". It would have broken the sequence of five.

ELEANOR: This letter – it's enough to send John Stockton to the electric chair.

VAN DUSEN: It would be.

ELEANOR: What do you mean "it would be"?

VAN DUSEN: I mean, it would be enough to send him to the electric chair – if it wasn't a forgery.

ELEANOR: A forgery? Didn't Pomeroy Stockton write it?

VAN DUSEN: Dear me, no. Indeed not, Miss Hatch.

ELEANOR: Then who...?

VAN DUSEN: Miss Elizabeth Devan, of course.

ELEANOR: Miss Devan? Then Miss Devan killed Pomeroy Stockton?

VAN DUSEN: Oh no. He died a natural death.

ELEANOR: Professor van Dusen, you have my head in a whirl. You seem to have sorted out this massive puzzle to your own satisfaction, but I'm at a loss. You simply must explain.

VAN DUSEN: Without going into too much detail, this is the sequence of events. Pomeroy Stockton died a natural death. The autopsy proved it. He had a heart attack.

ELEANOR: That *is* a relief. So Dr Benton is in the clear.

VAN DUSEN: A minor matter.

ELEANOR: Not to him.

VAN DUSEN: Maybe not. Well, Miss Devan found him dead. After John Stockton had left the house that fatal night, she decided to speak with her father – perhaps to ask for a part of the fortune he would be earning from his discovery of how to harden copper. Perhaps just to ask for a larger inheritance.

ELEANOR: She knocked – but got no answer.

VAN DUSEN: Exactly. Now this is supposition, but I presume that as his secretary she'd been given her own key to that door. Either that, or she'd had a spare key cut. Anyway, she bends down to look through the keyhole. Perhaps Mr Stockton's key was in the lock. If it was, she manoeuvres it out. In any case, she unlocks the door from the outside. She finds her father dead. Shocked, no doubt – for she certainly had feelings for her adopted father – she also saw a golden opportunity to remove the one person who stood between her and his fortune, a person, moreover, she hated. She spent some time concocting this letter…

ELEANOR: She couldn't have done that in a hurry…

VAN DUSEN: No indeed. That cipher – getting a hidden message into the body of a much longer letter – that took a good deal of working out. But once she's written the letter, forging his handwriting, she puts it into his pocket. Don't forget she'd been his secretary for years. She knows his handwriting very well – perhaps she even signed his cheques for him from time to time. Anyway, she places a drop of prussic acid on his tongue, smashes the bottle of acid, leaves the room with both keys in her possession, locks the door from the outside, and next day had it broken down. That was why neither a key, nor any pen and ink, were found.

ELEANOR: So when we were down in the cellar, it really was Miss Devan who shot Stockton.

VAN DUSEN: It was. And she was the one who tore page 7 from the family Bible, and then hid the Bible in John Stockton's room.

ELEANOR: But why? Why that page?

VAN DUSEN: My guess is that Pomeroy Stockton had written the secret of his copper hardening process on that page in invisible ink. I think he told John Stockton about it, and that Elizabeth Devan overheard the conversation. That's why she included a reference to it in her coded message. She knew I'd break the code, and she arranged matters so that maximum suspicion would fall on her step-brother. The Bible was to be found hidden in his room, with the vital page missing. She put it there.

ELEANOR: She was determined to get rid of him.

VAN DUSEN: Indeed she was.

ELEANOR: I'm beginning to get a grip on this case. But what I don't yet understand is the why? Why on earth did a perfectly respectable young woman devise and carry out such a fiendish plot?

VAN DUSEN: Well, I'd broken the code in that letter very shortly after I received it. Miss Devan had given me a tale of disagreement between father and son, quarrelling and all that. But I'd picked up a certain underlying animosity against her step-brother, despite her cleverness. Mind you, she'd so mingled fact with fiction that it wasn't altogether easy to weed out the truth.

ELEANOR: Well, she was the first to suggest that the letter might contain a cipher.

VAN DUSEN: Yes she planted that idea very early on.

ELEANOR: And didn't she propose at one time that her stepfather had been forced to write the letter?

VAN DUSEN: That was another ploy. But men who are being murdered don't write intricate letters in code, nor do people contemplating suicide. Among all the oddities in the letter, one sentence is particularly silly: "I dare not speak." Pomeroy Stockton wasn't a prisoner. If he'd feared there was a plot to kill him, why shouldn't he speak?

ELEANOR: You sent me to see John Stockton, and to get hold of the Bible, or at least page 7.

VAN DUSEN: I apologize, Miss Hatch. I already knew that page 7 had been torn out and that Miss Devan had it.

ELEANOR: And I suppose you knew that the vault was empty when we went down into the cellar?

VAN DUSEN: I did. Suspecting Miss Devan as I did, I knew that page 7 of the bible, and whatever had been in the vault, were already in her possession. Even then

I could see that the coded message that directly accused John Stockton, and the letter itself, might have been forged by Miss Devan – and that she'd brought the letter to me so that I might be an unwitting accomplice in her scheme.

ELEANOR: She'd have known that the Thinking Machine would crack the cipher easily.

VAN DUSEN: Exactly. At that early stage I thought that if Pomeroy Stockton had been murdered, she was the one who'd done it – whereas I could easily understand John Stockton's motive in trying to cover up the disgrace of his father's supposed suicide.

ELEANOR: All right, you've demonstrated in great detail how Miss Devan seized on her father's death to concoct an elaborate plot to implicate her stepbrother, John Stockton in his supposed murder. But the motive, the motive. What on earth induced her to embark on such a scheme?

(CROSSFADE)

VAN DUSEN: The time for prevarication is passed, Mr Stockton. There's nothing to be gained from it. You can tell me the truth. What lies behind Miss Devan's hatred of you?

STOCKTON: The hatred, as you put it, is one-sided. I don't hate Elizabeth. If anything I like and admire her. What I can't do is marry her. We more or less grew up together as children. Then I went away to college for a few years. When I returned to start work in the family firm, we tried to resume our old friendship. Unfortunately, her feelings ran much deeper than mine. I'd met a girl while away at Harvard, and we'd fallen very much in love. We'll be announcing our engagement very soon. But the time came when I had to tell Elizabeth that we couldn't go on meeting, that there was someone else.

VAN DUSEN: She took it badly?

STOCKTON: Very badly. That was when I decided to leave the house and go into lodgings.

VAN DUSEN: But down in the cellar that time – why did you say that you had shot yourself?

STOCKTON: I'd hurt Elizabeth enough. I certainly didn't want her to be charged with attempted murder.

VAN DUSEN: You didn't realize that she was planning to send you to the electric chair?

STOCKTON: I certainly did not. I went to the house that night to retrieve whatever was in that vault. My father had told me that he'd hidden his secret formula in two places. He'd written it in invisible ink on page 7 of the family Bible. By the way, that page has very little printing on it. Genesis starts on page 24. The other copy he'd hidden in the vault.

VAN DUSEN: The problem was that Miss Devan had been outside the door of your father's workroom, listening to your discussion. So *she* knew, too. She wove that knowledge into the plan she devised to entrap you.

STOCKTON: Poor Elizabeth.

VAN DUSEN: Poor Elizabeth indeed. If she'd succeeded, you'd be sitting in the condemned cell at this very moment.

(FADE OUT. FULL UP)

ELEANOR: Well, prison is where Elizabeth Devan should be. Where is she?

VAN DUSEN: I'm afraid the bird has flown the coop, Miss Hatch. I told my friend Detective Sergeant Devery the whole story a few days ago, and he went out to arrest her. She'd vanished without a trace. The police are searching for her. I doubt they'll find her. She's probably somewhere in Europe, by now.

(FADE IN MUSIC, PRE-SET TO END AFTER THE CLOSING ANNOUNCEMENT, UNDER THE FOLLOWING. KEEP IT LOW TILL END OF DIALOGUE)

ELEANOR: I don't suppose John Stockton would have pressed charges, anyway.

VAN DUSEN: I don't suppose he would.

ELEANOR: And Pomeroy Stockton's formula for hardened copper? What's happened to that, do you think?

VAN DUSEN: Well, Eleanor certainly can't make any commercial use of it now, that's for certain. I reckon she's destroyed both versions. I'm afraid that the end of this sad affair is that the world has lost a great scientific achievement – the secret of hardening copper. The secret that Pomeroy Stockton had rediscovered after four thousand years.

ELEANOR: This case has been full of secrets, hasn't it? A secret formula, a secret love that turned into a secret hate...

VAN DUSEN: ...and a secret cypher that was very nearly fatal.

(UP MUSIC. HOLD A LITTLE. DOWN FOR CLOSING ANNOUNCEMENT. UP MUSIC TO END)

CHARLEY'S AUNT

BY BRANDON THOMAS

DRAMATISED FOR RADIO
BY NEVILLE TELLER

Running Time: 90'

FIRST BROADCAST ACROSS
THE USA ON 25 FEBRUARY 2015
IN A PRODUCTION BY SHOESTRING
RADIO THEATRE, SAN FRANCISCO
DIRECTED BY STEVE RUBENSTEIN

CHARACTERS

SPETTIGUE	*50s. Lawyer type. Dusty.*
SIR FRANCIS CHESNEY	*50s. Hale and hearty type*
JACK CHESNEY	*20s. Upper-class English accent*
CHARLEY WYKEHAM	*20s. Upper-class English accent*
FANCOURT BABBERLEY	*20s. Upper-class English accent*
BRASSETT	*Butler type – affects upper class accent, but it continually slips*
DONNA LUCIA D'ALVADOREZ	*Middle aged English lady*
AMY	*20s. Upper-class English accent*
KITTY	*20s. Upper-class English accent*
ELA DELAHAY	*20s. Upper-class English accent*

NARRATOR: Oxford University, England, during the last golden years of Queen Victoria's reign – a time when young ladies were never permitted to visit young gentlemen in their rooms without being accompanied by a chaperone – a lady of impeccable respectability. Anything else would be scandalous in the extreme. But the rule doesn't apply to us, and we *are* able to peek in on a young Oxford undergraduate, Jack Chesney, as he sits at his desk, pen in hand. It's not some essay he is struggling to write, but a letter to the young lady he has fallen in love with. And he's not finding it easy...

JACK: (*as if writing*) "My Dear Miss Verdun..." No, too formal and not a bit what I really feel.

(PAPER RIPPED)

I wish to goodness I'd spoken to her at the dance the other evening, when she told me they were all going away for the summer. Instead, I've gone and left everything till the very last minute, and now I'm stuck.

(*as if writing*) "My Darling"! Rather strong, perhaps, to begin with.

(PAPER RIPPED)

Come on, Jack, here we are, in love with the dearest girl on earth—tackle her like a man, and tell her so, or they'll be off north and you'll have lost your chance for ever.
Hang it, why not? (*as if writing*) "My Dear Kitty"! That's great! Now I can get ahead like a house on fire. "My Dear Kitty, I …"

BRASSETT: (*coughs*) I beg pardon, sir, but would you mind—?

JACK: Go away, Brassett. I'm busy.

BRASSETT: Yes, sir, but—

JACK: I'm busy with the most important affair; get out!

BRASSETT: Yes, sir. Only…

JACK: Confound it all, Brassett, what do you want?

BRASSETT: You have a visitor, sir. Mr Charley Wykeham is here to see you.

CHARLEY: (*remote, advancing*) I say, Jack old man! Busy, are you?

JACK: What is it, Charley?

CHARLEY:	Nothing. I don't want to interrupt you if you're busy.
JACK:	It's all right, Charley, don't go.
BRASSETT:	(*retreating*) Excuse me, sir.

(DOOR CLOSES)

JACK:	That fool Brassett's driving me crazy.
CHARLEY:	What's he doing?
JACK:	Packing. And worrying me like Old Harry while I'm trying to write a most important letter. Don't mind me today; I'm all nerves.
CHARLEY:	And so am I, Jack.
JACK:	Why?
CHARLEY:	I've also been trying to write a letter.
JACK:	Who are *you* writing to?
CHARLEY:	To—to Miss Spettigue.
JACK:	How far have you got?
CHARLEY:	Oh! I began awfully well – "My Dear Amy " – and then words failed me, and I've come to you for advice. You always know what to say.

JACK: Oh! Do I?

CHARLEY: Well, I'm shy. You're not.

JACK: Aren't I?

CHARLEY: So tell me, old chap. What am I to say?

JACK: (*to himself*) I know – I'll tell him, and do the same myself.

        Now then, let's see. You're in love with Amy Spettigue, and you want to know if there's any hope for you and if so—

CHARLEY: You see, they're all off to Scotland tomorrow.

JACK: Yes, I know, and you want to see her at once. When and where? Do I diagnose the case accurately?

CHARLEY: To a "Tee," old chap!

JACK: Very well then; you'll want to say something to this effect. (*as if writing*). "My Dear Kitty—"

CHARLEY: No, not Kitty. Amy.

JACK: Of course, what am I thinking of?

(PAPER RIPPED)

"My Dearest Amy. Forgive me, darling, for thus addressing you, but I love you so deeply." Underlined.

CHARLEY: Rather strong, Jack.

JACK: Shut up! "That I must write and tell you so. All I ask is—"

CHARLEY: But there's one obstacle to my putting it quite as straight as that, much as I'd like to.

JACK: What's that?

CHARLEY: Well—er—I've an aunt.

JACK: My dear Charley, most of us have; what about her?

CHARLEY: I feel I ought to tell her first.

JACK: Well if you're going to drag an aunt into the business, we may as well wait till they all come back from Scotland.

CHARLEY: Why?

JACK: You know what aunts are like when they step in.

CHARLEY: No I don't. That's just it; I don't know her. I've never even seen her.

JACK: In that case we won't be too hard on that particular aunt; she hasn't interfered much in your affairs up to now.

CHARLEY: Except to find out that I was an orphan and have me sent to the best school in England. And then to Oxford. And now she writes that she's coming here this morning by an early train, and will take luncheon with me at one o'clock.

JACK: And you've never seen her?

CHARLEY: No. She went to Brazil before I was born, and became a sort of secretary to a very rich old Brazilian chap out there, called Dom Pedro d'Alvadorez. And now, by the merest chance, this is what I saw in this morning's paper. Just read that...

JACK: (reads) "Donna Lucia d'Alvadorez, the Brazilian millionaire, who has taken Lord Toppleby's magnificent mansion in Belgravia, is an Englishwoman, and a financial genius. Indeed it was her capacity in this direction that earned the gratitude of her late husband, and led to a romantic deathbed marriage." Well I don't see much in that!

CHARLEY: Go on, Jack, read the rest.

JACK: "Her only relation is a nephew at Oxford." Lucky nephew!

CHARLEY: That's me.

JACK: A millionaire – and you're her only relative? By George, Charley, this is a startler! And she may be here any minute?

CHARLEY:	Yes. And I wanted to write that letter to Amy. But it's all awfully difficult. Fearfully complicated.
JACK:	Why?
CHARLEY:	Well, you see, I've no parents or relatives or anything.
JACK:	No relatives? With an aunt like that!
CHARLEY:	But I've no reason to expect anything from her, more than she's already done for me, for which, of course, I'm very grateful and all that. But I want Amy, and … and…
JACK:	Charley! I've got a clinking good idea! Not only for you – for us both. You're gone on Amy; I'm in love with Kitty.
CHARLEY:	Really?
JACK:	Madly. I was writing to tell her so when you came in. There's the letter.
CHARLEY:	So what's your idea?
JACK:	Hang letter-writing! We'll give a luncheon party for your aunt, tea afterwards in the garden.
CHARLEY:	But my rooms are so small.
JACK:	Never mind, I'll lend you mine. Brassett will see to it. (*Calling*) Brassett! Now, come on! First

write and ask the girls to come here for luncheon and to meet your aunt.

CHARLEY: Do you think they'll come?

JACK: They'll jump at it. Come on, sit down here – and write. "My Dear Miss Spettigue—" (*calling*) Brassett, where are you?

(DOOR OPENS)

BRASSETT: (*advancing*) You called, sir?

JACK: Oh-er, Brassett, fetch someone to take a note to Mr Spettigue's house.

BRASSETT: Yes, sir. (*retreating*) Right away, sir.

(DOOR CLOSES)

CHARLEY: "My Dear Miss Spettigue—" Yes, Jack, I've got that.

JACK: "Would you and Miss Verdun do me the honour—"

CHARLEY: (*repeating*). "the honour"

JACK: "to lunch with me and Mr Chesney at his rooms, St. Olde's College, today at one o'clock, to meet my aunt…" What did you say her name was, Charley?

CHARLEY:	Donna Lucia d'Alvadorez.
JACK:	"Donna…" Alright, stick it down. "An answer by bearer will greatly oblige."
CHARLEY:	"Yours sincerely, Charles Wykeham." Splendid, Jack, you're a genius!

(DOOR OPENS)

BRASSETT:	(*remote*) The messenger, sir.
JACK:	Give him this, and tell him to look sharp.
BRASSETT:	(*retreating*) Yes, sir.

(DOOR CLOSES)

CHARLEY:	Now we shall have them all to ourselves.
JACK:	Yes, and we couldn't have asked them if it hadn't been for your aunt. They'd never have come without a chaperone. I'm beginning to love that dear old lady already. (*calling.*) Brassett!

(DOOR OPENS)

BRASSETT:	(*remote*) Yes, sir?
JACK:	Lunch for five.
BRASSETT:	(*advancing*) For five, sir?

JACK:	Why are you grinning?
BRASSETT:	Well, sir, I'm afraid our credit in the kitchen is somewhat exhausted.
JACK:	Really? Never mind, Brassett, get it outside. Go to Bunter's.
BRASSETT:	I'm afraid, sir, we owe Bunter's.
JACK:	Oh, do we?
BRASSETT:	However, sir, I've no doubt it will be all right if I say it's for me.
JACK:	*(laughing)*. Oh, all right, Brassett; lunch for five at one o'clock.
BRASSETT:	What wine, sir?
JACK:	Well the champagne, of course. It's in the sideboard.

(CUPBOARD DOOR OPENS)

BRASSETT:	Very little left, sir.
JACK:	There's half a dozen bottles there to my certain knowledge!
BRASSETT:	I think not, sir. Only four.

(BOTTLES. CUPBOARD DOOR CLOSES)

CHARLEY: Oh, four's quite enough.

JACK: There were six bottles there, I'll swear. (*softly to Charley*) He's pinched those other two.

CHARLEY: (*softly*) My fellow's just the same.

JACK: Now, while you and your dear old aunt are looking at the chapel and cloisters, Kitty and I can have our little talk.

CHARLEY: Yes, Jack, that's all very well, but what about Amy and me, and *our* little talk? My aunt will be in our way horribly.

JACK: I never thought of that.

CHARLEY: She's all very well as an excuse to get the girls to come here, but by herself she'll be an awful bore.

JACK: What shall we do?

CHARLEY: Couldn't we ask someone to meet her?

JACK: Jolly good idea. Someone we can depend upon. Let me see... What about Fanny Babbs! We'll ask him. He's a cheerful chap. He'll amuse your aunt like the deuce and keep her in a rattling good humour. (*calls*) Brassett!

BRASSETT: (*remote*) Yes, sir.

JACK: Go to Lord Fancourt Babberley's rooms, give him my compliments, and ask him to come here at once.

BRASSETT: Yes, sir.

CHARLEY: Say it's very important.

BRASSETT: Yes, sir. *(retreating)* I'll be as quick as I can.

(DOOR CLOSES)

CHARLEY: By the by, Jack, talking of Babbs's cheerfulness, haven't you noticed something about him lately? Ever since he was so ill and had to go off to the Mediterranean?

JACK: I've noticed he's been jolly hard up.

CHARLEY: I fancy, from a few hints he's dropped, that he's a bit hard hit himself.

JACK: What, Lord Fancourt Babberley in love?

CHARLEY: Yes; and if I'm not much mistaken, he's as soft-hearted over a girl as...

JACK: We are. All the better; he'll feel for us. He'll see the necessity of keeping the old lady well out of the way.

CHARLEY: By George, Jack, you'll be Prime Minister one of these days.

(DOOR OPENS)

BRASSETT:	*(remote, advancing)* His lordship's compliments, sir, and he says he can't come, he has a luncheon party, and could you lend him a few bottles of champagne?
JACK:	Lend him a few bottles of champagne! Of all the cheek!
CHARLEY:	Who's he got coming?
JACK:	Oh, Freddy Peel, I expect, and a lot of idiots like himself. And they'll be howling comic songs all the afternoon.
CHARLEY:	It'll sound awfully bad, won't it?
JACK:	He mustn't! Brassett, lay luncheon for six.
BRASSETT:	Yes, sir.
CHARLEY:	What are we going to do?
JACK:	Go to him and make him come. He can't upset all our plans in this selfish way. *(retreating)* Put the remaining four bottles of champagne on ice, Brassett. And tidy up my room. *(remote)* Come on, Charley, come on!

(DOOR CLOSES)

BRASSETT: Luncheon at one! Lay six places! Tidy the room. Hurry, scurry. No time for anything. Everything bang, bang, bang – except for paying their bills. Hm'm. Never thought he'd miss that champagne. Pity.

FANCOURT: *(remote, calling, advancing)* Jack! I say, Jack old man. Hello! It's Brassett, isn't it? Don't mind my coming in by the window, do you?

BRASSETT: That's perfectly in order, my lord.

FANCOURT: Where the Dickens is Jack? I wanted to borrow some fizz.

BRASSETT: I believe Mr Chesney and Mr Wykeham have gone in search of you, m'lord.

FANCOURT: Four bottles of fizz. The very thing. I'll just pop these into my bag and be on my way.

(BOTTLES CLINK)

BRASSETT: Excuse me, your lordship, but I believe Mr Chesney has earmarked that champagne for a small luncheon he is giving today.

FANCOURT: I can't worry about that. He shouldn't leave it lying about in this ostentatious way when I'm so beastly hard up. He'll have to make out with whisky and soda,

(DOOR OPENS)

JACK: (*remote, advancing*) Hallo, Babbs. We've just been over to your rooms to find you. We've been talking about you.

FANCOURT: No, really? Well, ta-ta!

JACK: Don't go, Babbs; you wanted to see us, didn't you?

FANCOURT: Oh yes! I just wanted to borrow some fizz, but...

JACK: Sorry, can't oblige. I did have six bottles, and I could have spared you a couple, but... Where *is* the champagne?

FANCOURT: In this bag of mine. Well, ta-ta!

JACK: No, you don't. We want you to stay and lunch with us today. Charley's aunt is going to pay him a visit.

LORD FANCOURT: No, really? What fun!

JACK: And you're just the sort of chap we want – jolly smart, with a fund of humour and lots of brilliant conversation.

FANCOURT: What's she like?

CHARLEY: Well, you see, Babbs, we don't quite know. I'm to see her today for the first time.

FANCOURT: But she may turn out to be an awful old 'croc'.

JACK:	She's a widow, and a millionaire, that's enough, isn't it?
FANCOURT:	Rather! What's her name?
CHARLEY:	Donna Lucia d'Alvadorez.
JACK:	You'll find her a charming old lady.
FANCOURT:.	Charming old lady! I say, look here, haven't you got anything younger coming?
CHARLEY:	Oh yes, two other ladies.
FANCOURT:	Nice? Young?
CHARLEY:	Yes.
FANCOURT:	That's more in my line. How many did you say?
JACK:	Two.
FANCOURT:	Oh, I see. One for each of you, and the old 'croc' for me. No thanks, I'm off.
JACK:	Now listen, Babbs. This is an awfully serious affair. We'll take you into our confidence. We're in love.
FANCOURT:	What, Charley as well?
CHARLEY:	If you knew the girls as well as we do, you wouldn'1 wonder at it.

JACK: And they're coming here to lunch today.

FANCOURT: I say, have you proposed?

JACK: No, that's just it.

FANCOURT: Oh, I see. You want me to propose for you?

JACK: No! We'll do that for ourselves. That's why we've asked them to come.

CHARLEY: You know, Babbs, you don't understand our feelings a bit.

FANCOURT: Oh, don't I, though? Haven't you noticed how sad I've been lately?

CHARLEY:. Yes.

JACK: What is it?

FANCOURT: Well, I think… I'm in love too.

JACK: Sit down and tell us all about it.

FANCOURT: You remember when they threw me out of college for the rest of term?

JACK: Beastly shame.

FANCOURT: No, not the last time they did it – the time before. I took the yacht round to the Mediterranean, and at Monte Carlo I came across an English officer named Delahay: quite penniless and dying. You know, Jack, he tried to commit suicide.

JACK: Bad luck at the tables, eh?

FANCOURT: Yes. He'd beggared himself – and also his only child, the sweetest little girl you ever saw, Jack. To amuse him and keep his spirits up, I used to play cards with him.

CHARLEY: And what became of him?

FANCOURT: He died, poor fellow!

JACK: And what became of the sweetest little girl you ever saw?

FANCOURT: I lost sight of her. A lady travelling home that way, from South America, I believe, took charge of her and brought her to England. You know, Jack, I tried to tell her that...

JACK: You loved her?

FANCOURT: But she was in such grief that...

JACK: You just couldn't do it.

FANCOURT: After all, you know, I might have been rejected – and a complete silly ass I'd have looked then.

JACK: At any rate, you can sympathise with us.

(KNOCK ON FRONT DOOR)

Brassett, just see who that is, will you?

BRASSETT: (*remote, advancing*) The messenger with a note, sir.

JACK: Give it here.

(ENVELOPE TEARS. PAPER)

They're coming! The girls are coming!

FANCOURT: By Jove!

JACK: You'll stop, Babbs? We won't let you go now that we've got you.

FANCOURT: But look here, Jack; I've something else to do.

JACK: What?

FANCOURT: I'm going to play in some amateur theatricals this afternoon. I've given my word.

JACK: What are you playing?

FANCOURT: An old lady. And I've got to try the costume on before those fellows come.

JACK: You can try the clothes on here. Where are they?

FANCOURT: In my rooms, in a box on the bed, but…

JACK: Fetch them, Brassett, quick !

BRASSETT: *(retreating, long suffering)* Yes, sir.

JACK: Our champagne may be in your bag, but I've still got a bottle of claret. Let's drink to the health of your lady love, wherever she is. Here's to the future Lady Fancourt Babberley. What did you say her name was?

FANCOURT: I haven't the slightest idea.

JACK: } *(laugh)*
CHARLEY: }

JACK: Go on with you. Miss Delahay!

BRASSETT: *(remote, advancing)* I believe this is the box your lordship was referring to.

FANCOURT: Thank you, Brassett. You're an awfully good chap. I say, Jack, could you lend me half-a-crown?

JACK: Charley! Have you half-a-crown?

CHARLEY: I have not.

JACK: *(softly)* Brassett, give me half-a-crown, will you?

BRASSETT: *(softly)* Yes, sir. Here you are, sir.

JACK: Babbs! Half-a-crown!

FANCOURT:	Thanks. Brassett, here you are. Now, these clothes – I'll try them on after lunch while you're all in the garden.
JACK:	You can't do that; we shall want you with us. Try them on now. Won't take long, will it?
FANCOURT:	Only a minute or two. (*retreating*) You know, I've lost an awful lot of time over these theatricals. But next term I mean to work. Shan't be long.

(DOOR CLOSES. KNOCK ON FRONT DOOR)

JACK:	That must be the girls for lunch, and your aunt's not come yet.
CHARLEY:	Good gracious! What shall we do?
JACK:	Oh, let them come in. We can explain. Show them in, Brassett.

(DOOR OPENS)

BRASSETT:	(*remote*) Miss Kitty Verdun and Miss Amy Spettigue.
JACK:	How do you do, Kitty?
CHARLEY:	So kind of you to come, Amy.
KITTY:	(*advancing*) Oh, we were very pleased to be able to come. Weren't we, Amy?

183

AMY: Oh, yes. Are we too early, Mr Wykeham?

KITTY: Yes, you didn't mention any time, Mr Chesney.

JACK: Oh, not at all, not at all! We're delighted!

AMY: But where's your aunt, Mr Wykeham?

CHARLEY: Oh around. She'll be back here very soon.

KITTY: And this is where you think and study and do all your work and everything?

JACK: Oh yes, Kitty, we do a lot of that sort of thing here.

CHARLEY: You know, Amy, I'm so glad you were able to come today. You're off to Scotland tomorrow, and we shall miss you so much.

AMY: Yes, Uncle always takes us to some dreadfully remote place at this time of the year, where we never see a soul, and it's so dreary. You know, it's lucky Uncle is away in town, or I don't think we could have come.

CHARLEY: Why's that?

AMY: Well, he raises such odd objections. And then you know he's so protective about Kitty.

CHARLEY: Why?

AMY: Well, she's an heiress, you know, and he's her guardian.

JACK: Kitty, have you forgotten that dance the other night? I never shall.

KITTY: No.

JACK: No! Those stolen moments in the garden by ourselves were the very happiest of all my life. Out there in the moonlight… There's nothing like moonlight, is there?

KITTY: I wonder how many people have said that?

JACK: Kitty, you're quite cynical today.

KITTY: I know; I'm thinking of that man.

JACK: What man?

KITTY: My guardian, Mr Spettigue. He has a habit of hurrying us away from all our best friends directly we get to know anyone really well.

JACK: Why's that?

KITTY: Because he's a selfish, wicked old man.

AMY: What a dear, sweet old lady your aunt must be, Mr Wykeham! I'm longing to know her. Where is she?

CHARLEY:	(*urgent, whisper*) Jack! Where's my aunt? (**to Amy**) Oh, she's hardly arrived yet.
AMY:	Oh, no! Kitty, Mr Wykeham's aunt hasn't come yet.
KITTY:	Hasn't come? Then we must… we'll run and do some shopping. And come back. Won't be long.
AMY:	Good-bye.
JACK:	Good-bye.
KITTY:	Good-bye.
AMY:	Good-bye.

(FRONT DOOR CLOSES)

CHARLEY:	Good-bye.
JACK:	See that? Off they shoot when they find your aunt isn't here. We either get that old lady here, or the girls won't stay.
CHARLEY:	Yes, it's a chaperone, or nothing.
JACK:	So Charley, you cut off to the station and bundle the old girl in here as quick as you can. Off you go!
CHARLEY:	(*retreating*) I say, Jack, I feel happier since I've seen them, don't you?

(FRONT DOOR OPENS AND CLOSES)

FANCOURT: *(remote, calls)* I say, old chap, have you got any hairpins?

JACK: Hairpins? Great Scot, no!

FANCOURT: May I send your man for some?

JACK: Certainly.

FANCOURT: I say, have you got sixpence?

JACK: Afraid not.

FANCOURT: You've never got anything! I say, Brassett, I gave you half-a-crown just now. Do you mind making it two shillings and getting me sixpennyworth of hairpins?

BRASSETT: Certainly, m'lord.

FANCOURT: You can keep the change.

BRASSETT: *(retreating)* Very good of you, m'lord.

(FRONT DOOR OPENS AND SHUTS)

FANCOURT: *(retreating)* I'll just go back and finish offI

(KNOCK ON FRONT DOOR)

JACK: Look out, Babbs! Someone's at the front door. Vanish!

(DOOR CLOSES. KNOCK ON FRONT DOOR)

Come in.

(FRONT DOOR OPENS)

SIR FRANCIS:	*(remote)* Jack!
JACK:	Dad!

(FRONT DOOR CLOSES)

SIR FRANCIS:	*(advancing)* My dear boy!
JACK:	Dear old dad! What brings you here? Wherever have you come from?
SIR FRANCIS:	From town, my lad. To have a chat with you and to bring you your cheque.
JACK:	Thanks, dad; you're a brick!
SIR FRANCIS:	A bit over-baked, my boy; after all my years in India. The old College is looking very spruce, though. New ivy, new paint.
JACK:	And so are you, dad. Fifty years ago you'd have been a stout, bald, domineering old boy. Yet here you are, a smart, bang up-to-date sort of chap. How have you done it? Do you drink?
SIR FRANCIS:	All I want.

JACK: Eat well?

SIR FRANCIS: Never noticed.

JACK: There you are! Consequently health good, temper perfect.

SIR FRANCIS: Now I have here…

(PAPERS RUSTLE)

… not only your cheque. There you are, to be going on with…

JACK: Thanks very much, dad.

SIR FRANCIS: … but also a handful of your unpaid bills. You've been very hospitable, I see, this term.

JACK: I hope, dad…

SIR FRANCIS: Never mind; same when I was a lad.

JACK: Let me see that one. I've been done over that wine monstrously.

SIR FRANCIS: Were you? Never mind, so was I. Done over everything monstrously at college, but settle up, settle up. I'm very satisfied with you. It's something to go down from college with a record like yours. And now, my lad, we must begin to think.

JACK: Think?

SIR FRANCIS: Now that I've come into the family title, as you know, I have also—which you don't know—come into the family debts and difficulties.

JACK: Debts!

SIR FRANCIS: Which are far more than I expected, with the result that all the money I've been saving for you in India goes to pay them. And in short, Jack, you and I, for the next few years, will be, comparatively speaking, poor.

JACK: Poor! (*to himself*) This settles me with old Spettigue.

SIR FRANCIS: However, I'm in hopes of a small appointment for you… in Bengal.

JACK: Bengal!

(FRONT DOOR OPENS)

What is it Brassett?

BRASSETT: (*advancing*) His lordship's hairpins, sir.

JACK: Confound his hairpins! Well, give them to him.

BRASSETT: (*retreating*) At once, sir.

(DOOR OPENS AND SHUTS)

JACK: Dad, I've an idea. Couldn't this financial problem be settled by a wealthy marriage?

SIR FRANCIS: No; that's the sort of thing I rather deprecate. I don't think, Jack, I'd…

JACK: Listen. You know my chum, Charley Wykeham? Well his aunt, Donna Lucia d'Alvadorez, is coming here to lunch today. She's a widow…

SIR FRANCIS: A widow?

JACK: And a millionaire.

SIR FRANCIS: And a millionaire?

JACK: And a charming woman.

SIR FRANCIS: No, Jack, I don't think I'd advise you to do a thing of this kind merely for the sake of money.

JACK: Not me, dad. You.

SIR FRANCIS: Me! You young rascal. No, no! I'll never marry again.

JACK: Don't be rash, dad. Think it over. Where are your things?

SIR FRANCIS: At the hotel.

JACK: Well, you go and change. Make yourself look as nice as possible. And come back here to lunch at one o'clock. Oh, and, dad – put a flower in your buttonhole.

CHARLEY: (*remote*) I say, Jack !

(FRONT DOOR CLOSES)

(*advancing*) Look what's just arrived… Oh…

JACK: Dad, you know Charley Wykham. Charley, my father.

SIR FRANCIS: Glad to meet you, my boy.

CHARLEY: Hullo, sir.

JACK: (*whispers*) Now, don't forget. A flower in your buttonhole.

SIR FRANCIS: All right, Jack. I'll have a look at her.

JACK: (*calls*) Remember – back here by one o'clock sharp.

SIR FRANCIS: (*remote*) I'll be here.

(FRONT DOOR OPENS AND CLOSES)

JACK: Well, Charley, what is it?

CHARLEY: Read that.

JACK: "Important business, don't expect me for a few days. Lucia d'Alvadorez." No!!!

CHARLEY: She's not coming!

JACK: But she must! Go—wire—telegraph—

CHARLEY: No use. There's no time.

JACK: But hang it! The girls won't remain without a chaperone. What are we to do?

CHARLEY: Oh my goodness! Look out there. Here they are! They're coming!

JACK: What on earth are we to do?

FANCOURT: (*remote*) I say, Jack, come in here and look at me!

JACK: What the deuce is it?

(INNER DOOR OPENS)

By George! Splendid! Charley, come here quickly! A miracle! The answer to all our prayers!

CHARLEY: (*approaching*) What is it?

JACK: Charley – allow me to present you. Your aunt. Babbs!

CHARLEY: Babbs! My aunt!

JACK:	It's the only one you've got, so you'll have to make the best of her.
FANCOURT:	(*advancing*) I say, look here…
JACK:	Just look at her. Isn't she splendid?

(KNOCK AT FRONT DOOR)

FANCOURT:	Who's that?
JACK:	The girls! And Charley's aunt can't come.
FANCOURT:	Can't she? Then I'll go and take these things off.
JACK:	No! They won't stop if you do.
FANCOURT:	Won't stop! What do you mean?
JACK:	You must be Charley's aunt!
FANCOURT:	Me? Certainly not. Under no circumstances!
JACK:	Charley, give me a hand. Now you just sit down there, Babs, and behave yourself.
FANCOURT:	Let me go!
JACK:	Charley, stand in front of him till he quietens down. Brassett!
BRASSETT:	Sir?

JACK:	Show them in.

(FRONT DOOR OPENS)

	Ah, you've got back. So glad!
KITTY:	Yes; we've been longer than we intended, but Amy wanted to get flowers for Charley's aunt. Has she come?
AMY:	Yes. Has she? I hope she's come.
JACK:	Oh yes, she's come.
CHARLEY:	And here she is. Auntie dear, may I present Miss Spettigue, Miss Verdun. Amy, Kitty, my aunt – Donna Lucia d'Alvadorez.
JACK:	(*whispers*) Well say something!
FANCOURT:	(*as aunt*) Er – er – How do you do, my dears?
KITTY:	We called upon you before, Donna Lucia, but you hadn't arrived.
AMY:	I hope your journey from town hasn't tired you.
FANCOURT:	(*as aunt*) Oh, no! It was very jolly.
JACK:	(*urgent whisper*) Babbs!
FANCOURT:	Pleasant, I mean.

AMY:	You look worried, Mr. Wykeham. Are you ill?
CHARLEY:	No; I'm anxious, I'm…
JACK:	He's a little affected at meeting his aunt today, for the first time. *(whispers)* Why the dickens don't you say something?
FANCOURT:	*(whispers)* What the dickens am I to say?
JACK:	*(whispers)* Talk about the weather.
FANCOURT:	*(as aunt)* Charming weather.
KITTY:} **AMY: }**	Oh, yes, delightful! Oh, yes, it is charming!
AMY:	After all, you know, we have some nice weather sometimes in poor old England.
FANCOURT:	*(whispers)* What on earth does she mean by that?
JACK:	*(whispers)* You're a foreigner.
FANCOURT:	*(whispers)* A foreigner! What did you say my name was?
JACK:	*(whispers)* Donna Lucia d'Alvadorez.
FANCOURT:	*(whispers)* What am I? Irish?
CHARLEY:	*(whispers)* No, English. Married a Portuguese abroad.

JACK: (*whispers*) A widow.

CHARLEY: (*whispers*) From Brazil.

JACK: (*whispers*) And a millionaire.

FANCOURT: I say, Charley, have I any children?

CHARLEY: (*whispers*) No, you fool!

FANCOURT: (*whispers*) Well, one ought to know. That's all right. Now I can go ahead. (*as aunt*) Yes, it is wonderful weather, for England.

KITTY: } Yes, it is.
AMY: } Yes.

FANCOURT: (*whispers*)Shall I take them to see the chapel and the cloisters.

JACK: (*whispers*)No. You leave that to me and Charley. We'll attend to them.

KITTY: Of course, Oxford is all very new to you, Donna Lucia, but it's a dear old place in any weather. Amy and I will show you all about.

FANCOURT: I shall be delighted.

KITTY: You're staying till tomorrow, are you not?

FANCOURT: (*whispers*) Am I staying until tomorrow?

JACK: *(whispers)* No.

FANCOURT: No.

CHARLEY: I'm afraid auntie can't stay after today.

FANCOURT: No; you see, it's my washing day.

CHARLEY: She has so much business to attend to—in town.

JACK: Yes, lawyers, stocks…

FANCOURT: Yes, stocks and socks… All very important, you know.

AMY: Oh, I'm so sorry. We have so longed to know you.

FANCOURT: Have you, my dear?

AMY: Mr Wykeham has told us so much about you, that he has made us quite love you.

FANCOURT: Has he, my dear? How very nice. And what a very tiny waist you have.

CHARLEY: *(whispers)* None of that!

AMY: And he's so grateful. He says he owes everything to you and never could repay you. It was noble of you!

FANCOURT: Of course, my dear. It was only my duty to see after the welfare of my poor brother's—

JACK: *(whispers)*Sister's, you fool!

FANCOURT: Sister's, you fool!... Sister's. And brother-in-law's orphan girl.

JACK: *(whispers)*Boy Boy!

FANCOURT: Boy—boy! *(whispers)* I'll say twins in a minute.

AMY: Yes, but it was so good of you to find out. you were so far away in a foreign land, and he might have been left to starve. But you have a good, kind, affectionate nature...

FANCOURT: Have I, my dear?

AMY: Anyone can see it in your face. I feel I could tell my whole heart to you!

JACK: *(whispers)* Don't let her.

FANCOURT: *(whispers)* I'm not going to. The dear little thing!

AMY: You don't mind my talking to you like this, do you?

FANCOURT: My dear, you are a very charming girl, and I'm sure I could soon grow very fond of you.

CHARLEY: *(whispers)* Babbs!

FANCOURT: And you must tell me all you like, some day, when you know me better.

AMY: Oh, I feel I've known you years and years already. (*kiss*) There!

CHARLEY: (*groans*)

BRASSETT: (*remote, approaching, calling*) Mr Chesney! Mr Chesney! I beg pardon, sir, but I heard Mr Spettigue enquiring at the gate for your rooms, sir.

KITTY } Oh dear, my guardian!
AMY: } Oh dear, my uncle back!

CHARLEY: Mr Spettigue!

JACK: Mr Spettigue back! I thought he was in London.

KITTY: Mr Chesney, I beg of you to send him away.

(KNOCK AT FRONT DOOR)

BRASSETT: Quick! If I draw the curtain across this recess…

(CURTAIN PULLED ON RAIL)

Mr Wykeham and the ladies can conceal themselves.

JACK: Brilliant, Brassett. Come along, quickly.

KITTY } (*giggling*)
AMY: }

CHARLEY: You stay where you are, Babbs.

FANCOURT: I'm not facing him alone.

CHARLEY: You certainly are.

FANCOURT: But what am I to say? What am I to do?

CHARLEY: Tell him what you like, only get rid of him. I'm joining the others. Bye-bye!

(LOUDER KNOCK AT FRONT DOOR)

SPETTIGUE: (*remote, muffled*) Why doesn't somebody answer this door?

(DOOR OPENS)

FANCOURT: What do you want?

SPETTIGUE: (*advancing*) I wish to see Mr. Chesney. At once.

FANCOURT: Well, you can't. He's not present. I am the only person present.

SPETTIGUE: But the porter told me that two young ladies— my niece and my ward—were here.

FANCOURT: As you can see, I am the only young lady present.

SPETTIGUE: But he told me he saw them come in.

FANCOURT: And didn't he tell you he saw them go out?

SPETTIGUE: No!

FANCOURT: Very well then, what more do you want? And now, sir, having got all the information you are likely to get, in your present condition…

SPETTIGUE: What *do* you mean, madam? I am annoyed, but perfectly sober.

FANCOURT: Well, you don't look it.

SPETTIGUE: (*retreating*) Madam, I wish you good morning.

(FRONT DOOR SLAMS)

FANCOURT: (*calling*) My dears… You may emerge. Our visitor has retired.

(CURTAIN PULLED ON RAIL)

KITTY: How sweet of you! (*kiss*)

AMY: You darling! (*kiss*)

CHARLEY: (*whisper*) Just look at him, Jack!

JACK: (*whisper*) I'll punch his head if he does it again!

(KNOCK AT FRONT DOOR)

JACK: And now here's my father! (*whisper*) Babbs, Take care. My father's arrived,

FANCOURT: (*whisper*) Am I related to him in any way?

JACK: *(whisper)* No; you're Charley's aunt, from Brazil.

FANCOURT: *(whisper)* Brazil! Where on earth's that?

JACK: *(whisper)* You know—er—where the nuts come from.

(FRONT DOOR OPENS)

BRASSETT: *(remote)*: Sir Francis Chesney.

JACK: Father, may I present Miss Verdun. Miss Verdun, my father.

SIR FRANCIS: Delighted.

JACK: And this is Miss Spettigue.

SIR FRANCIS: Charmed. Now, Jack, has she come?

JACK: Oh yes, she's come. Go on, Charley, introduce your aunt.

CHARLEY: Donna Lucia d'Alvadorez, Sir Francis Chesney, Jack's father.

FANCOURT: How do you do, Sir Francis?

SIR FRANCIS: How do you do?

FANCOURT: I'm Charley's aunt from Brazil. Where the nuts come from.

CHARLEY:	*(whispers)* Shut up, Babbs.
SIR FRANCIS:	I say, Jack!
JACK:	Yes?
SIR FRANCIS:	Is that the lady?
JACK:	Er – Yes.
SIR FRANCIS:	Oh, by George! I've just remembered. A pressing engagement…
JACK:	Oh, don't go, dad! *(whispers)* Well, say something, Babbs. Go on. Charley's told you all about him.
FANCOURT:	Charley's told you all about him.
JACK:	No, no!
FANCOURT:	No, no!
JACK:	My nephew Charles.
FANCOURT:	My nephew Charles has told me so much about you.
JACK:	*(whispers)* In his letters
FANCOURT:	In his letters. In his letters… *(whispers)* That's all right, isn't it?
JACK:	*(whispers)* No, it isn't.

FANCOURT: *(whispers)* Do it yourself, then!

SIR FRANCIS: I'm much obliged to Mr Wykeham.

JACK: *(whispers)* Remember you've only just come to England, and you've never seen Charley till today.

FANCOURT: *(whispers)* Why the deuce didn't you say so before?

SIR FRANCIS: *(confidential)* Jack! My dear boy, it's impossible. Just look at her!

BRASSETT: *(remote)* Excuse me, sir. Luncheon is ready.

JACK: Jolly good, Brassett. Now come along everyone. *(whispers)* Babbs, you take my father, and be careful how you talk him. Dad, will you take Donna Lucia?

SIR FRANCIS: Allow me, Donna Lucia.

FANCOURT: You'll sit beside me, won't you, Sir Francis?

(CHAIRS SCRAPE)

SIR FRANCIS: I shall be delighted. You've travelled a great deal, I suppose?

FANCOURT: Oh yes, I've been a great traveller, Sir Francis. i came all the way from London only this morning.

CHARLEY: Open the wine, Brassett.

(CORK. POURING. GLASSES)

KITTY: You have very pleasant rooms here, Mr. Chesney.

JACK: Oh yes.

AMY: Oh yes, they're awfully nice rooms, Mr. Chesney, I'm sure. Don't you think so, Sir Francis?

SIR FRANCIS: Pleasanter today than usual, i fancy. (*sips wine*) Jack, my boy, where did you get this stuff?

FANCOURT: Champagne is what we need, isn't it. How very fortunate that I brought some with me in my bag. In my bag, Brassett.

(FRONT DOOR OPENS)

SPETTIGUE: (*remote, advancing*) Ah-ha! What do I find?

KITTY: }	Mr Spettigue
AMY: }	Uncle!
JACK: }	Mr Spettigue
CHARLEY: }	Mr. Spettigue.

SPETTIGUE: So, I was right after all. And that old fool of a woman told me they weren't here.

JACK: Mr. Spettigue...

SPETTIGUE:	Don't address me, sir! Is this the way you take advantage of my absence!
JACK:	Mr. Spettigue!
SPETTIGUE:	Don't address me, sir! I have no wish to hold any converse with you.
CHARLEY:	But won't you allow us to explain?
SPETTIGUE:	My business is with this young man, sir, and not with you.
FANCOURT:	But you won't listen to either of them!
SPETTIGUE:	Go away, madam, and don't interfere.
FANCOURT:	Where did you get that hat? Take it off, sir!
SPETTIGUE:	You're a very foolish old woman, and I must beg of you not to interfere. Ladies, come with me!
AMY:	Yes, uncle.
SIR FRANCIS:	Sir, you cannot put such an affront upon Mr Wykeham's friends.
SPETTIGUE:	I don't know them. And I don't want to know them.
SIR FRANCIS:	Introduce me, Mr Wykeham.
CHARLEY:	Mr. Spettigue, this is Sir Francis Chesney.

SIR FRANCIS:	Mr. Chesney is my son, sir and this lady is…
FANCOURT:	Pray don't introduce me to him. I've been sufficiently insulted by the old boun… er… gentleman, already.
SPETTIGUE:	I have only this to say. I am deeply annoyed to find, on prematurely returning from town, my niece and my ward lunching, without my permission, with these two young gentlemen.
SIR FRANCIS:	To meet Mr. Wykeham's aunt.
SPETTIGUE:	Indeed!
SIR FRANCIS:	There is no "Indeed" about it, sir. I repeat, to meet Mr. Wykeham's aunt. Now, allow me to introduce you. Donna Lucia d'Alvadorez _ Mr… What's his confounded name, Jack?
SPETTIGUE: } **JACK: }**	Donna Lucia! Spettigue.
SIR FRANCIS:	Mr Spettigue.
SPETTIGUE:	The celebrated millionaire? Oh, *how* do you *do?*
FANCOURT:	How do you do. Yes, I'm Charley's aunt from Brazil, where the nuts come from.
SPETTIGUE:	I've been indiscreet. I'm very, very sorry.

(FADE UP MUSIC BENEATH FOLLOWING)

FANCOURT: Your apology is accepted. You'll stay to lunch, won't you?

SPETTIGUE: If you wish it. And I am forgiven?

FANCOURT: Forgiven.

(UP MUSIC. HOLD A LITTLE. FADE BENEATH FOLLOWING)

BRASSETT: *(to himself)* Well, we're sailing along. He makes a wonderful lady, not a doubt about it. A bit odd to look at, perhaps, but then look at some of your old ladies! Both the old gents have got their eye on her. Lor'! If only they knew. I fancy Sir Francis is favourite, although old Spettigue fancies himself.

JACK: *(approaching)* And here we back again!

AMY: That was most instructive, Mr Wykeham.

JACK: I say, Charley, why not show Miss Spettigue round the college gardens?

CHARLEY: What a good idea. *(retreating)* They are quite delightful, Miss Spettigue, I do assure you.

JACK: *(calls)* And don't forget, Miss Spettigue, tea here in half an hour. At last, Miss Verdun, my dear Kitty, we are alone.

KITTY: Don't you think it was rather selfish of us, Mr. Chesney, to send them away like that?

JACK: Well, they'll be much happier together, alone, and it seems as if could never get five minutes with you safe from some miserable interruption. Indeed, I was beginning to fear you'd think me very rude, neglecting you as I have done.

KITTY: Oh, not at all, I quite understand. I couldn't expect you to devote yourself entirely to me.

JACK: My dear Miss Verdun, won't you sit down? I have something to say to you of importance.

KITTY: *(sitting)* Indeed, Mr. Chesney?

JACK: Yes. You know, Miss Verdun, there are times when a fellow's got to think a lot and think long.

KITTY: I suppose so.

JACK: And there are times when a fellow mustn't stop to think, or if he does, he'll spoil his chance!

KITTY: Yes.

JACK: Well, then, Miss Verdun, Kitty, my dear Kitty…

SIR FRANCIS: *(remote, advancing)* Ah, there you are. Oh, I beg pardon. No, don't mind me, Miss Verdun. I only wanted a word with my boy here.

KITTY: Oh, then, I'll have a look round the gardens. *(retreating)* Goodbye. I'll be back in time for tea.

JACK: Well, dad, anything important?

SIR FRANCIS: Yes, Jack, it is. Now you know, my boy, I'd do anything to see you get on in the world, and make a mark. As I know you will, if you get your chance…

JACK: You needn't tell me all this, dad.

SIR FRANCIS: Well, Jack, having thought it over I've decided that you shall continue the career I originally mapped out for you, and seeing a way out of the difficulty, I've determined to take your advice, my boy, and marry a lady of wealth.

JACK: I see, you've fallen a victim to the fascinations of some young and lovely…

SIR FRANCIS: No, Jack, she's not "lovely". And I'm afraid she is not over "young". But she has one thing in her favour, she has money, which, after all, is the real object in this instance.

JACK: All right, dad, as long as you are satisfied, go in and win!

SIR FRANCIS: And I have to thank you, my boy, for the tip.

JACK: Well, who is she? What's her name?

SIR FRANCIS: Can't you guess?

JACK: No, dad, I can't!

SIR FRANCIS: Donna Lucia d'Alvadorez!

JACK: What? The deuce! Dad, this is impossible!

SIR FRANCIS: Impossible? Why, you yourself suggested it, and for your sake, my lad, I'm going to do it.

JACK: But, dad, you can't!

SIR FRANCIS: Can't? Why not? I flatter myself she's taken rather a fancy to me. And as for old Spettigue, in spite of his marked attentions, I don't think he has the ghost of a chance. *(retreating)* So wish me luck, Jack.

JACK: Spettigue's attentions? What can he mean? *(calling)* Take time, dad, think it over.

CHARLEY: *(remote, advancing)* Jack! Jack! I wish you'd speak to Babbs, he's carrying on disgracefully. He's taken Amy away from me, and gone off round the garden with her.

JACK: Well, that's nothing to what's going on here. My Dad's just gone off to find Babbs in order to propose marriage.

CHARLEY: I knew something awful would come of this. We'll be found out and disgraced. How could you let it go on?

JACK: Don't blame me. It's all because of your muddle-headed aunt not knowing her own mind, and leaving us in the lurch. I could strangle her.

CHARLEY: What shall we do?

JACK: We must find Babbs, and put him up to the governor's game. Come on, *(retreating)* We can go round the gardens different ways until we've got him. Come on.

(FADE OUT. FADE IN GARDEN, BIRDS)

SIR FRANCIS: Ah, Mr Spettigue. Are you in search of anything?

SPETTIGUE: Nothing particular, Sir Francis. Are you looking for anyone?

SIR FRANCIS: Dear me, no. But I was thinking perhaps it would be as well if you rejoined the ladies. They might think it rude, both of us being away.

SPETTIGUE: Perhaps so, perhaps so. *(to himself)* So, she's somewhere in the gardens. *(retreating)* Quite right, Sir Francis. I'm on my way.

SIR FRANCIS: Well, here's where she promised to meet me, but she doesn't appear to be coming.

JACK: *(remote, approaching, calls)* I say, dad, you haven't seen Donna Lucia, have you?

SIR FRANCIS: No, Jack, I've not.

JACK: *(to himself)* That's fortunate.

SIR FRANCIS: I'm waiting for her here.

JACK: Waiting for her. Here?

SIR FRANCIS: Yes, I've an appointment with her. I didn't tell you before, Jack, but she's due. In fact, she's overdue! So get out, my boy, get out!

JACK :   (*to himself*) They mustn't meet till I've seen Babbs. (*to Sir Francis*) Now I come to think of it, dad, I saw her only a moment ago.

SIR FRANCIS: Oh, where?

JACK: Over in the rose garden.

SIR FRANCIS: Hang it, I've just sent old Spettigue there! (*retreating*) See you later, my boy.

JACK: I know Babbs isn't there, but where on earth has he got to?

CHARLEY: (*approaching, calling*) Well, have you found him?

JACK: No, and I've looked all over the place.

CHARLEY: So have I, and the worst of it is he's got Amy with him.

JACK: I'll kill the little monkey when I get hold of him!

CHARLEY: Now's your chance. Here he is, strolling arm in arm with Amy. By heavens!

AMY: *(approaching)* Ah, Mr. Wykeham, there you are. Did you think you'd lost us?

CHARLEY: Yes, I'm afraid I did.

JACK: *(whisper)* Where have you been with that girl, you fool?

FANCOURT: *(whisper)* Nowhere.

JACK: *(whisper)* Stop where you are. I've something to tell you. *(to Charley)* Charley, has Miss Spettigue seen the college dining room? *(whisper)* Take her away while I tell Babbs. *(to Amy)* You must see the college dining room. It's awfully impressive. Full of portraits and whatnot.

CHARLEY: *(retreating)* Yes, come along Amy. There are one or two statues scattered about as well. Wonderful place to have dinner...

AMY: *(retreating)* It must be...

JACK: What the deuce do you mean by this game?

FANCOURT: What game?

JACK: Your job was to look after those two old chaps. And here you are canoodling with Miss Spettigue – but I've no wish to argue. I want to put you on your guard.

FANCOURT: On my guard! Oh, thank you!

JACK: Yes. My dad's going to propose to you.

FANCOURT: Oh, is he? Well, I'm not going to marry him for you or anybody else. I'll see you hanged first.

JACK: Of course not, you idiot. All you've got to do is to be calm and refuse him.

FANCOURT: Be calm and refuse him! But a proposal puts anyone in a flutter. You know that.

JACK: All you've got to do is to remember that you're a real old lady.

FANCOURT: How the dickens am I to remember that I'm a real old lady with my trousers on under this dress?

JACK: Never mind your trousers. Look out, here's dad! I'm off!

FANCOURT: Yes, but what am I to say? I've never been proposed to before.

JACK: Oh, say he's taken you by surprise. *(retreating)* But whatever you do, mind you refuse him. 'Bye.

FANCOURT: Oo! Oo!

SIR FRANCIS: Ah, dear Donna Lucia, here you are! It's so good of you to come. Won't you sit down?

FANCOURT: As you wish.

SIR FRANCIS: Donna Lucia, you'll pardon the rude metaphor of an old campaigner, I'm sure, but to meet you today for the first time, as I have done, is to me like a lonely traveller coming across some, er… bright little flower by the wayside.

FANCOURT: Do you mean me?

SIR FRANCIS: Yes, Donna Lucia, yes.!

FANCOURT: (*to himself*) What am I to say to that, I wonder? (*to Sir Francis*) That's very nice and very kind of you.

SIR FRANCIS: (*to himself*) By George, she looks anything between fifty and a hundred! (*Clears throat*)

SIR FRANCIS: Donna Lucia, do you know what a man longs when he's lonely, desolate, and wretched?

FANCOURT: A drink?

SIR FRANCIS: No, Donna Lucia, this is what he longs for. He longs to plant in his own heart that bright little flower. And I have come all the way from India to find that little flower.

FANCOURT: You must be tired. Take a chair.

SIR FRANCIS: Thank you. And I have found it. Dear Lucia… That flower must sit at the head of my table. Walk by my side. Dwell in my heart for ever. I'll waste no more words; come to the point with a soldier's bluntness. Will you be my wife? Will you be my little flower?

FANCOURT: Well, you… You've taken me so much by surprise.

SIR FRANCIS.: Then I may hope?

FANCOURT: I'm afraid not. No, don't hope. I must refuse you. The fact is, I am another's.

SIR FRANCIS: Another's? Then it is quite useless our prolonging this interview. And you will accept my regrets and apologies for ever having broached the subject?

FANCOURT: Oh, certainly! Any time you're passing.

SIR FRANCIS: *(to himself)*. Refused. What a relief! I'm sorry, though, for the boy's sake. I must take myself off and tell him the news. **(loud, retreating)** Good-bye, Donna Lucia.

JACK: *(approaching)* You fool, what did you want to make a fool of my dad like that for?

FANCOURT: Were you there all the time? Not very sporting to eavesdrop on other people's conversations. And I didn't make a fool of the fool, you fool! Did you hear what he called me?

JACK: Yes, a flower.

FANCOURT: A nice thing.

JACK: Why didn't you cut him short, and refuse him at once?

FANCOURT: I couldn't refuse him until he'd proposed. No lady could. I'll find myself in the divorce court before I know where I am. Look out, here's old Spettigue. *(retreating)* I'm off!

SPETTIGUE: *(approaching)* Ah, Mr. Chesney, have you seen…? Is that Donna Lucia I see? *(retreating)* I must catch her.

JACK: What a sorry mess! Why on earth couldn't Charley's aunt behave like a lady and turn up as she promised, instead of giving us all this trouble. Now, I must find Kitty, before it's too late.

(FADE OUT. FADE IN)

DONNA LUCIA: *(approaching)* First door to the left? Thank you very much. Now, Ela, the first door to the left.

ELA: Yes, Donna Lucia, here it is. "Mr. John Chesney." Shall I knock?

DONNA LUCIA: Yes, do, my dear.

(KNOCK ON DOOR)

"Chesney." The name sounds familiar. Why couldn't my nephew remain in his rooms, and not compel me to follow him about like this.

ELA: You telegraphed to say you couldn't come.

DONNA LUCIA: I know, my dear.

ELA: And then you changed your mind.

DONNA LUCIA: Yes, for about the first time in my life.

ELA: Why?

DONNA LUCIA: Some vague desire to see him without his knowing. Knock again, dear.

(KNOCK ON DOOR)

ELA: The porter said they might all be in the gardens. I could roam about these old places all day. Isn't it all beautiful?

DONNA LUCIA: Dream away.

ELA: Oh, to live among these ancient spires. Like silent music, a scholar's fairyland! And how lovely it must be by moonlight.

DONNA LUCIA: What has put all these fancies into your head today?

ELA: Oh, I don't know.

DONNA LUCIA: I think I do. I can trace it all back to moonlight seen from the bridge of a certain yacht. I remember a certain "someone" who told you that you looked like "the angel of the watch." He was a flattering-tongued person, that "someone." What was his name again? Ah yes – Lord Fancourt Babberley. But I don't want your mind fixed on these things, my dear. Why, I'd almost forgotten to tell you, I've invested your poor father's money for you, and thanks to his forethought for his little girl he has rendered you independent for life – and what is worse, independent of me.

ELA: Independent!

DONNA LUCIA: But you won't be, Ela?

ELA: No.

DONNA LUCIA: For I've grown to love the little orphan I met in such grief in a strange land. So let's make a bargain. Be my little girl and call me "Auntie," will you?

ELA: Darling auntie. (*kiss*)

DONNA LUCIA: How did your poor father come to have so large a sum of money by him like that? I thought he'd lost it all.

ELA: Papa won it at cards.

DONNA LUCIA: But from whom?

ELA: Lord Fancourt Babberley. Auntie, if ever we meet, may I give it back?

DONNA LUCIA: I don't think he'd take it. Ah, my dear, you've set me thinking now.

ELA: Have I? What about?

DONNA LUCIA: Oh, it was before I went abroad, to Brazil. I was very young and he was very shy. He got as far as a stammering compliment and a blush, and then…

ELA: And then?

DONNA LUCIA: Then he was ordered off with his regiment.

ELA: Oh, Auntie!

DONNA LUCIA: It was at a dance the evening before he went away.

ELA: And you've never loved anyone since? What was his name, auntie?

DONNA LUCIA: Frank Chesney.

ELA: And here we are outside the door of a Mr Jack Chesney. How strange.

SIR FRANCIS: *(approaching)* Good afternoon ladies.

ELA: I'm afraid we're intruding.

SIR FRANCIS: Not at all. The college grounds are open to everyone. I am, so to speak, at home here merely because these are my son's rooms

DONNA LUCIA: Mr…?

SIR FRANCIS: My name is Chesney. I'm afraid it's Sir Francis, now.

DONNA LUCIA: Pardon my asking, but were you, Lieutenant Frank Chesney?

SIR FRANCIS: I was.

DONNA LUCIA: And do you remember the day, twenty years ago, when you embarked for India?

SIR FRANCIS: Indeed I do, madam.

(FADE IN BENEATH FOLLOWING OLD FASHIONED WALTZ)

DONNA LUCIA: But you've forgotten the evening before?

SIR FRANCIS: No, not altogether.

DONNA LUCIA: Then?

SIR FRANCIS: Lucy! Good gracious! And to think that at that very dance... but you don't remember that of course.

DONNA LUCIA: No?

SIR FRANCIS: No, because you never knew. But that night, by George, I nearly made you an avowal that... Ah! And we've never met in all that time! Over twenty years.

DONNA LUCIA: I'm afraid so.

SIR FRANCIS: I remember the dance perfectly, you were in white, tied up with blue.

(FADE OUT MUSIC)

DONNA LUCIA: Tied with blue! Like a chocolate box!

SIR FRANCIS: You must see my son, he's a splendid fellow! These are his rooms, or rather, he has lent them to a college friend, a young fellow named Wykeham.

DONNA LUCIA: Yes, Wykeham?

SIR FRANCIS: Who is entertaining some ladies. Two young ladies and his aunt. A lady from Brazil.

DONNA LUCIA: From Brazil?

SIR FRANCIS: Yes. Donna Lucia d'Alvadorez. I must introduce you.

DONNA LUCIA: Do I understand you to say that Donna Lucia d'Alvadorez is here. Actually here?

SIR FRANCIS: In the garden. Or was five minutes ago. Do you know her?

DONNA LUCIA: I… I've heard of her.

SIR FRANCIS: Then I'll find Donna Lucia, and the boys, or perhaps you wouldn't mind coming into the garden to them?

DONNA LUCIA: With pleasure. I'm quite curious to see them. This, Sir Francis, is my niece, Miss Delahay.

SIR FRANCIS: How do you do?

DONNA LUCIA: Come, Ela.

SIR FRANCIS: This way, ladies. (*to himself*) Ah, Jack, my boy, if this had been Donna Lucia, things might have been very different.

(FADE OUT. FADE IN)

JACK: And now here we are at last, Kitty. No one here, and I can speak to you. Kitty, my dear Kitty...

KITTY: But, Jack, look! Isn't that your manservant?

JACK: Brassett? What are you doing, Brassett?

BRASSETT: Laying the table for tea, sir.

JACK: Go away!

BRASSETT: But you gave orders, sir.

JACK: Put it back for half an hour. Quick, man, can't you see I'm engaged?

BRASSETT: Really, sir? I congratulate you.

JACK: Get out and don't come back!

BRASSETT: (*retreating*) Just as you wish, sir.

JACK: And now, my dear Kitty...

KITTY: Yes, Jack, you've said that before.

JACK: Now don't interrupt me. I go straight at most things, and I'm not going to hesitate over this. Kitty, in a few hours you'll be hundreds of miles away, and it may be years before we meet again, unless… unless…

KITTY: Unless… what?

JACK: Will you listen?

KITTY: I can't help myself.

JACK: I've told you how my father intended me for Parliament and all that?

KITTY: Yes.

JACK: Well, he tells me now, that for the next few years I shall have to give up all that, and earn my own living.

KITTY: Well, that will do you no harm, Jack.

JACK: No, that's how I look at it. But the question is, will you wait?

KITTY: Wait? What for?

JACK: What I really mean is, that… before I say anything further… I should like you to understand what I've been telling you.

KITTY: Oh, yes. What was that?

JACK: Well, to be practical and lay everything fairly before you, my position in life will be something in, er...

KITTY: The City.

JACK: Thanks. My home, er...

KITTY: Suburban.

JACK: Thanks. Exactly! Transit...

KITTY: Bus or rail.

JACK: My salary...

KITTY: Small.

JACK: Any extra income...

KITTY: Precarious.

JACK: But under certain conditions my fears would be nil and my hopes tremendous.

KITTY: (*to herself*) The dear fellow! (**loud**) Well, I hope those happy conditions will be realised to your heart's content.

JACK: Kitty, my dear Kitty. They will never be realised, without you.

KITTY:	Without me?
JACK:	Now you're vexed with me. You hate the City!! You despise the suburbs!! You loathe buses!
KITTY:	Why should you say that, Jack? As if I hadn't the heart to do what thousands of better girls than I have done. As if I couldn't guess all the happy fun that is to be got out of cooking and mending, and ministering to the wants and happiness of the man who will work and strive for the woman he loves!
JACK:	Then, Kitty.?
KITTY:	Try me, Jack; for I love you dearly.
JACK:	My dear, darling Kitty (*kiss*)
KITTY:	Oh, but what about my guardian, Mr. Spettigue?
JACK:	I'll see him at once.
KITTY:	No, that won't do. I must have his consent in writing.
JACK:	In writing, why?
KITTY:	So that he can't retract. You don't know him as well as I do. Now, there's only one person who can get that written consent for us, so be a good boy and send her to me at once.

JACK: What, Amy?

KITTY: No, Charley's aunt. Donna Lucia.

JACK: Donna Lucia? But…

KITTY: Now, don't ask questions, there's a good boy. (*retreating*) I'm going off to find Amy. Meanwhile you get hold of Charley's aunt, and send her to me at once.

JACK: Where on earth are we now? This simply can't go on.

(MUSIC. FADE BENEATH FOLLOWING)

NARRATOR: While the real Donna Lucia, accompanied by Ela Delahay, has arrived in the college, Lord Fancourt Babberley, dressed as Charley's aunt, is being pursued round the college gardens by Mr Spettigue, In the meantime Jack Chesney has found time to propose to Kitty and has been accepted. Now it's Charley's turn…

(EXTERIOR, BIRDS)

CHARLEY: (*remote, approaching*) I've done it, Jack, I've done it!

JACK: Done what?

CHARLEY: Told her that I love her.

JACK: Oh, is that all?

CHARLEY: Yes, but Jack, she knows her uncle's with Donna Lucia, and she's gone off to get old Spettigue's consent. We shall be in the dickens of a mess yet.

JACK: Well, keep cool, man, keep cool! We're all right up to now. We're all right up to now! Hey. Babbs, what are you up to?

FANCOURT: *(moving across the mic)* Don't mind me. Spettigue's after me. I must find somewhere to Hide. Quick.

SPETTIGUE: *(remote, approaching)* Now where can she be? I'm sure I saw her coming this way. *(retreating)* I'll try the rose garden.

CHARLEY: Now, Babbs, explain yourself. You're going to land us in the most awful trouble.

FANCOURT: You don't know the things he keeps saying to me.

CHARLEY: What, for example?

FANCOURT: You're too young, Charley. I'll whisper it to Jack. *(whispers)*

JACK: Goodness gracious. Does he?

FANCOURT: And it's very embarrassing.

CHARLEY: Oh, I wish to goodness you'd bring it all to an end.

FANCOURT:	So do I! I'm damned if I'm going to go on wearing this ridiculous costume. Come on, Jack, help me out of this dress. Here, Charley, take this wig. I want a drink!
JACK:	You just put yourself back into that dress, Babbs, or you'll ruin everything. We must have old Spettigue brimming over with good cheer. He's got to give his consent to our marrying the girls. Now you don't want to ruin everything, do you? You just play along with him for a bit, until he's said yes. Come on, this wig suits you very well.
FANCOURT:	It's damned hot. And if you think I'm going to marry old Spettigue, you're much mistaken. I could never be happy with a man like that.
CHARLEY:	You know, Babbs, if it was your girl, we'd do anything for you.
FANCOURT:	Oh, well. Charley, am I all right behind?
CHARLEY:	Let me see. Perfect.
JACK:	Look out. Here are the girls!
KITTY:	(*approaching*) Oh, Donna Lucia, we've been looking for you everywhere. Amy and I want so much to speak to you.
AMY:	We have a problem, you see...

KITTY:	...and we want you to be an angel. Now Jack, do go away!
AMY:	Yes, Charley, do go away.
FANCOURT:	(*as aunt*) You two, go away. They want me to be an angel.
KITTY:	Now, dear Donna Lucia, you know that Amy's uncle, Mr. Spettigue, is my guardian, and under my father's will, gets nearly all my money if I marry without his consent. And Amy and Charley are in love with each other, too. You don't object, do you?
FANCOURT:	Oh, no, my dears.
KITTY:	You old dear! (*kiss*)
AMY:	You dear thing! (*kiss*)
JACK: **CHARLEY:**	} Now then, now then. Stop all that. }
KITTY:	Jack, do go away.
AMY:	Yes, go away, Charley.
FANCOURT:	(*as aunt*) Yes, go away. We three girls want to be alone.
JACK: **CHARLEY:**	} (*retreating*) Well, really. } (*retreating*) This is too much

KITTY: Now, you know where we left off, don't you?

FANCOURT: Yes, you're all in love, and want to get married.

AMY: And we need uncle's consent.

KITTY: And your help.

FANCOURT: My help? To do what?

KITTY: Why, get Mr Spettigue's consent.

AMY: For both of us.

FANCOURT: Would you like me to be one of your bridesmaids?

KITTY: And his consent must be in writing.

FANCOURT: Oh, but my dears, I've no influence over him.

AMY: But you're so clever and so kind.

KITTY: And so rich.

AMY: Oh, dear Donna Lucia, do say you'll try.

FANCOURT: Well, I'll do my best.

KITTY: Then we'll find Mr Spettigue and send him to you
         at once. *(retreating)* Come along, Amy. There's no
         time to lose.

FANCOURT:	Well, here's a deuce of a mess. And another one approaching.
SPETTIGUE:	(*approaching*) Ah, there you are, dear Donna Lucia. I've been looking for you all the afternoon. I have so much to say to you.
DONNA LUCIA:	(*approaching*) Ah, Mr. Spettigue. Here you are again. Won't you introduce me to this lady – or this lady to me?
SPETTIGUE:	Oh, certainly! Donna Lucia d'Alvadorez.
FANCOURT:	How do you do? I'm Charley's aunt from Brazil, where the nuts come from.
DONNA LUCIA:	How do you do? Do you know I'm most interested in meeting you.
FANCOURT:	Really?
DONNA LUCIA:	I knew your late husband. Intimately!
FANCOURT:	Oh, Lord. Did you?
JACK:	(*remote, approaching*) Well, how is everyone getting on? Everything all right, is it?
FANCOURT:	(*whispers*) No! She knew my late husband intimately!
JACK:	(*whispers*) The deuce! Oh, hullo! Here's Brassett with the tea. On the table, Brassett.

BRASSETT: Indeed, sir. I would not dream of putting the tray anywhere else.

JACK: Now, Donna Lucia, will you pour out tea?

FANCOURT: Oh, certainly.

(CROCKERY, CUTLERY, POURING)

DONNA LUCIA: You haven't been in England long, have you?

JACK: Ah! Here's my father. *(calls)* Hullo, Dad. Come and join us for some tea.

SPETTIGUE : *(to himself)*. I must see her alone. I have it! They must come to dinner. After dinner, that's the time for my purpose. Pardon me, but I have a little proposition to make. Now I want you, all of you, to come and dine at my house tonight.

AMY: } Oh, yes, uncle. How nice of you.
KITTY: } That will be delightful.
JACK: } Grand idea.
CHARLEY: } Thanks awfully, sir.

(FADE IN JOLLY MUSIC BENEATH FOLLOWING)

DONNA LUCIA: Well, I have my niece with me. And here she comes. Miss Delahay.

FANCOURT: *(incredulous, own voice)* Miss Delahay!

SPETTIGUE: Bring her along. Delighted!

ELA: (*approaching*) That voice! Who called my name? It is. It is...

FANCOURT: (*as aunt*) Miss Delahay? Charmed to meet you.

ELA: Oh! Oh! I'm so sorry. How do you do?

DONNA LUCIA: This, my dear, is Donna Lucia!

(UP MUSIC TO END. FADE IN)

NARRATOR: And here we are in Spettigue's drawing room. Dinner in the next room is drawing to a close.

(BURST OF LAUGHTER FROM DINING ROOM)

Brassett is engaging in turning up the oil lamps, but hearing the laughter from next door, puts his ear to the door.

BRASSETT: There they go! They'll all be in here pretty soon. Fancy old Spettigue getting me to come here tonight and butler for him. I suppose he's too mean to have a butler of his own. Well, all I can say is, it's simply marvellous the way his lordship's kept it up! He's played the perfect lady something wonderful!

(LOUD LAUGHTER AND TALKING)

Hullo! What's up now?

(DOOR OPENS)

FANCOURT:	(*approaching*) Brassett, get me a cab, quick; I'm going home.
BRASSETT:	(*retreating*) At once, sir.
JACK:	(*approaching*) You've been going along all right, Babbs. If you'd only paid more attention to old Spettigue. Why did you bolt from the dinner table like that?
CHARLEY:	(*approaching*) It's so awfully dangerous and unkind of you, you know.
JACK:	Instead of behaving in a dignified manner as Charley's aunt, here you are going on like some disgraceful old... old...
FANCOURT:	Oh, go on, finish it. Don't spare me.
CHARLEY:	Think of the girls and the solemn promise you gave to help us, for their sakes.
FANCOURT:	Yes, but Miss Delahay wasn't here then.
JACK:	What, the girl with Mrs... what's-her-name?
FANCOURT:	Yes. She's the girl I met at Monte Carlo, and this woman is the woman who took her away. I want to tell her what you fellows have been telling your girls. Hang it! I'm just as much in love as you are.

CHARLEY: Quiet! They'll hear everything.

FANCOURT: *(loud)* And what's more, you can tell those confounded girls of yours to leave off kissing me before her. I won't stand it!

JACK: *(shouting).* Don't shout, you idiot! *(To Charley)* We'll make some excuse. Say she's ill, put him in a cab, and be done with him.

FANCOURT: And, Charley, you can make some excuse to Miss Verdun for me.

JACK: Miss Verdun! What have you got to say to Miss Verdun? Come, out with it!

FANCOURT: Haven't I promised to get old Spettigue's consent in writing, you idiot? You're as helpless as a couple of babies, you want your mothers with you!

BRASSETT: *(remote, advancing)* This way, madam.

CHARLEY: They're coming!

JACK: Here, Babbs, sit down, quick! Let's all sit down.

DONNA LUCIA: *(advancing|)* How is your aunt, Mr. Wykeham? We were afraid she might be ill.

ELA: Yes, is there anything the matter?

CHARLEY: Er... Auntie's been a little upset by the... by the heat of the dining room, that's all. Oh, hullo Miss Spettigue, Miss Verdun.

AMY: *(advancing)* I hope Donna Lucia is all right?

KITTY: Yes, is she?

ELA: Oh, yes, Mr. Chesney says she all right now.

KITTY: Well, Jack, will you and Mr Chesney go and tell Mr Spettigue? He's most anxious.

AMY: Yes, we'll look after her now.

ELA: *(quietly to Donna)* I wonder who she really is, auntie?

DONNA LUCIA: *(quietly)* Oh, some old thing they got after receiving my telegram.

ELA: Say something to her, auntie. I like to hear her talk.

DONNA LUCIA: I would, my dear, but look at her. If I thought they intended that to be like me, I'd never forgive them. *(loud to Fancourt):* Do you know, I remember a very funny story...

FANCOURT: *(to himself)* That's just what I expected.

DONNA LUCIA: ...that Dom Pedro was very fond of telling.

FANCOURT: *(to himself)* I must put a stop to this. Won't one of the young ladies play something, please?

DONNA LUCIA: *(quietly)* How rude to interrupt like that!

ELA: Oh, she couldn't have heard you, auntie.

KITTY: Oh, do tell us the story.

AMY: Yes, anything about Dom Pedro would be so interesting. Do tell us.

DONNA LUCIA: But perhaps Donna Lucia would prefer to tell Don Pedro's story herself?

FANCOURT: Tom Pedro?

DONNA LUCIA: Your late husband, you know, Dom Pedro d'Alvadorez.

FANCOURT: Oh, yes, of course I know his name. But I don't remember his stories. I don't hold with such frivolity.

ELA: Auntie, don't tease her so, tell the story yourself.

DONNA LUCIA: Well, Dom Pedro, who was the kindest soul in all the world, but... Will Donna Lucia give me permission?

FANCOURT: if I must, I must!

DONNA LUCIA: Well, as I said before: Dom Pedro, who was the kindest soul in all the world, once found one of his cellarmen tipsy, very tipsy. So Dom Pedro said to the man, "What would Dom Pedro say if he saw you like this?"

FANCOURT: And what did the man say?

DONNA LUCIA: The man said, "Oh, that's all right, Dom Pedro's often like this."

KITTY: }
AMY: } (*laugh*)
ELA: }
DONNA LUCIA: }

FANCOURT: What was the man's name?

DONNA LUCIA: Really, I don't know the man's name.

FANCOURT: Oh, that's a pity!

DONNA LUCIA: But don't you remember the story? It was a favourite one of Dom Pedro's.

FANCOURT: Oh, perfectly! I shrieked when I heard it first. Won't one of the young ladies play something, please?

KITTY: Oh, I'm so out of practice. You sing something, Amy!

AMY: Oh, I can't. I know nothing new.

FANCOURT: Sing that charming little ballad. Ta-Ra-Ra-Boomdeay.

AMY: I'm afraid I can't, Donna Lucia.

DONNA LUCIA: Won't you sing something for us, Donna Lucia?

FANCOURT: Me?

DONNA LUCIA:	Yes, one of those charming little Brazilian songs I've heard Dom Pedro was so fond of.
FANCOURT:	Oh, no. I haven't sung since I had the measles.
DONNA LUCIA:	*(to Ela)*. What?
FANCOURT:	Over forty years ago.
DONNA LUCIA:	*(to Ela)*. Another libel! I was the merest infant.
FANCOURT:	But I play a little. What shall I play? A little Beethoven or the Blue Bells of Scotland?

(PIANO – CHOPSTICKS)

	Do you know that?
SPETTIGUE :	*(remote, calls)* I'm on my way, Donna Lucia!
KITTY:	Here they are! Now don't forget the letter!
FANCOURT:	Oh, no, I won't forget.
KITTY:	Let's get them all out into the garden, Amy, and leave her alone with Mr Spettigue. *(retreating)* Come along, everyone.
SPETTIGUE:	*(advancing)* Charming! Charmingly played, Donna Lucia.

(MUSIC STOPS)

CHARLEY: Look at him, Jack.

JACK: What's he doing?

CHARLEY: Staring at her like he did all through dinner.

JACK: The fool!

SIR FRANCIS: You've been enjoying yourselves capitally, Miss Verdun, we heard the music.

KITTY: Yes, Donna Lucia has been playing for us.

SPETTIGUE: How charming of you, Donna Lucia. What should we have done without your dear aunt, Charley?

CHARLEY: *(groans)*

AMY: Is something the matter, Charley?

CHARLEY: No, no.

AMY: Then let's go out into the garden. It's a lovely evening. *(retreating)* Coming, Charley?

CHARLEY: *(retreating)* Lead on!

JACK: Are you fond of music, Mr. Spettigue?

SPETTIGUE: I... I hope to be.

FANCOURT: *(whispers)* Why's he looking at me like a boiled owl?

JACK: Dad, I'm glad you know about Kitty now, she's a splendid girl, isn't she?

SIR FRANCIS: I like her very much, I must say, Jack.

JACK: You've taken a load off my mind, Dad. I thought I was quite without means.

SIR FRANCIS: Not altogether, my boy.

SPETTIGUE: But why won't you listen to reason?

FANCOURT: Of course, I'll listen to reason, but where is the letter?

SPETTIGUE: Ah, I remember. I've not written it yet.

FANCOURT: Not yet!

SPETTIGUE: We must find an opportunity to talk it over, alone!

FANCOURT: That will be nice!

JACK: Kitty, I've told Dad straight out, and he's delighted! But, Kitty, you won't regret turning your back on "Society" and everything…?

KITTY: And have something real to think about? Jack, the vista is too heavenly. Come into the garden.

(SOFT PIANO MUSIC)

SIR FRANCIS:	Shall we join them?
DONNA LUCIA:	Yes, it's a charity to leave those two people alone.
SIR FRANCIS:	Indeed, why?
DONNA LUCIA:	Only a little match-making mischief, that's all.
SIR FRANCIS:	On Spettigue's account?
DONNA LUCIA:	No. On Donna Lucia's. *(retreating)* Come along – let's leave them to each other's company.
SPETTIGUE:	Ah at last! They've gone. Lucia! They've gone! Lucia, how I have longed for this moment.
FANCOURT:	*(to himself).* He's at again.
SPETTIGUE:	Lucia, I must speak to you, I—
FANCOURT:	No. I am very angry with you.
SPETTIGUE:	Lucia, you wound me; don't say that!
FANCOURT:	But I do say that. After the promise you made me, to treat me like this.
SPETTIGUE:	Promise?
FANCOURT:	The consent you promised in writing.
SPETTIGUE:	Lucia, how can you, when we have so much to say that more nearly concerns ourselves.

FANCOURT: No, we have not. You don't know me! I'm no ordinary woman.

SPETTIGUE: Lucia, I beg of you to listen to me!

FANCOURT: I'll listen to you with pleasure, but where is the letter you promised me?

SPETTIGUE: Will you hear me, Lucia?

FANCOURT: Until you give me the letter, all is over between us.

SPETTIGUE: Lucia, that decides me. I go to my room. A brief note...

FANCOURT: With full consent and signed, don't forget.

SPETTIGUE: (*retreating*) Then say you will be mine?

FANCOURT: I'll say anything you like, only don't be too long in the study.

SPETTIGUE: (*remote*) Darling!

(DOOR OPENS, CLOSES)

FANCOURT: That's all right! I say, what devils we women are! It's too bad of those fellows! Why, I'll be an old woman for the rest of my life. I haven't had a drink or a smoke all day! By George, the cigar box! Here's a find! I Wonder how long he'll be? Hanged if I don't chance it!

(MATCH STRIKES)

(puffing on cigar) Beautiful! Beautiful!

DONNA LUCIA: *(remote, advancing, to Ela)* She's smoking! Ahem!

FANCOURT: *(coughs, splutters)*

ELA: Auntie, did you find it chilly?

DONNA LUCIA: Yes, my dear, I thought I'd get a wrap of some kind.

ELA: *(retreating)* I'll just go upstairs and get you something. I know where your things are!

DONNA LUCIA: Are you alone?

FANCOURT: Yes, I'm all alone. And so sad.

DONNA LUCIA: Dear me, what a dreadful smell of smoke.

FANCOURT: Yes, I noticed it myself. I'll go and find out who it is.

DONNA LUCIA: No, don't go. I wanted to talk to you.

FANCOURT: Yes.

DONNA LUCIA: About your late husband, Dom Pedro.

FANCOURT: Oh, that will be nice.

DONNA LUCIA: Do you know, when I met Dom Pedro, he told me he had no wife.

FANCOURT: Oh, the wicked story-teller. Ah, but he was a cruel husband.

DONNA LUCIA: The Dom Pedro I knew was noble, kind and gentle.

FANCOURT: That was his father, the old gentleman with the white moustache.

DONNA LUCIA: *(to herself)* I never knew such effrontery! *(loud)* Do you know, Donna Lucia, I'm surprised you don't indulge in the habit of smoking. So many Brazilian ladies do, you know.

FANCOURT: Well, to tell you the truth, that's just what I was doing when you came in. See. A cigar.

DONNA LUCIA: Then, pray don't let me interrupt you.

FANCOURT: Can I offer you one?

DONNA LUCIA: No thanks.

FANCOURT: Will you have a drink of any kind?

DONNA LUCIA: No thanks. Oh, Donna Lucia, pardon my curiosity, but have you any children?

FANCOURT: Only a few. None to speak of.

ELA: *(approaching)* Here's your wrap, auntie.

DONNA LUCIA: Thank you, dear. I'm going into the garden. I fancy Sir Francis has something to say to me and it's rather chilly. *(retreating)* Perhaps you'd better stay in!

ELA: I fancy Auntie wants to speak to Sir Francis. Years ago, you know, she and Sir Francis were sweethearts.

FANCOURT: Were they?

ELA: But he went away, without telling her he was ever and ever so fond of her. Auntie says he was shy, and he went away without knowing that she was ever and ever so fond of him. But the noblest man I ever knew was shy, and oh, so kind. He got to know how papa had become so ill, and so poor, and lost a large sum of money to him at cards, auntie thinks, on purpose. I often wondered why they played cards, and papa so ill too, but when I asked the doctor if it wasn't doing harm, he said, "Not the game that was being played." But I've got all the money and if ever we meet, I mean to give it back.

FANCOURT: Oh, no, you must never think of doing that. It would be like accusing him of sort of cheating, you know.

ELA: But it was so much. Enough, auntie says, to make me independent for life.

FANCOURT: And do you think he'd take it back if he knew that?

ELA: Oh, but I should feel it my duty.

FANCOURT: It's too late now.

ELA: But he went away before I had time to tell him how much I... I... loved him... for ...for his kindness to my poor father. You don't mind my telling you all this, do you? I don't know why, but I like to talk to you. I like you and I do so long to see him again. *(retreating)* I must go to my aunt. Hullo, Mr Spettigue.

SPETTIGUE: *(remote, advancing)* Miss Delahay. Ah, Lucia!

FANCOURT: Have you got the letter?

SPETTIGUE: Yes, here it is. But first, make my happiness complete. Say that from this blissful moment we are engaged?

FANCOURT: We are engaged. Got it! We are engaged.

SPETTIGUE: Darling!

FANCOURT: Mr Spettigue!

SPETTIGUE: *(calls)* Call me Stephen.

FANCOURT: *(retreating)* Yes, I will. Very shortly. After I have delivered this letter.

SPETTIGUE: Ah, Sir Francis. Mrs – er ... Madam. Congratulate me! I'm the happiest man in the world, but where are the dear children? This must be a day of happiness and rejoicing for us all!

SIR FRANCIS:	*(approaching)* What on earth does he mean? What's all this excitement about?
DONNA LUCIA:	Can't you guess?
SIR FRANCIS:	No.
DONNA LUCIA:	Don't you understand? She's accepted him.
SIR FRANCIS:	What?
DONNA LUCIA:	Yes, Donna Lucia d'Alvadorez!
SIR FRANCIS:	You don't mean that?
DONNA LUCIA:	I fancy he'll find out his mistake before long.
SIR FRANCIS:	By George, what a fool I've been!
DONNA LUCIA:	Why? Are you sorry?
SIR FRANCIS:	No, but that rascal of a boy of mine made some sort of a stupid suggestion that I should…
DONNA LUCIA:	That you should offer your hand and heart to Donna Lucia d'Alvadorez, from Brazil, where the nuts come from.
SIR FRANCIS:	When I think of what a fool I was… might have been… should…
DONNA LUCIA:	Then you don't envy him – Spettigue?

SIR FRANCIS: Envy him!

DONNA LUCIA: But think of her millions.

SIR FRANCIS: Ah, Lucy, when I saw your face—

DONNA LUCIA: You didn't recognise it!

SIR FRANCIS: No, but when I did… But I told you all that in the garden just now, you'll be content for a while with a cottage and your old sweetheart?

DONNA LUCIA: And you? You would take me, a penniless widow?

SIR FRANCIS: Nothing could make me happier!

DONNA LUCIA: Frank!

SIR FRANCIS: Lucy! Why, what are you smiling at?

DONNA LUCIA: I was only thinking of…

SIR FRANCIS: Of what?

DONNA LUCIA: Of Donna Lucia d'Alvadorez. Oh, here's my niece. Hullo, Ela, my dear.

ELA: (*approaching*) Auntie, dear/

SIR FRANCIS: Well, Donna Lucia's a quaint little figure, I must own!

ELA:	Auntie, How pretty you look tonight! *(whispers)* Has Sir Francis…?
DONNA LUCIA:	Ssh!
SPETTIGUE:	*(remote, advancing)* Come along, my dear children. Come along! Kitty, Amy, you sit there.
JACK:	Charley – over here. Brassett, is there anything in the way of refreshments in this establishment?
BRASSETT:	I believe something could be found, sir.
SPETTIGUE:	Now, everybody, I have something to tell you. Something you will all be very pleased to hear. Where is Donna Lucia?
BRASSETT:	Donna Lucia's gone to her room, sir!
SPETTIGUE:	Ah, perhaps it's just as well! Now, before she returns, I have a little secret to tell you.
ALL:	*(murmuring)* A secret? Really? How intriguing. Wonder what the old boy is about to reveal. I like secrets. Don't you? Etc., etc
SPETTIGUE:	I am sure you will pardon me if I ask your attention for a few moments.
CHARLEY:	Good gracious, Jack, what's he going to say?
JACK:	How do I know till he's said it?

SPETTIGUE:	Situated as I am, a lonely widower, a mateless uncle, surrounded with grave responsibilities – my ward, my niece – a good fairy has, I may say, tripped in among us, bringing with her unexpected light and joy!
CHARLEY	Who does he mean?
JACK:	Shut up!
SPETTIGUE:	Under her influence, I have consented to the engagement of my niece to a gentleman in whose honour and probity I have the fullest confidence: Mr. Charles Wykeham.
AMY:	Charley, how sweet of your dear aunt.
SPETTIGUE:	Furthermore, charmed by irresistible spells, I have consented to the union of my ward with John, only son of my friend, Sir Francis Chesney.
KITTY:	Jack, we have my guardian's approval…
SPETTIGUE:	But what will you say to a third engagement?
JACK:	} A third?
CHARLEY:	} What?
SPETTIGUE:	Our good fairy— nay, let me add without further metaphor —one whose name is honoured in the South-Western hemisphere, has consented to become Mrs Stephen Spettigue. I allude to our dear friend, Donna Lucia d'Alvadorez.

(CLATTER OF DROPPED TRAY AND GLASSES)

What is that?

BRASSETT:	Beg pardon, sir. The tray, sir.
SPETTIGUE:	Be more careful, Brassett
CHARLEY:	Mr. Spettigue, I can listen to this ghastly farrago no longer.
SPETTIGUE:	Mr. Wykeham, sir. What do you mean?
CHARLEY:	I say, sir. And I don't care what the result may be. I can listen to this ghastly—
SPETTIGUE:	I presume, sir, in espousing my niece—
CHARLEY:	I can't. I won't espouse her under these false and lying pretences. That woman...
SPETTIGUE:	Do you allude in such a manner to—
CHARLEY:	I say that woman—
SPETTIGUE:	I must beg of you to speak with more respect of your aunt.
CHARLEY:	She is not my aunt!
SPETTIGUE:	Not your aunt! What do you mean?
CHARLEY:	I love Amy far too sincerely to—

SPETTIGUE: Never mind that, sir. Explain your words!

JACK: Mr. Spettigue, will you allow me to say that the blame is mine and let me explain?

SPETTIGUE: I am addressing this person. Answer me, sir, explain your words.

BRASSETT: *(to himself)*. I must tell his lordship of this! At once!

CHARLEY: At the last moment, this morning, my aunt—on whose account we had invited Miss Verdun and Miss Spettigue— telegraphed to say she couldn't come. The ladies arrived and we—

JACK: And I, sir, prevailed upon another person, to... well...

SPETTIGUE: To impersonate her. I've been treacherously, infamously deceived!

CHARLEY: That was not our intention, sir!

SPETTIGUE: Don't lie to me, sir.

JACK: I beg your pardon, sir, you forget you were not expected.

SPETTIGUE: A frump like that, with a wig!

JACK: Well you can't blame her for that.

FANCOURT:	*(remote, advancing, as himself)* May I come in?
SPETTIGUE:	Turn that woman out of my house!
FANCOURT:	I say, may I come in?
SPETTIGUE:	Turn that woman out of... Who are you, sir?
FANCOURT:	I'm Charley's aunt from Brazil where the nuts come from.
JACK:	May I present Lord Fancourt Babberley!
FANCOURT:	That is who I am, Mr Spettigue, despite these remnants of my costume. And I beg your pardon.
ELA:	Oh, auntie! And I told him everything!
SPETTIGUE:	What does this mean, sir?
FANCOURT:	It means that we've all done very wrong and we're all extremely sorry, and tender you our humblest apologies. My apologies, I should say, for if I hadn't offered the temptation, the whole thing would never have occurred.
CHARLEY:	And if Mr Spettigue will allow us to add our—
JACK:	And say we have no words to express our contrition—
SPETTIGUE:	It's infamous, infamous! But where is the document obtained from me under these fraudulent pretences?

FANCOURT: Oh, the letter, I have the letter. Here it is!

KITTY: It's mine, mine!

SPETTIGUE: Give it to me, Miss Verdun!

DONNA LUCIA: Allow me to take charge of it. Thank you!

SPETTIGUE: I shall dispute it, under her father's will. I shall dispute it.

DONNA LUCIA: This letter is addressed, and has been delivered to Donna Lucia d'Alvadorez.

SPETTIGUE: But she... I mean he, is not Donna Lucia d'Alvadorez.

DONNA LUCIA: No, but I am!

ALL. You!! Never! You are Donna Lucia? How is that? Etc., etc.

SIR FRANCIS: Lucy!!

CHARLEY: My aunt!

SPETTIGUE: You will pardon me if I retire. As for you, sir, Lord Fancourt, if that is indeed who you are, I shall inform the college authorities in the morning about your totally unacceptable conduct, and I trust they will administer a suitable punishment. Goodnight, sir.

(DOOR SLAMS SHUT)

FANCOURT: Charley, can he have me up for breach of promise?

AMY: Charley, how dare you? I'll never forgive you! I'll never forgive any of you, for treating uncle Stephen like that.

DONNA LUCIA: Be patient with us, my dear. Your uncle shall have the most profound reparation my influence can make. For my own part I only shared in the deception when I found another lady established in my place.

FANCOURT: No wonder she knew all about my late husband.

KITTY: Well, I'm as sorry as anyone, but I'd trust Jack with my life.

DONNA LUCIA: Indeed? Then he must wait till I'm his mother.

JACK: Mother?

SIR FRANCIS: Yes, Donna Lucia, in deceiving me as much as anybody, has, however, done me the honour to recollect an old affection, and has promised to assume that authority. So look out, Jack!

DONNA LUCIA: Lord Fancourt Babberley. I am afraid you have gained one confidence that nothing could excuse.

FANCOURT: I know, and I reproach myself beyond expression, but I wouldn't part with the memory of that confidence to save my life, and if Miss Delahay will allow me to say so, I am willing to atone for it, with a life-long devotion.

(FADE MUSIC BENEATH FOLLOWING)

DONNA LUCIA: Now, where's my son?

JACK: Here, Mama!

DONNA LUCIA: I shall have to talk to you very seriously before I give you this letter. And Charley, I'll never forgive you if you deceive that sweet girl again! And as for you, Lord Fancourt,,,

FANCOURT: Oh no, never again, I give you my word. I'll give you the clothes if you like, I've done with them. Miss Delahay has consented to think me over as a husband, and in future I resign to Sir Francis Chesney all claims to "Charley's Aunt."

(UP MUSIC. DOWN FOR CLOSING ANNOUNCEMENT. UP MUSIC TO A RESOUNDING END)

THE VALLEY OF FEAR

BY SIR ARTHUR CONAN DOYLE

DRAMATISED FOR RADIO
BY NEVILLE TELLER

Running Time: 60'

FIRST BROADCAST ACROSS THE
UNITED STATES ON 1 FEBRUARY 2017
IN A PRODUCTION BY SHOESTRING
RADIO THEATRE, SAN FRANCISCO
DIRECTED BY MELISSA FLOWER

CHARACTERS

MALE:

SHERLOCK HOLMES

DR WATSON

INSPECTOR MACDONALD   *30s. Scottish*

CECIL BARKER   *40s. English*

SERGEANT WILSON   *50s. English country policeman*

AMES   *60s. English butler*

JACK DOUGLAS   *40s. American, light East coast accent*

SCANLAN   *30s. American blue collar*

JACOB SHAFTER   *50s. American. Ettie's father*

TED BALDWIN   *30s. American blue collar*

JACK MCGINTY   *40s. American union boss*

CAPTAIN MARVIN   *30s. American police.*

MORRIS   *50s. American.*

FEMALE:

MRS HUDSON   *50s. English*

MRS ALLEN   *50s. English. Housekeeper*

MRS DOUGLAS   *40s English*

ETTIE   *20s. American*

(MUSIC. DOWN FOR OPENING ANNOUNCEMENT. UP MUSIC. CROSSFADE TO SLOW TICKING OF GRANDFATHER CLOCK. FADE CLOCK SLOWLY BENEATH FOLLOWING)

WATSON: You know, Holmes, I'm inclined to think…

HOLMES: (*distracted*) Think? Yes, yes, my dear Watson. Do that.

WATSON: Really, Holmes, you are a little trying at times.

HOLMES: You know, this *is* Porlock's handwriting. That Greek "E" with the peculiar flourish – it's very distinctive. And if it's Porlock, then this letter must be of the first importance.

WATSON: Porlock? Who's Porlock?

HOLMES: Porlock, Watson, is the pen-name of a shifty individual. He told me in a previous letter that Porlock isn't his real name, but he defied me to trace him among the teeming millions of London. He's of no importance in himself. His importance lies in the towering personality with whom he's in touch. You've heard me speak of Professor Moriarty?

WATSON: The famous scientific criminal?

HOLMES: The greatest schemer of all time, the controlling brain of the underworld – but also the celebrated author of works which ascend to the rarefied heights of pure mathematics. If I am spared by lesser men, one day Professor Moriarty and I will surely cross swords.

WATSON: May I be there to see it! But you were speaking of this man Porlock.

HOLMES: Ah, yes. The so-called Porlock is a link in the chain. I encourage him with a small remuneration from time to time, and he provides me with inside information about Professor Moriarty. Now this letter – I have no doubt that if we knew the code, we'd find it of the greatest importance. Take a look.

WATSON: I can make nothing of it. It's mostly a series of numbers. Oh no – there's a name. "Douglas".

HOLMES: And down here?

WATSON: Birlstone – twice. What do you make of it, Holmes?

HOLMES: Well, it's obviously an attempt to convey secret information. If this first number – 534 – is the page of a book, most of the rest could be the words on the page. But which book? That's the question.

WATSON: Why are "Douglas" and "Birlstone" spelled out?

HOLMES: Obviously, Watson, because those words do not appear on the page.

WATSON: But why on earth has this Porlock not told you what book he's using?

HOLMES: My dear Watson, who in their right mind would enclose both a cipher and its key in the same envelope? Unless I'm very much mistaken, the next post will provide us with some enlightenment.

              (DISTANT DOUBLE KNOCK ON FRONT DOOR)

              And that will be it. No doubt Mrs Hudson is collecting the post at this very moment. Now she will be mounting the stairs. *(calls)* Enter, Mrs Hudson. Do not bother to knock.

              (DOOR OPENS)

              You have a letter for me, I believe?

MRS HUDSON: How on earth did you…? Oh, well, I'm past being surprised at anything you say, Mr Holmes. Here it is.

WATSON: Thank you, Mrs Hudson.

              (ENVELOPE TORN OPEN. DOOR CLOSES)

HOLMES: Dear me, this is very disappointing! "Dear Mr Holmes. I will go no further in this matter. It is too dangerous. I can see he suspects me. He nearly caught me sending you the key to the cipher in this envelope. Please burn the coded message. It can now be of no use to you, Fred Porlock."

WATSON: I presume he's referring to Professor Moriarty. It's pretty maddening to think that an important secret may lie on this slip of paper, and that it's beyond human power to unravel it.

HOLMES: Why don't we try, Watson, using our powers of deduction, and see how far we can get? Now this book – what do we know about it?

WATSON: Nothing.

HOLMES: Surely not. The cipher message begins with 534. Assuming that's the page number, our book has already become a large book. The next sign is C2. What do you make of that, Watson?

WATSON: The second chapter?

HOLMES: Hardly that, Watson . Why would we need to know the chapter? We're given the page.

WATSON: Column!

HOLMES: Brilliant, Watson. So now, we can visualize a large book printed in double columns, each of considerable length. Look, one of the words numbered in the cipher is the two hundred and ninety third.

WATSON: I see.

HOLMES: Have we reached the limits of what reason can supply?

WATSON: I fear we have, Holmes.

HOLMES: You do yourself an injustice. Our friend Porlock did not intend to send us the volume itself. He was going to give me the name of the book – he says so himself in his note. What does that tell you, Watson?

WATSON: I'm at a loss.

HOLMES: Why, that he assumed I would have the book in question. In short, Watson, it is a large book, printed in double columns, and in common use.

WATSON: The Bible!

HOLMES: Good, Watson, but not good enough. There are too many editions of Holy Writ. Don't forget that his page 534 must coincide with my page 534. So our search is narrowed down to a standardized book that anyone might be supposed to possess.

WATSON: An almanac!

HOLMES: Excellent, Watson. Let's consider the claims of Whitaker's Almanac. It's in common use. It has the requisite number of pages. It is in double columns. Would you be so kind as to hand me the current edition – on the bookshelf by your left hand.

WATSON: Here you are. My word, it weighs a ton.

HOLMES: Not quite!

(PAGES RUFFLED)

Page... 534...column two ... A substantial block of print – dealing, I perceive, with the trade of British India. Jot down the words, Watson. Number 13 is "There". Number 127 is ... "is". "There is". Next – "danger". Put this down, Watson. "There – is – danger. May – come – very – soon. One..." Then we have the name Douglas. "Rich – country – now – at – Birlstone House. Birlstone. Confidence – is – pressing." There.

WATSON: "There is danger. May come very soon. One Douglas. Rich. Country now at Birlstone House, Birlstone. Confidence is pressing." It doesn't all quite make sense, Holmes.

HOLMES: I disagree. The meaning is perfectly clear. Some devilry is intended against a certain Douglas, living in Birlstone House. Porlock is sure – confidence is as close as he could get – that it will all happen very soon. There is our result – and a very workmanlike little bit of analysis it was.

(KNOCK ON DOOR. DOOR OPENS)

MRS HUDSON:	*(distant)* Mr Holmes, there's an Inspector MacDonald here to see you. He says he's from Scotland Yard.
HOLMES:	And so he is. You're a suspicious soul, Mrs Hudson. Show him in, show him in. *(calls)* Ah, my dear Mac. Good to see you. I believe this is the first time you have bearded us in our den.

(DOOR CLOSES)

MACDONALD:	*(advancing)* And a very cosy den it is, to be sure. Mr Holmes. Dr Watson.
HOLMES:	Seat yourself, Mr MacDonald. I fear your call means that there is some mischief afoot.
MACDONALD:	Excuse me... This piece of paper... What is this, Mr Holmes, witchcraft? Douglas! Birlstone! Where in the name of all that's wonderful did you get these names?
HOLMES:	It's a code, a cipher, that Dr Watson and I have had occasion to solve. But what's so special about these names?
MACDONALD:	Just this, gentlemen. Last night Mr Douglas of Birlstone Manor in the county of Sussex was brutally murdered.
HOLMES:	Remarkable!

MACDONALD: You don't seem surprised, Mr Holmes.

HOLMES: Why should I be? I receive a communication from a source in the criminal underworld who goes by the name of Porlock. He warns me that danger threatens a certain person. Within the hour, I learn that this person is dead. I am interested but, as you observe, not surprised. What surprises me is your visit.

MACDONALD: I called because I propose going down to Birlstone this morning, and I wondered if you and Dr Watson would care to come with me.

HOLMES: We seem to be involved in the case already. What say you, Watson?

WATSON: I'm game if you are.

MACDONALD: One moment. This source of yours – this Porlock. You believe there is someone behind him?

HOLMES: I know there is.

MACDONALD: This professor that I've heard you speak of? Moriarty?

HOLMES: Exactly.

MACDONALD: Mr Holmes, we at Scotland Yard think you have a bee in your bonnet over this professor. After you spoke of him, I made it my business to see him. We had a wee chat. A pleasanter, more

THE VALLEY OF FEAR

THE VALLEY OF FEAR

knowledgeable gentleman you'd never meet. He'd have made a grand minister, with his thin face and gray hair and solemn manner. When he put his hand on my shoulder as we were parting, it was like a father's blessing.

HOLMES: Tell me, friend MacDonald, this pleasing and touching interview was, I suppose in the professor's study?

MACDONALD: That's so.

HOLMES: Did you happen to observe a picture over the professor's head?

MACDONALD: Yes. A young woman with her head on her hands, peeping at you sideways.

HOLMES: That painting, Mac, is by Jean Baptiste Greuze, a French artist who flourished in the eighteenth century. Some twenty years ago it was sold at auction to an anonymous buyer for one million two hundred thousand francs. May I remind you that the professor's salary – it's a matter of public record – is seven hundred pounds a year.

MACDONALD: Then how could he…?

HOLMES: Exactly. He clearly has access to some alternative source of income. And I can assure you, he inherited no family fortune.

MACDONALD: But I thought you told me that you had never met Professor Moriarty.

HOLMES: I never have.

MACDONALD: Then how do you know about his rooms?

HOLMES: That's quite a different matter. I've been to his rooms three times. How or when – that I will not elaborate to a Scotland Yard detective. The important point is that he is obviously a very wealthy man. How does he acquire his wealth?

MACDONALD: You think, illegally.

HOLMES: Exactly. Of course I have many other reasons for believing him to be the mastermind behind a vast criminal empire. As to the reason for Mr Douglas's death, we can speculate a little. Moriarty rules his people with a rod of iron. There is only one punishment in his book – death. If this murdered man – this Douglas, whose approaching fate was known by one of the arch-criminal's subordinates – had in some way betrayed him, his death was inevitable.

MACDONALD: Well, that is one suggestion, Mr Holmes. There may be others. In any event – to Birlstone we must go!

(BURST OF MUSIC. CROSSFADE TO INTERIOR OF TRAIN DRAWN BY STEAM LOCOMOTIVE.

DRUMMING OF WHEELS ON TRACK. DOWN AND HOLD BENEATH FOLLOWING)

MACDONALD: Well, since you ask, Mr Holmes, a letter arrived at Scotland Yard by special messenger very early this morning. It had been sent by the milk train from Birlstone. One of the night staff came round to my house at 5 a.m.

HOLMES: And the letter was from…?

MACDONALD: Sergeant Wilson of the Sussex police– an old friend of mine. I have it here. See.

HOLMES: "Dear Mac, wire me the train you can catch to Birlstone. This case is a snorter. I enclose the official report. If you can bring Mr Holmes, please do so, for he will find something after his own heart." And the official report?

MACDONALD: Here, Mr Holmes

(PAPER)

HOLMES: Interesting. I will pass you each page, Watson, as I complete it. I think we should both be fully apprised of the facts.

(UP TRAIN. FADE FAST BENEATH FOLLOWING AND OUT)

WATSON: (*as narrator*) In the light of knowledge that came to us later, let me describe events which occurred before Sherlock Holmes and I arrived upon the scene.

The village of Birlstone lies on the northern border of the county of Sussex. About half a mile away, standing in an old park, is the ancient manor house of Birlstone, surrounded by a moat. The only approach to the house was over a drawbridge which was actually raised every evening and lowered every morning. So during the night the Manor House was converted into an island.

The house had been occupied by John Douglas and his wife for some years. Douglas was very popular among the villagers, subscribing handsomely to local projects, and attending their concerts and other functions. He appeared to have plenty of money, which rumour said he had gained in the California gold fields. In any case, it was clear from what he and his wife said that he'd spent part of his life in America.

His wife was known to be an English lady who'd met Mr Douglas, then a widower, in London. She was a beautiful woman, tall, dark, and slender, some twenty years younger than her husband.

Someone else lived at Birlstone from time to time. Cecil James Barker, of Hales Lodge, Hampstead, was a frequent visitor. Undoubtedly English himself, it was clear from his conversation with local people that Cecil Barker had first known Douglas in America. Rather younger than Douglas – forty-five at most – he was a tall, broad-chested fellow with a clean-shaven, prize-fighter face.

As to the other inhabitants of the old building, it will suffice to mention the respectable and capable butler – Ames – and Mrs Allen, a buxom and cheerful person, who relieved the lady of some of her household cares. The other six servants in the house bear no relation to the events of the night of January the 6th.

It was at eleven forty-five that the first alarm reached Sergeant Wilson of the Sussex Constabulary.

(EXTERIOR. DOOR BELL CLANGING REPEATEDLY)

BARKER: *(agitated, calling)* Sergeant! Sergeant Wilson! Wake up, man! For heaven's sake.

WILSON: *(remote from inside house, advancing)* All right, sir. All right, sir. I'm coming.

(DOOR OPENS)

It's Mr Barker, isn't it? What's happened, sir?

BARKER: It's Mr Douglas, up at the manor. He's been murdered!

WILSON: What?

BARKER: Murdered! Murdered! Douglas is dead! Come along Wilson, for heaven's sake.

WILSON: You go back to the house, Mr Barker. I have to telegraph the county police. I'll follow in a few minutes.

(FADE OUT. FULL UP)

WATSON: (*as narrator*) On reaching the Manor House, Sergeant Wilson found the drawbridge down, and the whole household in a state of wild confusion. Cecil Barker led him to the fatal scene.

The dead man lay sprawled on his back in the centre of the room. A dressing gown covered his night clothes. He had been horribly injured. Lying across his chest was a shotgun with the double barrel sawn off a foot in front of the triggers. This had clearly been fired at close range, and he had received the whole charge in the face, blowing his head almost to pieces.

(INTERIOR)

WILSON: My God! I've never seen anything like this. We'll touch nothing until my superiors arrive.

BARKER: Nothing has been touched so far. This is exactly as I found him at half-past eleven. I was in my bedroom when I heard the gunshot. I rushed down. I don't suppose it was thirty seconds before I was in the room.

WILSON: Was the door open?

BARKER: Yes. Poor Douglas was lying as you see him. His bedroom candle was alight on that table. I lit this lamp a few minutes later.

WILSON: And did you see anyone, Mr Barker?

BARKER: No. But I heard Mrs Douglas coming down the stairs. I rushed out to prevent her from seeing this dreadful sight. Mrs Allen, the housekeeper, came along almost at once, and took her away.

WILSON: I understand the drawbridge is kept up all night.

BARKER: Yes, sergeant. It was up until I lowered it.

WILSON: Then how could any murderer have got away? It's out of the question. Mr Douglas must have shot himself.

BARKER: That was my first idea. But look here. This window is wide open. And there – on the sill. Do you see?

WILSON: Blood. A shoe-print.

BARKER: Someone stood on that window-sill to get out, sergeant.

WILSON: You mean he waded across the moat?

BARKER: Exactly.

WILSON: That's all very well, Mr Barker. But if the drawbridge was up, how did he get into the house in the first place? When was it raised?

BARKER: I asked the butler that same question. He says he raised it at about six o'clock last evening.

WILSON: So it comes to this. If anyone came in from outside, they must have been in the house before six, and been in hiding until Mr Douglas came into this room after eleven.

BARKER: That's how I read it. Mr Douglas went round the house every night last thing before he turned in. The man was waiting in here, and shot him. Then he got away through the window and left his gun behind him. Nothing else fits the facts.

WILSON: What's this card lying beside the body?

BARKER: I hadn't noticed. The murderer must have left it.

WILSON: Something's written on this side. V.V. and the number 341. Does that mean anything to you, Mr Barker?

BARKER: Not a thing.

WILSON: And this tattoo on Mr Douglas's arm. It *is* a tattoo, I suppose. A triangle within a circle. Is this anything to do with the crime?

BARKER: It's not a tattoo. I saw this type of mark often when I was in the western states of America. It's branding – they do it to mark cattle. And yes, I knew that Douglas had this on his arm. He never told me how he came by it. And now I come to look at him, I see that his wedding band is missing. He always wore his wedding band beneath that ring he has on that finger – the twisted snake ring.

WILSON: Do you mean the wedding ring was below the other?

BARKER: Always.

WILSON: Then the murderer, or whoever it was, first took off this snake ring, then the wedding ring, and afterwards put the snake ring back. No, no, no. This is a deal too thick for the likes of me. I'll be pleased to hand this over to Detective Inspector MacDonald, when he gets here.

(FADE OUT. FADE IN. INTERIOR)

HOLMES: Remarkable, Sergeant Wilson. I can hardly recall any case where the features have been more peculiar. What say you, Watson?

WATSON: Most puzzling.

WILSON: I thought you'd say so, Mr Holmes. I examined the gun. I found the two triggers were wired together, so that, if you pulled on the back one, both barrels were discharged. Whoever fixed that up was going to take no chances of missing his man. There was no complete maker's name, but the printed letters P.E.N. were on the fluting between the barrels.

HOLMES: Ah – the Pennsylvania Small Arms Company. A well-known American firm.

WILSON: Wonderful, Mr Holmes. Do you carry the names of all the gun makers in the world in your memory?

HOLMES: A chance piece of knowledge.

MACDONALD: I'm really not convinced that all this was done by someone from outside. It's clean against common sense. This is no burglar. The ring business and the card point to premeditated murder.

WILSON: But on the other hand, would someone planning a murder bring the noisiest weapon imaginable, knowing it would fetch everyone in the house to the spot as quick as they can run?

HOLMES: Both arguments are irrefutable, gentlemen. The question is – can they be reconciled? Sergeant Wilson, I think perhaps we should proceed to the house.

(FADE OUT. FADE IN HOUSE INTERIOR)

WILSON: Well, this is where the murder took place. Now after the gunshot was heard only a minute at the most passed before most of the household were down here – not only Mr Cecil Barker, but the butler Ames, Mrs Douglas and the housekeeper. Could the murderer in that time have taken a ring off the dead man's finger, removed the wedding band beneath it and replaced the first one, opened the window, marked the sill with blood, left a card, and all the rest of it? It's impossible.

HOLMES: I'm inclined to agree with you.

WILSON: Then it was done by someone who got into the house before six – someone with a private grudge against Mr Douglas. Since Mr Douglas spent much of his life in America, and the shotgun is an American weapon, this murder may be connected with his past. He enters the house by this window, and hides behind the curtain. Just after eleven Mr Douglas enters the room. It was a short interview.

HOLMES: The candle shows that. It has not burned more than half an inch.

WILSON: Mr Douglas enters and puts the candle down on the table. The man appears from behind the curtain, armed with this gun. He demands the wedding ring – heaven knows why. Mr Douglas gives it. Then either in cold blood, or during the course of a struggle, he shoots Mr Douglas. He drops the gun, flings down this strange card – V V 341, whatever that means – and makes his escape through the window and across the moat. How's that, Mr Holmes?

HOLMES: Interesting, but just a little unconvincing. Dear me, these injuries are really appalling. Mac, can we have the butler in for a moment?

MACDONALD: *(calls)* Mr Ames! Mr Ames, would you be good enough to join us.

AMES: *(approaching)* Certainly, sir. Can I be of assistance?

HOLMES: This unusual mark – this branding, here on Mr Douglas's forearm. I understand you have seen it often, this triangle within a circle?

AMES: Frequently, sir.

HOLMES: I also see a small piece of plaster at the angle of Mr Douglas's jaw.

AMES: Yes, sir. He cut himself shaving yesterday morning.

HOLMES: That may point to some nervousness. Perhaps this attack was not entirely unexpected. Let us pass to this card – V.V. 341. Does this mean anything to you, Ames?

AMES: Nothing, sir.

HOLMES: What do you think, Mac?

MACDONALD: Well, it feels like some sort of secret society. That also goes for the branding on his forearm.

HOLMES: Watson?

WATSON: I agree.

HOLMES: All right, let's adopt that as a working hypothesis. An agent from this secret society makes his way into the house, waits for Mr Douglas, nearly blows his head off with this shotgun, and escapes by wading the moat, leaving his calling card beside the dead man. When that fact is reported in the papers, it will tell other members of the gang that vengeance has been done. That all hangs together. But why this gun, of all weapons? And why the missing ring? Ames, what's this under the table?

AMES: Mr Douglas's dumb-bells.

HOLMES: Dumb-bell. There's only one. Where's the other?

AMES: I don't know, Mr Holmes

HOLMES: One dumb-bell...

BARKER: (*remote, advancing*) Hullo there. Sorry to interrupt. My name's Barker. I just wanted to let you know that the grooms have found the bicycle the fellow must have used. It was dumped in the bushes, a hundred yards from the front door.

HOLMES: Mr Cecil Barker, I presume?

BARKER: Indeed.

MACDONALD: What on earth induced the fellow to leave it? And how did he get away without it?

HOLMES: Questions that will no doubt be answered in the fullness of time. Meanwhile, I think it would be useful if we heard what the housekeeper has to tell us. Could you arrange that, Inspector?

(FADE OUT. FADE IN)

MRS ALLEN: I was about to go to bed when I heard a bell ringing down in the pantry. So I put on my dressing gown, and hurried out. I met Mr Ames in the corridor, and we went downstairs together. As we reached the front of the house, we saw Mr Barker coming out of the study. He saw Mrs Douglas on the stairs, and urged her to go back.

BARKER: *(urgent, calling)* Poor Jack is dead! You can do nothing. For God's sake, go back!

MRS ALLEN: I took Mrs Douglas's arm, and went back to her room with her. I stayed with her most of the night.

HOLMES: Very clear, Mrs Allen. Thank you. Just one point – did you hear the gunshot?

MRS ALLEN: No sir. I can't say I did. But a good deal earlier, just as I entered my bedroom, I do remember hearing something like the slamming of a door.

(CROSSFADE)

BARKER: I suppose I knew Douglas better than any man alive, but there were some chapters in his life he never spoke of. He'd emigrated to America as a very young man. I first met him in California, where we became partners in a successful mining claim at a place called Benito Canyon. We'd done very well, but Douglas had suddenly sold out and started for England. He was a widower at that time. Later I too realized my money and followed him – and so we renewed our friendship.

HOLMES: Thank you, Mr Barker. Tell me, had Mr Douglas been at all uneasy over the recent past?

BARKER: It's odd you should ask that, Mr Holmes. For quite a few weeks he'd given me the impression that some danger as hanging over him. I believe that some secret society was on his track, and had planned to kill him. I think that the card left by his body is a message from that organization.

WATSON: What makes you believe that?

BARKER: Because when he left California so suddenly, I think he'd had a warning of some sort. Within a week of his departure half-a-dozen men were inquiring for him – a mighty hard-looking crowd.

HOLMES: But that was how long ago?

BARKER: Six years.

HOLMES: And by then you'd been together for what? ... Five years.

BARKER: That's right.

HOLMES: So all this business dates back at least eleven years.

BARKER: That is correct. I think it shadowed his whole life. He always went about armed, you know?

HOLMES: Really?

BARKER: Oh yes. His revolver was never out of his pocket. It was bad luck that last night he was in his dressing gown, and had left it in the bedroom. Once the drawbridge was up, I guess he thought he was safe.

MACDONALD: I have a different question for you, Mr Barker. Did Mr Douglas entirely approve of your friendship with his wife?

BARKER: (*pause*) Well, I guess you gentlemen are only doing your duty. Let me put it this way. Douglas was fond of me, and he was devoted to his wife. Yet if his wife and I spoke together, a kind of wave of jealousy would pass over him. More than once I've sworn off coming here for that reason, but then he'd write me such imploring letters that I just had to.

MACDONALD: You are aware that the dead man's wedding ring has been taken from his finger. Does that not suggest that the marriage and the tragedy are connected?

BARKER: I don't know what it means. But this I must say – no man ever had a more loving, faithful wife.

(CROSSFADE)

MRS DOUGLAS: Yes, I first met him in London, shortly after his return from America. We have been married five years.

MACDONALD: Have you heard him speak of anything which occurred in America that might bring some danger on him?

MRS DOUGLAS: Yes, I have. I've always felt that some sort of danger was hanging over him. He refused to discuss it with me. And he always kept secret certain episodes of his life in the States. I noticed the way he looked at unexpected strangers. In the end I was perfectly convinced that he had some powerful enemies, that he believed they were on his track, and that he was always on his guard against them. Then there were certain words he sometimes let slip.

HOLMES: What words, Mrs Douglas?

MRS DOUGLAS: The Valley of Fear. That was what he sometimes said when I questioned him. "I have been in the Valley of Fear. I am not out of it yet."

WATSON: (*as narrator*) For some time after Mrs Douglas had left us, my friend sat sunk in thought. Then he rose and rang the bell. "Ames," he said, when the butler entered, "was Mr Douglas at all disturbed yesterday?"

"He did seem out of sorts, sir. He spoke scarcely a word since he returned from Tunbridge Wells the day before."

"And when you joined Mr Barker in the study last night, can you remember what he had on his feet?"

"Oh yes, Mr Holmes. Bedroom slippers. They're still under the chair in the hall. I may say that I noticed they were stained with blood – so indeed were my own."

"Very good, Ames. We'll ring if we want you."

A few minutes later we were in the study. Holmes had brought with him the carpet slippers from the hall. As Ames had observed, the soles of both were dark with blood.

Stooping, Holmes placed the slipper upon the blood mark on the sill. It exactly corresponded. He smiled at his colleagues. The inspector was transfigured with excitement.

MACDONALD: Man, there's not a doubt of it! Barker marked the window sill himself with those slippers. But what's the game, Mr Holmes – what's the game?"

(MUSIC. DOWN FOR FOLLOWING AND OUT UNDER)

WATSON: (*as narrator*) The three detectives were occupied with their enquiries, so I took a stroll in the old-world garden which flanked the house. Yew trees circled the garden. At the end farthest from the house they thickened into a continuous hedge. On the other side, concealed from anyone approaching from the house, there was a stone seat. As I drew near I became aware of voices. An instant later I had come round the hedge and my eyes lit upon Mrs Douglas and the man Barker before they were aware of my presence.

Her appearance gave me a shock. In the dining-room she had been demure and discreet. Now her face was quivering with amusement at some remark of her companion. He sat forward, an answering smile upon his face.

In an instant – but it was an instant too late – they resumed their solemn masks as I came into view. A hurried word passed between them, and Barker rose and came towards me.

BARKER: Excuse me, Dr Watson, would you mind coming over and speaking to Mrs Douglas?

WATSON: (*as narrator*) I followed him with a dour face. In my mind's eye I saw that shattered figure on the floor. Here, within a few hours of the tragedy, were his wife and his nearest friend laughing together.

(OPEN AIR)

WATSON: Mrs Douglas?

MRS DOUGLAS: Dr Watson, you know Mr Holmes better than anyone else. Tell me, if something was told him in complete confidence, would he find it absolutely necessary to pass it on to the detectives?

WATSON: Mr Holmes is an independent investigator. He is his own master, and he would act as his judgment directed. At the same time, he would not conceal anything which would help the police bring a criminal to justice. I suggest you speak to Mr Holmes himself.

(FADE OUT. FULL UP. INTERIOR)

HOLMES: I want none of their confidences. Confidences, Watson, are mighty awkward if it comes to an arrest for conspiracy and murder.

WATSON: You think it will come to that?

HOLMES: Very possibly. When we have traced the missing dumb-bell…

WATSON: The dumb-bell?

HOLMES: Dear me, Watson, is it possible you have not realized that the case hangs upon the missing dumb-bell?

WATSON: Holmes, you amaze me…

HOLMES: A lie, Watson, a big, thumping lie – that's our starting point. The whole story told by Barker is a lie. But Barker's story is corroborated by Mrs Douglas. So she is lying also. They are in a conspiracy. But why are they lying – and what is the truth they are trying to conceal? Let us try, Watson, to reconstruct the truth. Let us start with the gunshot. What is Barker's story?

WATSON: He hears the explosion in his bedroom, and rushes downstairs.

HOLMES: How long do you think elapsed from the sound of the shot and Barker appearing in the study?

WATSON: A minute, perhaps. No more than two.

HOLMES: Precisely. Yet we are asked to believe that in that time the assassin took a wedding ring, which was underneath a serpentine ring, from the dead man's finger, replaced the serpentine, put that strange card beside the victim, and left by the window.

WATSON: Not very likely.

HOLMES: indeed not, Watson. On the contrary, I have no doubt that the assassin was alone with the dead man for some time, with the lamp lit. So it follows that the gunshot must have been fired much earlier than we are told, and therefore...

WATSON: ...therefore both Barker and Mrs Douglas are lying.

HOLMES: Exactly. And since I've shown that the blood mark on the windowsill was deliberately placed there by Barker to mislead the police, the case grows dark against them.

WATSON: So when did the murder take place?

HOLMES: Well, just after a quarter to eleven, for that's when the servants all went to their rooms – all, that is, except Ames who was still in the butler's pantry. I carried out a brief experiment this afternoon, and I find that no noise from the study can be heard in the pantry when the doors are shut. This is not the case in the housekeeper's room. Noise does penetrate up there. You will recall that Mrs Allen told us she'd heard something like the slamming of a door half an hour before the alarm was given.

WATSON: And you believe that was the sound of the gun?

HOLMES: I do indeed, Watson. That was the real moment of the murder. Now the interesting question is what were Barker and Mrs Douglas doing from a quarter to eleven – when they say that the sound of the shot brought them downstairs – until a quarter past, when they summoned the servants?

WATSON: So do you believe that Barker and Mrs Douglas are guilty of the murder?

HOLMES: I think they know the truth about the murder and are conspiring to conceal it. Whether they committed it is not so clear. I think that an evening alone in that study would help me a great deal.

WATSON: An evening alone in the study?

HOLMES: Indeed. I propose going up there before too long. I've arranged it with the estimable Ames. I shall sit in that room this evening, and see if its atmosphere brings me inspiration. You smile, friend Watson. Well, we shall see. By the way, you have that big umbrella of yours, have you not?

WATSON: Yes. It's here.

HOLMES: Well, I'll borrow that, if I may.

WATSON: Certainly – but what a wretched weapon.

(DOOR OPENS)

WILSON: (*remote, advancing*) Ah, I'm pleased to find you together, gentlemen. Inspector MacDonald and I have some good news.

MACDONALD: Yes, we've identified the bicycle – the one left behind by the assassin.

HOLMES: Well done indeed. I congratulate you both.

WILSON: I started from the fact that Mr Douglas had seemed disturbed since the day before, when he'd been at Tunbridge Wells. I assumed that it was there that he'd become aware of some danger. So we took the bicycle with us, and showed it at the hotels. It was identified at once by the manager of the Eagle Commercial. He said it belonged to a man named Hargrave, who'd taken a room there two days before. The man was an American. He left the hotel after breakfast yesterday morning on his bicycle, and no more was heard of him.

MACDONALD: We obtained a good description, though. About five foot nine, aged fifty or so, hair slightly grizzled, a greyish moustache.

HOLMES: That might almost be a description of Douglas himself. Well, Mac, I am now certain that the crime was committed an hour earlier than reported, that Barker and Mrs Douglas helped the murderer escape, and that they are both conspiring to conceal something.

MACDONALD: If that's true, we only tumble out of one mystery into another.

HOLMES: Tonight I propose to spend some time alone in Mr Douglas's study, the scene of the murder. Tomorrow morning I hope to be able to throw some light on these apparent mysteries. Good evening, gentlemen.

(FADE OUT. FADE IN)

WILSON: Well, Mr Holmes?

HOLMES: While sitting in the Manor House last night – I spent a good few hours there, incidentally – I took the opportunity to browse through this interesting account of the old building. Have you come across it? It costs the modest sum of one penny, and is available at several local stores.

MACDONALD: You're making fools of us, Mr Holmes.

HOLMES: I assure you I am not. I found it most interesting.
           For example, there is a moving account concerning
           poor unfortunate King Charles the First. When
           fleeing from the Roundhead troops who would
           later capture and behead him, he was concealed
           for several days in the Manor House. Do you not
           find that of interest?

MACDONALD: I dare say it is, Mr Holmes, but what on earth has
           it to do with this case?

HOLMES: Breadth of view, my dear Mac – breadth of view is
           one of the essentials of our profession. Well, well,
           I'll drop past history and get down to present day
           facts.

WATSON: Besides browsing through the local history, what
           else did you do in Mr Douglas's study?

HOLMES: To the point, as ever, Watson. I was looking for
           the missing dumb-bell.

WATSON: That dumb-bell. You're quite obsessed with it.

HOLMES: And with good reason. It has always bulked
           rather large in my estimate of the case. I ended by
           finding it.

MACDONALD: I'm pleased for you, Mr Holmes, but you're clearly
           not telling us everything. You're holding things
           back. That's hardly fair of you.

HOLMES: Inspector MacDonald – gentlemen – I undertake to hold nothing back from you one moment longer than is necessary. But I would ask you to do something for me, first.

WILSON: Willingly, Mr Holmes.

HOLMES: And after that, I promise to share with you everything I know and everything I suspect.

MACDONALD: That sounds more like it.

WILSON: And what is it you want me to do?

HOLMES: Just this, Sergeant Wilson. Please write a note to Mr Barker, telling him that the police intend draining the moat, starting tomorrow morning. Send it by hand about four o'clock this afternoon.

WILSON: I'll willingly do that.

(FADE IN MUSIC BENEATH FOLLOWING)

HOLMES: Please spend the rest of today as you will. But let us all meet up here, in this room, at four o'clock. Come in your warmest coats. It gets very cold at this time of year, and tonight we shall be spending a long time out in the open.

(UP MUSIC. FADE BENEATH FOLLOWING)

WATSON: (*as narrator*) Slowly the shadows darkened over the old house. There was a single lamp over the gateway, and a steady globe of light shone through the window of the fatal study. Everything else was dark and still.

MACDONALD: *(whisper)* We've been here an hour. What we are waiting for?

HOLMES: *(whisper)* Hold fast, Macdonald. Hold fast... Any minute... There! That's what I expected to see.

WATSON: *(as narrator)* As he spoke the study window was thrown open, and we saw the outline of a man's head. He leaned forward, and seemed to be stirring up the moat with something he held in his hand. Then, just as a fisherman lands a fish, he hauled in some large, round object and dragged it through the open window.

HOLMES: *(calls)* Now! Come on, gentlemen. Quickly! Follow me!

(OPEN AIR. FOUR RUNNING)

To the house!

WATSON: *(as narrator)* We staggered after him as he ran across the bridge and rang at the bell. A rasping of bolts, and the amazed Ames stood in the entrance. Holmes brushed him aside and, followed by all of us, hurried into the study. Cecil Barker stood facing us, a lamp in his hand. Holmes took a swift glance round, and then pounced upon a sodden bundle tied with cord lying under the writing table.

HOLMES: This is what we are after. This bundle, weighted with a dumb-bell, which you have just raised from the bottom of the moat, Mr Barker.

BARKER: How in thunder do you know anything about it?

HOLMES: Because I retrieved it yesterday and replaced it there. Your umbrella, Watson, was an invaluable aid both in fishing up the bundle last night, and in putting it back.

WATSON: I couldn't imagine what you wanted my umbrella for, Holmes.

HOLMES: You will recall, gentlemen, that I was struck from the start by the fact that only one dumb-bell was present in this room. When water is near and a weight is missing, it's not far-fetched to suppose that something has been sunk in the water. By announcing that the moat would be drained tomorrow, Inspector MacDonald, I expected that whoever had hidden the bundle would attempt to retrieve it without delay. Now, Mr Barker, I think you owe us an explanation – but first let us examine what you attempted to conceal from us.

WATSON: (*as narrator*) Sherlock Holmes undid the cord that bound the sopping bundle. From it he extracted a dumb-bell. Next he withdrew a long sheathed knife. Finally he unravelled a bundle of clothing, including a gray tweed suit and an overcoat.

HOLMES: See the inner pocket of this coat. It has been extended into the lining, leaving ample space for the sawn-off shotgun. And here is the tailor's tab. "Neal. Outfitter. Vermissa USA."

MACDONALD: USA?

HOLMES: Indeed, Mac. I've spent an instructive afternoon in the rector's library. Vermissa is a town at the head of a flourishing coal and iron vallery in the United States. It is not too far-fetched to infer that the V.V. on the card by the dead body stands for Vermissa Valley – or, indeed, that this valley may be that Valley of Fear which Mrs Douglas referred to. But I seem to be standing rather in the way of your explanation, Mr Barker.

MRS DOUGLAS: *(remote, advancing)* No, no, Cecil. You've done enough for now.

HOLMES: Mrs Douglas. I urge you to take the police into your complete confidence. There is much that is unexplained.

MACDONALD: There most certainly is. If you have information about the murder, you would do best to impart it.

HOLMES: In fact, Mrs Douglas, I strongly recommend that you ask your husband to tell us his own story.

MACDONALD: Mr Holmes, what on earth can you possibly…

HOLMES: You seem astounded, Mac. Yet look behind you. The gentleman standing by the wall is, if I am not mistaken, Mr Douglas himself.

MACDONALD: Where on earth have you sprung from, sir?

MRS DOUGLAS: Jack! Oh, Jack!

BARKER: My dear fellow!

MRS DOUGLAS: It's best this way, Jack. I am sure it's the best.

HOLMES: Indeed it is, Mr Douglas.

DOUGLAS: Are you Dr Watson?

WATSON: Indeed I am, sir.

DOUGLAS: Then I would like to deposit these papers with you.

WATSON: With me? But what are they?

DOUGLAS: I've heard of you, Dr Watson. You're the historian of this bunch. Well, you've never had such a story as that pass through your hands. Tell it in your own way, but the facts – all the facts – are in that document. I've spent two days cooped up and all alone, and I spent the time writing the complete story of the Valley of Fear. It is all there, Dr Watson.

HOLMES: But that's the past, Mr Douglas. What we want now is to hear your story of the present.

MACDONALD: Excuse me just a minute. If you are Mr John Douglas of Birlstone Manor, then whose death have we been investigating? And where in the world have you spring from?

HOLMES: Ah Mac, you thought me frivolous when I commended that excellent history of Birlstone Manor. It provided a vivid account of how King Charles the First was concealed inside the manor for several days, when he was fleeing from the troops of Oliver Cromwell. In those days many country residences had places of concealment built into the walls. They're often called "priests' holes", because Catholic families often assisted their priests to escape the authorities in time of religious conflict.

DOUGLAS: Here, in the wainscot behind me – you see this sliding panel? Behind it is a small chamber – very small indeed, when you are stuck in it for forty-eight hours.

HOLMES: My commiserations. But I've suspected for some time that you had to be concealed somewhere in the house. Those clothes in the moat with the American tailor's tag – they made it clear that the dead body must be that of the cyclist from Tunbridge Wells. He'd been dressed in your garments, and his had to be disposed of.

DOUGLAS: Yes, well you've figured it out. It was like this. When I was in Tunbridge Wells the day before all this happened, I caught sight of my worst enemy, just by chance, in the street. I knew there was trouble coming. But after the drawbridge was up that night, I felt pretty safe, never dreaming that he'd got into the house and was waiting for me.

I go round the house at about eleven. I'd no sooner entered the study, than I spotted a boot under the curtain. The next instant he sprang at me, a gun in his hand. We grappled with each other, and I tried to wrestle it from him. How the trigger went off I'm not certain – but the result was that he got both barrels in the face. And there I was, staring down at all that was left of Ted Baldwin.

BARKER: That was the moment I came hurrying down. Douglas let me in, and we stood by the body for a few minutes, expecting some of the servants to join us. But nobody came, and we gathered they'd heard nothing. All that had happened was known only to ourselves.

DOUGLAS: It was then the idea came to me. The man's sleeve had slipped up, and there was the branded mark of the lodge on his arm. He was similar to me in height and weight, and his face was unrecognizable. I brought down some clothes of mine, and in a quarter of an hour Barker and I dressed him and put my dressing gown on him, and he lay as you found him.

BARKER: Yes, we tied all his own clothes in a bundle, and I weighted them with the dumb-bell and put them through the window. We found the card he'd intended to lay beside my body in his pocket.

HOLMES: And now we come to the rings.

DOUGLAS: Indeed. The serpentine ring that I wore above my wedding band came off easily enough, and we slipped it on his finger. But look – my wedding ring is so firmly lodged that it would take a file to remove it.

BARKER: Don't forget the plaster. I went upstairs to fetch it.

DOUGLAS: Ah, you slipped up there, Mr Holmes, clever as you are. If you'd removed the plaster from poor Baldwin's jaw, you'd have found no cut underneath. That would have aroused your suspicions at once.

HOLMES: A minor point. I assume you hoped that the newspapers would report that Baldwin had got his man, and that those who wanted you dead would be satisfied.

DOUGLAS: Yes, I thought I'd lie low for a while, and wait for the story to die down. I knew all about the priests' hole, so I retired into it, and I left it to Barker to do the rest.

BARKER: Well, I opened the window, and I dipped a slipper in the blood and made a mark on the window sill. Then when everything was fixed, I ran the bell for the servants. The first thing we heard was Mrs Douglas coming down the stairs. I ran to the door and stopped her. By then Mrs Allen was at the head of the stairs with Ames. So I got Mrs Allen to take Mrs Douglas back to her bedroom and stay with her.

DOUGLAS: Yes, gentlemen, that's the truth of what happened. Tell me, how do I stand with the English law on all this?

HOLMES: English law is in the main a just law. You will get justice.

(FADE IN MUSIC BENEATH FOLLOWING)

But I fear you are facing far worse dangers than the English law – worse even than your enemies from America. I fear you are somehow tied into a conspiracy operated by a ruthless master criminal. How did this man Baldwin know that you lived here? Or how to get into your house? Or where to hide, and for how long? No, Mr Douglas, all I can see before you is trouble.

(UP MUSIC. HOLD A LITTLE. FADE AND LOSE BENEATH FOLLOWING)

WATSON: (*as narrator*) And now I will ask you to come away with me for a time, far from the Sussex Manor House of Birlstone and the strange story of the man known as John Douglas. I want you to journey back some twenty years in time, and westward some thousands of miles, so that I may lay before you a tale so strange and terrible that you may find it hard to believe. When I have recounted those distant events, and you have solved this mystery of the past, we shall meet once more in those rooms in Baker Street, where this, like so many other wonderful happenings, will find its end.

It was the fourth of February in the year 1875, and the snow lay deep in the gorges of the Gilmerton Mountains in Virginia, USA. The evening train was slowly groaning its way up the steep gradients which lead to Vermissa, the central township which lies at the head of Vermissa Valley.

(FADE IN INTERIOR OF STEAM TRAIN CHUGGING ALONG SLOWLY. KEEP IN BACKGROUND UNDER FOLLOWING)

In the leading passenger car, a long, bare carriage, some twenty or thirty people were seated. Most were workmen returning from their day's toil in the lower part of the valley. In a corner by himself sat one young man. A working man came up and seated himself on the adjoining bench.

SCANLAN: Hullo, mate! A stranger in these parts?

DOUGLAS: That's right.

SCANLAN: Got any friends?

DOUGLAS: Not yet – but I'm soon able to make them.

SCANLAN: How's that, then?

DOUGLAS: I'm a member of the Eminent Order of Freemen. There's no town without a lodge, and where there's a lodge I'll find my friends.

SCANLAN: My hand, friend. Ah ha, I see you speak the truth. I'm Brother Scanlan, Lodge 341, Vermissa Valley. Glad to know you.

DOUGLAS: What luck to meet a brother so early. I'm Brother Jack McMurdo, Lodge 29, Chicago.

SCANLAN: Where are you planning to stay in Vermissa?

DOUGLAS: I'm lodging at Jacob Shafter's on Shendan Street.

SCANLAN: We can walk together. I'm passing Shafter's on the way to my own shack.

(UP TRAIN. CROSSFADE TO OPEN AIR. TWO WALKING ON PAVEMENT)

SCANLAN: See that saloon – that's the Union House. Jack McGinty's the boss there.

DOUGLAS: What sort of a man is he?

SCANLAN: I thought his name was known clear across the country. It's been in the papers often enough over the Scowrers.

DOUGLAS: Yes, I read of the Scowrers in Chicago. A gang of murderers, aren't they?

(WALKING STOPS SUDDENLY)

SCANLAN: Man, you won't live long in these parts if you speak in the open street like that. Many a man has had the life beaten out of him for less. the lodging house you're after is over there. You'll find old Jacob Shafter that runs it as honest a man as lives in this township.
I'll bid you goodnight.

DOUGLAS: Goodnight – and thanks.

SCANLAN: (*retreating, calls*) I'll see you around.

(KNOCKER ON DOOR. DOOR OPENS)

ETTIE: Oh, I thought it was father. Did you come to see him? He's downtown. I expect him back any minute.

DOUGLAS: No, miss, I'm in no hurry to see him. But I was told I'd find board and lodging here.

ETTIE: And so you can. Come right in, sir. I'm Ettie Shafter. I run the house for my father – and there he is. (*calls*) Hi, Dad.

SHAFTER: (*advancing, calls*) Hullo, Ettie. Who have we here?

DOUGLAS:	My name's John McMurdo. I'm after board and lodging with you.
SHAFTER:	And you're very welcome. Come along in. We'll soon get you fixed up.

(MOVEMENT. DOOR CLOSES)

WATSON:	There were a dozen boarders at Shafter's, but McMurdo was a man who made his mark quickly. When they gathered together of an evening, his joke was always the readiest, his conversation the brightest. And he made no secret that the daughter of the house had won his heart. Early on he told her that he loved her, and although she tried to discourage him, he went on telling her so. After a while in Vermissa, McMurdo found a temporary job as bookkeeper which kept him busy all day long. After a week or so he'd still not found time to report himself to the head of the lodge of the Eminent Order of Freemen. One evening, he had a visit from Mike Scanlan.

(FADE A LITTLE. FULL UP)

SCANLON:	Say, McMurdo, I'm surprised you've not reported to the Bodymaster. Why haven't you seen Boss McGinty yet?
DOUGLAS:	Well, I had to find a job. I've been busy.
SCANLON:	You must find time for him, if for nothing else. You should have gone down to the Union House

on your first morning. You go and see him, my lad!

(FADE A LITTLE. FULL UP)

WATSON: (*as narrator*) But by chance that very evening McMurdo had another, more pressing, interview...

(INTERIOR. DOOR CLOSES UNDER FOLLOWING)

SHAFTER: Just come in here with me, mister. Plant yourself down here.

DOUGLAS: Thanks very much. Well, Mr Shafter?

SHAFTER: I won't beat about the bush. It seems to me that you're getting set on my Ettie. Ain't that so?

DOUGLAS: Yes, that is so.

SHAFTER: Well, I want to tell you right now that it ain't no manner of use. There's someone slipped in afore you. It's Teddy Baldwin.

DOUGLAS: And who the devil's Teddy Baldwin?

SHAFTER: He's a boss of the Scowrers.

DOUGLAS: So what? Everybody keeps talking about the Scowrers. What are they all afraid of?

SHAFTER: Round these parts the Scowrers are the Eminent Order of Freemen.

DOUGLAS: But I'm a member of that order myself.

SHAFTER: Are you, by God? If I'd a-known that, I'd never have had you in my house.

DOUGLAS: What's wrong with the order? It's for charity and good fellowship. The rules say so.

SHAFTER: Maybe in some places. Not here in Vermissa.

DOUGLAS: What's it here then?

SHAFTER: Here it's a murder society. And there are murders to prove it.

DOUGLAS: Put yourself in my place. I belong to a society known through the length and breadth of the States as an innocent one. Now, when I'm counting on joining it here, you tell me that it's the same as a murder society called the Scowrers.

SHAFTER: I can only tell you what the whole world knows, mister. The bosses of the one are the bosses of the other. And since you're one of them, you'll soon be as bad as the rest. You'll find other lodgings, mister. I can't have you here.

(FADE IN. INTERIOR)

ETTIE: It's no good, Jack. I told you, you're too late. There's someone else – and even if I haven't promised to marry him at once, I can promise no one else.

DOUGLAS: Suppose I *had* been first, Ettie – would I have had a chance?

ETTIE: I wish to heaven you had been first.

DOUGLAS: In that case, say you'll be mine and we'll face it out together.

ETTIE: Not here? Not here in Vermissa?

DOUGLAS: Yes, here. Aren't we free folks in a free country? If we love each other, who'll dare to come between us?

ETTIE: Jack, you don't know this Baldwin. You don't know McGinty and his Scowrers. They're killers.

DOUGLAS: I don't know them, Ettie – but I don't fear them. And if they've committed all these crimes, and everyone knows it, how come that none are brought to justice?

ETTIE: Because no witness dares to appear against them. He wouldn't live a month if he did. Jack, let's get out of Vermissa. We could take father with us, and make our lives together far away from the power of these evil men.

DOUGLAS: Ettie, no harm shall come to you, nor to your father either. I promise.

(DOOR BURSTS OPEN)

BALDWIN: (*calls, advancing*) Hullo, hullo. Who's this?

ETTIE: Mr Baldwin! You're earlier than I'd thought.

BALDWIN: I can see that! Well, who is he?

ETTIE: A new boarder here. Mr McMurdo – this is Mr Baldwin.

BALDWIN: Maybe Miss Ettie has told you how it is with us? This young lady is mine – and you'll find it a very fine evening for a walk.

DOUGLAS: Thank you, but I've no mind to take a walk.

BALDWIN: Really? Then perhaps you've a mind for a fight, Mr Boarder.

(CHAIR KICKED OVER)

DOUGLAS: That I am!

ETTIE: For God's sake, Jack. He'll hurt you!

BALDWIN: So it's Jack, is it? You've come to that already?

DOUGLAS: Maybe, Mr Baldwin, you'll take a turn down the street with me. There's some open ground beyond the next block.

BALDWIN: I won't need to dirty my hands to get even with

you. You'll wish you'd never set foot in this house
before I'm through with you.

DOUGLAS: No time like the present.

BALDWIN: I'll choose my own time, mister. You can leave
the time to me. Here, see this on my arm – this
brand? Know what that means?

DOUGLAS: I don't know and I don't care.

BALDWIN: Well, you'll know soon enough, I can promise you
that. *(retreating)* Within the hour. Within the
hour.

(DOOR SLAMS)

ETTIE: Oh, Jack, if you are a Freeman, go down and make
a friend of Boss McGinty. Hurry! Get your word
in first, or the hounds will be on your trail. Hurry!

(FADE OUT. FULL UP CROWDED BAR)

DOUGLAS: Let me through, there. Let me through. Hey,
which one's the Boss? Where's McGinty? Yeh, I
see. Mr McGinty?

MCGINTY: Well, young man? I can't call your face to mind.

DOUGLAS: I'm new here, Mr McGinty. My name's McMurdo.
I was advised to see you.

MCGINTY: And who advised you?

DOUGLAS: Brother Scanlan of Lodge 341, Vermissa.

MCGINTY: We don't take folk on trust in these parts, Mr McMurdo. Come in here for a moment behind the bar.

(MOVEMENT. DOOR OPENS.)

This way. Now.

(DOOR CLOSES. BAR BACKGROUND SUDDENLY LOW)

Sit down. I've got you covered, and if I'm not satisfied with your answers, you're a dead man. Understood?

DOUGLAS: Fire away.

MCGINTY: Where were you made?

DOUGLAS: Lodge 29, Chicago.

MCGINTY: When?

DOUGLAS: June the 24th, 1872.

MCGINTY: What bodymaster?

DOUGLAS: James H Scott.

MCGINTY: Why did you leave Chicago?

DOUGLAS: I've a newspaper clipping here. Can I show you? Here…

MCGINTY: (*pause*) You shot this Jonas Pinto?

DOUGLAS: Fraid so. It was him or me.

MCGINTY: Why did you shoot him?

DOUGLAS: I was helping Uncle Sam make dollars. They looked just as good as his, and were much cheaper. This man Pinto helped me pass them into circulation. Then he got greedy – wanted a bigger share. When I said no way, he threatened to split on the whole operation. I wasn't going to stand being blackmailed forever. I just killed him and lighted out for the coal country.

MCGINTY: Why the coal country?

DOUGLAS: Cause I'd read they weren't too particular in those parts.

MCGINTY: First a coiner, then a murderer – and you come here because you thought you'd be welcome.

DOUGLAS: That's about the size of it.

MCGINTY: I guess you'll go far. Say, can you still make those dollars?

DOUGLAS: Hold it a second. Just take a look at these. These never passed the Philadelphia mint.

MCGINTY: Let's see. Well, I couldn't tell they were fake. Gar! you could be a mighty useful brother. And you seem to have a good nerve. You didn't squirm when I shoved this gun at you.

DOUGLAS: It wasn't me that was in danger.

MCGINTY: Who then?

DOUGLAS: You, Mr McGinty. Yes, see this? I was covering you all the time. I guess my shot would have been as quick as yours.

MCGINTY: (*roars with laughter*) Say, we've had no such holy terror come to hand for many a year. I reckon the lodge will learn to be proud of you.

BALDWIN: (*remote, calling*) Councillor McGinty! I want to see him!

(DOOR BURSTS OPEN)

                (*close*) Mr McGinty! Oh, so you got here first, did you? I've a word to say to you about this man…

DOUGLAS: I've offered to fight him if he thinks I've wronged him. I'll fight him with fists, or whichever way he chooses.

MCGINTY: What's it all about, then?

DOUGLAS: A young lady. She's free to choose for herself.

BALDWIN: Is she?

MCGINTY: As between two brothers of the lodge, I'd say she was.

BALDWIN: That's your ruling, is it?

MCGINTY: Yes it is, Ted Baldwin. Are you going to dispute it?

BALDWIN: You'd throw over someone who's stood by you this five years for a man you've never seen before in your life? You're not Bodymaster for life, you know.

MCGINTY: Take that!

(CRACK TO THE JAW)

BALDWIN: (*roar of pain*)

MCGINTY: You've been asking for this many a day, Ted Baldwin. As long as I'm chief, I'll have no man lift his voice against me or my rulings.

DOUGLAS: Here's my hand, Brother Baldwin. I'm quick to quarrel and quick to forgive. It's over for me, and I bear no grudge.

MCGINTY: Take his hand, Ted. Call it a day.

(FADE OUT. FULL UP)

WATSON: (*as narrator*) The next day McMurdo took up lodgings at the widow MacNamara's, on the outksirts of town. Scanlan, his original acquaintance on the train, also lived there. Old Shafter had relented to the extent of letting McMurdo come to his meals when he liked, so he continued to see Ettie, and they grew closer.

There were few evenings when McMurdo did not find his way to McGinty's saloon. His dashing manner and fearless speech made him a favourite with everyone – but a certain incident raised him even higher in their estimation. One night a man entered wearing the blue uniform and peaked cap of the mine police.

(FADE IN CROWDED BAR)

MARVIN:	Straight whisky.
MCGINTY:	You'll be the new captain?
MARVIN:	That's so. Captain Marvin's the name. We're looking to you, Councillor McGinty, to help us in upholding law and order in this township. Hullo. Here's an old acquaintance! Jack McMurdo of Chicago, isn't it? Don't deny it.
DOUGLAS:	I'm not. And you're Marvin of Chicago Central.
MARVIN:	We haven't forgotten the shooting of Jonas Pinto.
DOUGLAS:	I never shot him.
MARVIN:	Really? Well his death came in uncommon handy for you.

DOUGLAS: That's as may be.

MARVIN: Still, they could get no clear case against you. But don't think it's forgotten, McMurdo. The file stays open.

(FADE OUT. BAR FULL UP)

WATSON: (*as narrator*) As Marvin left the bar-room, the bar loafers crowded round McMurdo, clapping him on the shoulder, shaking his hand, filling his glass again and again. If his mate Scanlan hadn't been at hand to lead him home, the hero would surely have spent the night under the bar.

That Saturday night McMurdo was introduced to the rites in Vermissa lodge. After he was sworn in, the sleeve and shirt on his right arm were rolled back.

"Can you bear pain?" he was asked.

"As well as another," he said.

And suddenly an agonizing pain shot through his forearm. He nearly fainted at the shock of it, but he bit his lip and clenched his hands to hide his agony.

"I can take more than that," he said.

(APPLAUSE. MEN SHOUTING "BULLY FOR YOU", "WELL DONE", "GREAT GUNS")

WATSON: A finer first appearance had never been made in the lodge. There, on the flesh of his forearm, was a circle with a triangle within in, deep and red, as the branding iron had left it.

321

MCGINTY: And now to tonight's business. Brothers, we've a problem to deal with. There's a man in this town wants trimming up. James Stanger of the Herald. He's been opening his mouth against us again.

(MURMURS OF AGREEMENT)

For anyone who hasn't read today's edition, here's his latest.

"Reign of Terror" – that's how he heads it. "It's twelve years since those first murders that proved a criminal organization exists in this community. From that day we've endured a series of assassinations, yet not one man has gone on trial for them. The leaders and followers of this organization are known to us. How long are we going to endure it?" Et cetera, et cetera. Brothers, what are going to do about him?

(SHOUTS "KILL HIM!" "KILL HIM"!)

You all seem of one mind about this. Is there anyone who thinks different? Ah, Brother Morris. What's your opinion?

MORRIS: James Stanger's an old man, and much respected. If he's struck down there'll be a stir through this state that will only end with our destruction.

MCGINTY: See here, Brother Morris, I've had my eye on you for some time. You've no heart yourself, and you try to take the heart out of others.

MORRIS:	I apologize, Eminent Bodymaster, if I have said too much. It was my fear that evil will come to the lodge that made me speak. I won't offend again.
MCGINTY:	Very well, Brother Morris. Let's say no more about it. In fact, I agree – if Stanger got his full deserts there'd be more trouble than we need. These editors hang together. And every journal in the state would be crying out for police and troops. But I guess we can give him a pretty severe warning. Will you fix it, Brother Baldwin?
BALDWIN:	Sure.
MCGINTY:	Take half a dozen men– and include our new brother. I promised him he'd go on our next expedition.
BALDWIN:	Well, he can come if he wants.

(EDGE OUT. FULL UP)

MCGINTY:	Well, how did it go last night?
DOUGLAS:	You'll have heard already. Ted Baldwin was on the point of beating the man to death. I had to push my revolver in his face to get him to stop. You'd said quite clearly he wasn't to be killed.
MCGINTY:	You did quite right, Brother McMurdo.

(DOOR BURSTS OPEN)

MARVIN: Right, on your feet, McMurdo. Can't keep out of trouble, can you? You're coming along with us.

DOUGLAS: What am I accused of?

MARVIN: Involvement in the beating of old Editor Stanger at the Herald office. You're lucky it isn't a murder charge.

MCGINTY: Well, if that's all you have against him, you can save yourself a deal of trouble. This man was with me in my saloon playing poker up to midnight. I can bring a dozen to prove it.

MARVIN: You can settle that in court tomorrow. Come along.

WATSON: (*as narrator*) Next morning the magistrate could not possibly hold McMurdo, or the three others arrested with him, for a higher court. None could be identified for certain, while six citizens, including Councillor McGinty, testified that all were at a card party at the Union House at the time of the attack. They were discharged, and the verdict was greeted with loud applause. Jack McMurdo's popularity soared – except with Ettie Shafter's father. He barred McMurdo from the house.

(FADE IN)

ETTIE: If my father knew I was here, he'd never forgive me.

DOUGLAS: But achushla I was acquitted. They have nothing against me. Surely your mind is easy again, isn't it?

ETTIE: How can it ever be easy, Jack, when I know you're a criminal among criminals – when I live in fear that one day you'll be up in court for murder? Oh, Jack, give it up! For my sake, give it up! I beg you – give it up!

DOUGLAS: There, there, my darlin'. How could I give it up when I'd be breaking my oath and deserting my comrades? And even if I wanted to, you don't suppose the lodge would let a man go free with all its secrets?

ETTIE: Jack, listen to me. My father has saved some money. He's ready to leave. We could all run away together – to the West Coast, or to England – anywhere, to get away from this Valley of Fear.

DOUGLAS: Ettie, I just can't leave at this moment. But give me time, and I'll find a way of getting out of it honourably. Just a little time. That's all I ask.

ETTIE: Is that a promise?

DOUGLAS: I swear it. Within a year at most, we'll leave the valley behind us.

(FADE OUT. FULL UP)

WATSON: (*as narrator*) Meanwhile the lodge reigned supreme in the valley, and any who crossed its path were beaten or killed. The early summer of 1875 saw the height of the reign of terror. McMurdo had been appointed Inner Deacon, and stood every chance of some day succeeding McGinty as Bodymaster. He stood so high in the lodge, that nothing was done without his help and advice. One Saturday night he had a visitor – Brother Morris.

(FADE IN)

DOUGLAS: You look thoroughly shaken, Brother Morris. Sit you down. Here have a whisky.

(POURING)

That'll put some heart into you. Now, what can I do for you?

MORRIS: I've a secret, and it's burning the life out of me. If I tell, it'll mean murder for sure. If I don't it may bring the end of us all.

DOUGLAS: Come on, Brother Morris. Let me hear it.

MORRIS: I can tell it in one sentence. There's a detective on our trail.

DOUGLAS: But man, isn't the place full of police and detectives, and what harm did they ever do us?

MORRIS: No, no, it's no man of the district. You've heard of Pinkerton's? When they're on your trail, you're finished. We're all destroyed.

DOUGLAS: Get a grip, man. Who is the fellow? How did you hear of him?

MORRIS: I left good friends behind me in the East when I came here. One's in the telegraph service. I had a letter from him today. Read it yourself.

DOUGLAS: "I expect to hear news of the Scowrers in your parts before long. Five big corporations and two railroads are after you in earnest. They've engaged Pinkerton, who's sent his best man, Birdy Edwards." By Gar, Morris, I know who that is. We'll fix him, before he can do any harm. Morris, will you leave this in my hands? Your name needn't even be mentioned.

MORRIS: That's just what I'd want.

DOUGLAS: Then leave it at that, and keep your mouth shut.

(FADE OUT. FULL UP)

ETTIE: Thank heaven father's not here, Jack. But something's happened. Oh, Jack, you're in trouble!

DOUGLAS: It's not very bad, my sweetheart. And yet it might be wise for us to make a move before it gets worse.

ETTIE: Make a move?

DOUGLAS: I had bad news tonight, and I see trouble coming. I may have to get out of here quick. And if I go, you must come with me. Will you come?

ETTIE: Yes, Jack, day or night I'll come.

(FADE OUT. FULL UP MEN CHATTERING)

DOUGLAS: *(calls)* Eminent Bodymaster!

(CHATTER DIES)

Eminent Bodymaster, I claim urgency.

MCGINTY: Brother McMurdo claims urgency. It's a claim that by the rules of this lodge takes precedence. Now, Brother.

DOUGLAS: You all see this letter? It contains bad news. A friend out East tells us that at this very moment a Pinkerton man – one Birdy Edwards – is at work in this valley collecting evidence which may put a rope round the necks of many of us.

MCGINTY: Does anyone know this Birdy Edwards?

DOUGLAS: I do. And I believe we hold him in the hollow of our hands. If we act quickly we can cut this thing short. And there's only one sure way.

MCGINTY: This can't be planned in open lodge. I'll select a small committee, and we'll meet upstairs in fifteen minutes.

(FADE OUT. FULL UP)

MCGINTY: Now McMurdo.

DOUGLAS: This Birdy Edwards – he's lodging at Hobson's Patch, pretending to be a newspaper reporter named Steve Wilson. I happened to meet him on the train on Wednesday. Kept asking about the Scowrers. Said he'd pay well for information. I fed him a line or two and he handed over a twenty dollar blll. "There's ten times that for you," he said, "if you can find me all I want."

MCGINTY: How do you know he isn't a newspaper man.

DOUGLAS: I chanced into the telegraph bureau just as he was leaving. The operator said: "I guess we should charge double rates for this." He'd filled a form with gobbledegook. It was code of course. No reporter uses code.

MCGINTY: You're right. What do you suggest?

DOUGLAS: I'll go over to Hobson's Patch tomorrow and offer him the secrets of the lodge for a price. I'll say the documents are at my house, and he should come over at ten tomorrow night. You can plan the rest yourselves. We'll get him, this Birdy Edwards.

MCGINTY: We'll be at your place at nine. Just get the door shut behind him, and you can leave the rest to us.

(FADE OUT. FULL UP. THREE LOUD KNOCKS)

DOUGLAS: (*whisper*) That's him. (*retreating*) I'll go to the front door, and show him in here.

(DOOR OPENS, CLOSES)

MCGINTY: *(whisper)* Not a sound, anyone.

(DOOR OPENS)

MCGINTY: *(calls)* Well, McMurdo, is he here? Is Birdy Edwards here?

DOUGLAS: *(remote, advancing)* Yes, Birdy Edwards is here. I am Birdy Edwards.

(SHATTERING OF GLASS)

MARVIN: Hands up, every mother's son of you. One move, McGinty, and you're dead. My men have the place covered – forty of them – every one with a twitching finger. Keep them covered, men.

MCGINTY: Blasted traitor!

DOUGLAS: No, no, no. I'm a hard-working employee of Pinkerton's. I was chosen to break up your gang. I had a dangerous game to play – and no one knew I was playing it except Captain Marvin here, and my employers. Take them in, Marvin, and get it over.

WATSON: *(as narrator)* There is little more to tell. Early next morning Ettie Shafter and her lover boarded a special train sent by the railroad company, and made a swift journey out of the land of danger. It was the last time either set foot in the Valley of Fear. Ten days later they were married in Chicago, with old Jacob Shafter as witness.

The trial of the Scowrers was held far from where the guardians of the law could be browbeaten, and the fortune spent on their defense was of no avail. They were broken and scattered. McGinty met his fate at the end of a rope, together with eight of his followers. Fifty or more had various degrees of imprisonment.

Yet the game was not over. Ted Baldwin escaped the death penalty, and so did several of the fiercest spirits of the gang. When they had all regained their freedom, some ten years later, they swore to have McMurdo's blood as vengeance for their comrades. Two attempts were made on his life in Chicago, so he and Ettie left for California under a changed name. There, with an English partner, he made a fortune in the gold rush, but it was there that the light went out of his life when Ettie died. Once again he was nearly killed. He escaped – this time calling himself Douglas – and made his way to England.

After the events at Birlstone Manor, the police had no alternative but to put him on trial for having killed Ted Baldwin, but he was acquitted. The jury accepted that he had acted in self-defense. Shortly afterwards, Sherlock Holmes wrote to his wife.

HOLMES: "Get him out of England at any cost, Mrs Douglas. There is no safety for your husband in England."

WATSON: Two months went by. Then, late one night, we had a visitor – Cecil Barker, Douglas's friend, whom we had last seen at Birlstone. His face was drawn and haggard.

BARKER: I've had terrible news, Mr Holmes. It's poor Douglas. He and his wife started together for South Africa in the *Palmyra* three weeks ago. The ship reached Cape Town last night. I received this cable from Mrs Douglas this morning. Look. "Jack was lost overboard in gale off St Helena. No one knows how accident occurred. Ivy Douglas."

HOLMES: Accident! I've no doubt it was well stage-managed.

BARKER: You mean it wasn't an accident?

HOLMES: Of course it wasn't. He was murdered.

BARKER: Those infernal Scowrers…

HOLMES: No, no. There's a master hand here. I can tell a Moriarty when I see one. This crime emanates from London, not America.

BARKER: But why?

HOLMES: Because this man Moriarty must succeed in everything he does. His whole position depends on it. A great brain and a huge organization have been turned to the extinction of one man.

BARKER: But how did he come to have anything to do with it?

HOLMES: We first came to hear of this business through one of his minions. These Scowrers still had immense wealth at their disposal. They came to an agreement with the greatest consultant in crime. From that moment John Douglas was doomed. First Moriaty found their victim for them. Then he showed them how to go about killing him. Finally, when he learned about the failure of their agent, he stepped in himself.

BARKER: Have we to sit down under this? Can no one get even with this monster?

HOLMES: I don't say that. But you must give me time.

WATSON: We sat in silence for some minutes, as my friend's eyes seemed to be looking far into the future.

(MUSIC.   DOWN   FOR   CLOSING ANNOUNCEMENT. UP MUSIC TO END)

CHIP OF THE FLYING U

BY B M BOWER
DRAMATISED FOR RADIO
BY NEVILLE TELLER

Running Time: 90'

FIRST BROADCAST ACROSS THE
USA ON 20 JANUARY 2020
IN A PRODUCTION BY SHOESTRING
RADIO THEATRE, SAN FRANCISCO
DIRECTED BY PAUL DOUGHERTY

CHARACTERS IN
ORDER OF APPEARANCE

[Note: There are 6 male and 4 female characters (two of whom have one speech only, and. are easily doubled)]

CHIP *Late-20s. Cowboy, ranch hand. Reticent type, but with an artistic soul. Talented artist, knows his Shakespeare. Both aspects need to be there – cowboy and artist.*

J.G. *35. Ranch owner. Shrewd, tough but affable enough.*

SHORTY *30. Ranch foreman.*

DELLA *25. JG's sister, just out of medical school. She falls for Chip as she claps eyes on him, but delights in keeping him guessing. At heart well suited as a doctor – gentle and caring.*

PATSY *40s. Motherly type. JG's housekeeper and cook.*

SLIM *Late 20s. Ranch hand. One of Chip's comrades.*

MRS DENSON *Mid-40s. Typical Montana ranch housewife. Accustomed to giving orders, and having them obeyed. One speech only.*

DUNCAN *Mid-30s. JG's "sleeping" partner. A business type.*

BLAKE *Late-40s. Senator. Assumes control naturally. Air of authority.*

CECIL *25. She's Della's great friend, and has one short speech only, but it's key in the play. She needs to have a warm, inviting voice, almost sexy. Her speech will galvanize listeners as much as Chip. It's what's known as a "coup de théatre"*

(FRISKY AMERICAN COUNTRY MUSIC OF AROUND 1900. DOWN FOR OPENING ANNOUNCEMENT. UP MUSIC. FADE BENEATH FIRST SPEECH, HOLD MUSIC UNDERNEATH IT)

CHIP: Hi. Guess I'd best introduce myself, though I ain't too proud of the name I been landed with. Don't mind the Bennett so much, it's the Claude they plunked in front that I squirm at. Thank heaven no one used it much at the Flying U ranch in Montana, where all this took place back in the early 1900s. The boys in the bunk-house called me Chip – don't ask me why. I wasn't no carpenter. Just a ranch hand like the others – Jack, Cal, Happy, Weary and Slim. The Family, we called ourselves. The ranch belonged to the old man, James G Whitmore, and his absentee partner, Duncan. As for us boys, we were all corralled by the foreman, Shorty.

(CROSSFADE MUSIC INTO)

J.G.: *(bawling)* Shorty! Hey Shorty! Hi – stop. Come back here! I want you.

(HORSE'S HOOVES APPROACH. STOP)

339

SHORTY: *(calls)* There's things waiting to be done, JG.

J.G.:   *(angry)* I suppose that's your excuse for this?

SHORTY: For what?

J.G.:   This goddamn letter, that's what.

SHORTY: What of it?

J.G.:   Where's it bin? That's what I wanna know. Where's it bin? Come on, now Shorty. Why have you bin sitting on this letter?

SHORTY: I don't know what you're on about, JG. And that's God's honest truth.

J.G.:   Doggone it, man. Where's it bin?

SHORTY: How the devil do I know? In the office, most like. It came with the rest today.

J.G.:   But it's two weeks old. Two weeks.

SHORTY: All right. You've got it now.

J.G.:   What's the good of it now, when it says my sister's arriving tomorrow for the summer? Tell me that.

SHORTY: OK, JG. Look on the bright side. You've bin spared two weeks of worry.

J.G.:   But the house. It's like a junk shop. Della's just out of medical school – she's not going to put up with all that mess. She'll be finding microbes everywhere. You just take those boys off whatever they're doing and get them up here. I need the whole shack and yard cleaning up. Today. Starting now.

SHORTY: OK boss. I'm on my way.

(HORSE, NEIGHS, STAMPS)

J.G.:   (*calls*) Oh, and someone will have to meet Dell off the noon train tomorrow. Get Chip on to that, wlll you?

(HORSE TROTS AWAY)

SHORTY: (*retreating, calls*) Sure thing, JG. Leave it to me.

(FADE OUT. FULL UP EXTERIOR. STEAM TRAIN MOVING AWAY, AND FADING UNDER FOLLOWING)

DELLA: (*as narrator*) Well, I surely expected someone to meet me off the train and give a hand with the cases. But there I was, watching the train chugging off into the distance, with not a soul in sight. Well, not at first. But then, way off, outside the station, I saw a cloud of dust which quickly turned into a buggy pulled by two cream horses, with a tousled headed young man driving them. He rode right onto the platform, and pulled up beside me.

(FULL UP EXTERIOR. CART, HORSES TROTTING TO A STOP. WHINNYING)

DELLA: *(calls)* You aren't from the Flying U ranch by any chance?

CHIP: Sure am, ma'am. You must be Miss Della Whitmore. I'm the one they chose to meet you. You certainly ain't a bit like the boys on the ranch pictured you. Chuck those cases in the cart. You can sit up here alongside me, if you choose.

DELLA: What about lifting these cases into the cart for me?

CHIP: Sure thing, ma'am. Pardon me. Don't get too many ladies round here.

(CLAMBERING DOWN. TWO CASES THROWN INTO WOODEN CART)

DELLA: Thank you. Now a hand to climb up, if you please.

(CLAMBERING UP)

CHIP: All settled, Miss Whitmore?

DELLA: You know *my* name. What's yours?

CHIP: They call me Chip.

DELLA: Well, Chip, as you may know, I've never visited with my brother before. How far is the Flying U?

CHIP:	Oh, about five miles. Some of it's quite rough country. Are you ready, ma'am?
DELLA:	One thing, first. I'd like to know the set-up. How many ranch hands are there?
CHIP:	Six, ma'am, including me. Then there's our foreman, Shorty.
DELLA:	And I dare say they've been wondering about the boss's sister. Tell me, how did they all picture me?
CHIP:	Not sure I'd like to say, ma'am.
DELLA:	Go on. I won't hold it against you.
CHIP:	Aw shucks. They were calling you "the old maid". They won't be doing that for long, that I can tell you.
DELLA:	*(laughs)* I hope not. Well, I'm ready, if you are.
CHIP:	Right. Then off we go.

(TWO-HORSE CART SETS OFF AT SPEED. FADE OUT. QUICK FADE IN. EXTERIOR, CART RATTLING ALONG, HORSES HOOVES)

DELLA:	Tell me, what's that dog doing over there? Do dogs wander over this wilderness alone?
CHIP:	That's no dog, Miss Della. That's a coyote. They're an awful pest out here, you know. Attack the cattle.

Wish I could get a shot at him. Do you think you could hold the horses for a minute or two…?

DELLA: No, no. I've never managed horses. But I can shoot.

CHIP: *(calls to horses)* Slow down. Slow.

(HORSES SLOW TO A WALK, CART WHEELS SLOW)

Really? They give you shooting lessons at medical school? Well, ma'am, here's the rifle. See what you can do. I'll stop the horses. *(calls)* Whoa there! Whoa!

(HORSES AND CART STOP. RIFLE IS COCKED)

OK, ma'am. Take your shot. I'll see you don't fall.

DELLA: Very considerate, Chip.

(SINGLE RIFLE SHOT. HORSES NEIGH)

CHIP: *(shouts)* Jumpin' Jehosophat! You got him. Fine shot. Throw another shell in, quick.

(RIFLE IS COCKED. SINGLE RIFLE SHOT)

DELLA: I think I finished him off that time.

CHIP:	I'll get out and pick him up, if you'll hold the horses.
DELLA:	No, you hold the horses. I'd much rather pick him up myself. I won't be a minute.

(CLAMBERING DOWN)

(*Pause. Remote. Calls, advancing*) My goodness, he's heavy.

CHIP:	(*calls*) He's been fattening up on Flying U calves.
DELLA:	Look, here's where I hit him the first time. The bullet went from the shoulder through to the other side. But it missed the heart. He'd have died, but slowly and in pain. That second shot finished him off.
CHIP:	You certainly seem well up in medical matters.
DELLA:	I ought to be. Been surrounded by them all my life. My Uncle John was a doctor. He helped get me into medical school. Oh, just look at that. Blood all over my mandolin case. I'll never get it clean.
CHIP:	Out, damned spot!
DELLA:	Shakespeare? Out here?
CHIP:	Why not?

(HORSES AND CART START UP. FADE OUT. FULL UP)

DELLA: (*as narrator*) I arrived at the Flying U to be greeted by my brother, James, and a spotlessly clean ranch house. Patsy the cook had prepared a slap-up dinner, and afterwards she came and sat by the fire with JG and me.

(INTERIOR. FIRE)

PATSY: Pleased you liked it ma'am. I ain't going to produce something like that every night, mind.

DELLA: I wouldn't expect it, Patsy. And do please call me Della.

PATSY: Don't seem right, somehow.

DELLA: No, Patsy, I insist.

J.G.: Better do as she says, Patsy. My sister usually gets her way.

PATSY: If you say so, JG.

DELLA: (*warning tone*) I'm no Gorgon – so just lay off, Jimmy!

J.G.: Sorry. But since we're on the subject, Dell, I'd be grateful if you'd drop the Jimmy. Don't want the boys getting ideas. Here at the Flying U I'm JG. Let's keep it that way.

DELLA: That's OK with me, Jimmy – I mean JG. Yes, names are strange things. Do you know how Chip got his?

J.G.: Haven't a clue. Perhaps because he's always got one on his shoulder?

DELLA: Why, is he at odds with the world?

PATSY: I wouldn't say so, Della. Not Chip. But he is just a bit into himself. Doesn't say much. Quiet. Just like his horse.

DELLA: Yes, I saw him riding her this evening.

PATSY: It's not a her. It's a colt called Silver. About a year ago Chip rescued him from starving out on the range. Bought him off the owner, and petted and cared for him. He loves that animal.

J.G.: Silver's now one of the best saddle horses on the ranch.

DELLA: I couldn't see them all that clearly. It was already getting dark. But I did notice he was a dark chestnut with a beautiful white, crinkly mane and tail. Oh, and white feet.

PATSY: That's Silver.

DELLA: (*as narrator*) After breakfast next morning, I stood at the window and looked down at the bunk house where Chip and the others lived.

DELLA: Where are the boys right now, JG?

J.G.:   They're all down at the corrals, branding our new calves.

DELLA: Say, I'd like to see that. Do you think I could go down there?

J.G.:   Most certainly not. They wouldn't want you there, and it's no place for a young lady either. You stay right here in the ranch house. But *I've* got to go down there. *(retreating)* Now keep yourself occupied. I'll be back in an hour or so.

(DOOR OPENS)

(remote, calls) Goodbye.

DELLA: Goodbye.

(DOOR CLOSES)

DELLA: *(as narrator)* But I wasn't going to stay cooped up all morning. I had a burning curiosity about that bunk house halfway down the hill. I wanted to see how the ranch hands – and especially Chip – lived. So I clapped an old hat of JG's on my head and went down the hill. You'll want to know what I found. Well, nothing unexpected. It was one very big room with six beds scattered around. A table, some chairs, a pack of cards, a sack of smoking tobacco. Then my eye fell on a pile of journals stacked up by the side of one of the beds. I went over, certain that this was where Chip must sleep. I flicked through the top journal.

(FADE ROMANTIC MUSIC IN BENEATH FOLLOWING. HOLD UNDER)

As I did so, a paper fluttered out. I picked it up – and stared. It was a pencil sketch, done on cheap, rough paper, but I couldn't tear my eyes away. In the background rose the blunt-topped hills of Montana that had already become familiar to me. But right in front stood – well, me. It was me to perfection, immediately recognizable, right down to the fanciful tucks on my sleeve. There I stood in the picture, clutching Chip's rifle. And at my feet lay a dead coyote. He'd given the drawing a title: "The Old Maid".

(FADE OUT MUSIC)

Whoever supposed that the fellow could draw like this?

CHIP: (*remote*) Excuse me.

DELLA: (*really startled*) Oh. Chip. You startled me.

CHIP: I could ask what you're doing in here. And how you got hold of that sketch.

DELLA: Yes. Erm… Curiosity, I guess. Just wondered how you boys managed down here in the bunk house

CHIP: Well, I've got no time for that right now. Excuse me, ma'am. I need to reach under my bed. Please move aside. Thank you.

DELLA: A revolver! What do you need a revolver for? Are you going to shoot something?

(LOADING REVOLVER – CLICKS, THEN CYLINDER WHIRLS)

CHIP: Just as soon as I've loaded up.

DELLA: Who – what are you going to shoot?

CHIP: Well, I'm not too fond of snoopers.

DELLA: What…what…?

CHIP: But I've no time for all that right now. It's a terrible thing, ma'am, but I have to put Silver out of his misery.

DELLA: Silver? Oh, no. What's happened?

CHIP: He broke a leg. He's rolling around in agony. I have to go. Excuse me.

DELLA: No Chip, wait. How did it happen?

CHIP: I don't know. Wish I did. He was in the little pasture. Got kicked, maybe, by one of the wild ones. Some of them aren't broken in. Excuse me.

(DOOR OPENS)

DELLA: Don't. Not yet. Let me go. If it's a straight break I can set the bone and save him.

CHIP: You're not a vet, are you?

DELLA: No. But a broken bone's a broken bone. Let me try. Or are you all set to shoot him?

CHIP: Well, come on then. See what you can do.

(FADE OUT. FULL UP)

CHIP: By dingo, Shorty, after some of the boys got him into a box stall, she found the break.

SHORTY: Where was it?

CHIP: In the front leg – the right one. Just above the fetlock. Broke straight across.

SHORTY: So she set it, did she?

CHIP: She sure did.

SLIM: Problem is, will it mend clean?

SHORTY: You're right, Slim. A crippled horse is less than useless on a working ranch.

SLIM: Just bait for the coyotes.

CHIP: She says she done this before, Slim, for a colt of hers, and now he's as good as new. No trace of a limp.

SLIM: Well, I sure hope it works out the same with Silver.

CHIP: So do I, Slim. So do I.

(EDGE OUT. FADE IN. CROCKERY, CUTLERY)

J.G.: Just as soon as you've finished your breakfast, Dell, we'll drive down to the Denson's.

DELLA: *(eating)* Whatever for?

J.G.: I'd like to get that grass widow of theirs to come over and keep house for us.

DELLA: Grass widow?

J.G.: Mary Denson's sister – Louise, or the Countess, as she's known.

DELLA: Come on, JG. I don't want any old grass widow keeping house. I'm getting along very well, just so long as Patsy does the cooking. In fact, it's rather fun. And it's all looking much better than when I arrived. You must admit that.

J.G.: I do, Dell.

DELLA: Well, then. And to tell you the truth, JG, even with the housework there's not enough to keep me busy. I've decided to apply for my licence to practise medicine here in Montana. The nearest doctor's 50 miles away. I could be of some real use in these parts.

J.G.: That's a great idea, Dell – and if you get your licence, dang me if I won't throw a dance in your honour to celebrate.

DELLA: Great!

J.G.: That's even more of a reason to get the Countess over here. But I'll give you the clincher. Once the round-up starts, Patsy just won't be here. She always goes out on the range with the boys to cook for them. The few men I keep back will have to eat with us here in the ranch house – and you don't think I'm going to have you stuck in the kitchen cooking for five or six people, do you?.

DELLA: All right, JG. Got the picture. I give in. Let's get down to the Denson's, then.

(FADE OUT. FADE IN)

MRS DENSON: Louise, you know JG. And this here's Miss Whitmore. They're after you to go and keep house for them right during the round-up. I guess you'd better go, seeing we got the house cleaned, all but whitewashing the cellar – and I'll make Bill do that. You will, Bill, won't you? It won't hurt you a mite. They'll give you twenty-five dollars a month, Louise, and keep you all summer and as much longer as Miss Whitmore here decides to stay. I guess you might as well go, for there's not a soul in the neighbourhood could do as good a job as you in keeping the place up in shape and be company for JG's sister – and I do believe in helping a neighbour out when you can. Now don't you worry about me. With the house cleaning done, I'll get along just fine. You go right and pack your trunk this very minute, Louise. You're going to join the family at the Flying U.

(FADE OUT. FULL UP)

DELLA: (*as narrator*) If I thought my housekeeping at the ranch house was up to scratch, I was in for a mighty surprise. No sooner had the Countess arrived, than she set to work with a will, scrubbing and dusting and cleaning from morning till night. I left two days later to attend the State medical examination in Helena.

CHIP: (*as narrator*) It was while she was away that Shorty passed on a snippet of news that disturbed me a lot more than it should have done. I mean, what was Della Whitmore to me, or me to Della Whitmore?

SHORTY: I know you're grateful to the little doctor for all she's done for Silver, Chip, but it wouldn't do you any good to throw a nasty loop at her, cause she's spoken for. There's some fellow back East got a long rope on her.

CHIP: How do you reckon that, Shorty?

SHORTY: Cause she's doing a lot of writing to some Doctor Cecil Granthum, of Gilroy, Ohio. A letter a week's been hitting the trail.

CHIP: Her business, I reckon.

(*as narrator*) It hit me hard, that bit of news, and I wondered why I cared so much. Then I remembered all those nights I'd spent standing guard over the cattle, thinking what hell it was being all alone in the world. Then I thought about Della Whitmore, and I remembered how gentle she'd been as she set poor Silver's broken leg. Then, I thought, to be fair it'd be odd if the little doctor had gone through life without some fellow falling in love with her. In fact, there'd probably been several Doctor Cecil Granthums. That evening, visiting Silver in his stall, I took my pad with me and drew a graphic version of what I imagined Doctor Cecil Granthum looked like. It wasn't a very flattering portrait.

(EXTERIOR. HORSE BOX. HORSEY SOUNDS)

DELLA: (*approaching*) Hi there!

CHIP: Miss Whitmore? Didn't expect you back till tomorrow. How did those medics treat you back in Helena?

DELLA: It was all over by mid-morning. Didn't see any sense in hanging around. How's Silver doing?

CHIP: Just great. See for yourself. Clearly on the mend – thanks to you.

DELLA: Good boy! Good old boy! What's that you're drawing? My goodness, I wouldn't like to meet him on a dark night. Who on earth is it?

CHIP: Dr Cecil Granthum.

DELLA: (*slowly overcome with helpless laughter*) Dr Cecil... Dr Cecil Granthum! (*roars with laughter*) Oh Silver ... you don't know ... just how funny this master of yours can be...

CHIP: I don't see what's so funny.

DELLA: How did you know about Cecil?

CHIP: I didn't know. And I don't want to know. I just heard the boys talking, that's all. Gather you write once a week.

DELLA: (*still amused*) Well, I don't think Cecil would be very flattered, that's all I can say. Where on earth did you learn to draw like this? You're very good.

CHIP: I've always made pictures, long as I can remember. Never had any lessons.

DELLA: Did you ever try painting?

CHIP: Nope. Never really tried colours at all. Never had the chance.

DELLA:	I tell you what, Chip. Why don't you come up to the house some evening? I'll show you some of my sketches. They're none of them as good as "The Old Maid". But I've paints and canvas, if you ever care to try that…

(FADE OUT. FADE IN)

DELLA:	JG, it's come!
J.G.:	What's come?
DELLA:	My licence. I'm allowed to practise as a doctor here in Montana.
J.G.:	Well done, little sister! Here, let me give you a big hug.
DELLA:	I'm just delighted.
J.G.:	Tell you what, we'll rig up that room off the dining-room for your office. And you just make up a list of what equipment and what dope you want, and I'll send for it. Make sure you order plenty of what you'll need.
DELLA:	I'll do just that, JG. But I want to hold you to something else. Remember you said you'd lay on a dance for me if I got my licence?
J.G.:	Course we'll have a dance. Let's make it Friday night. Great timing, The round-up starts early next week. A dance will send the boys off in the right mood.

(SLOW FADE IN BENEATH FOLLOWING, FIDDLE AND BANJO, 1900 RURAL DANCE MUSIC)

Why don't you and the Countess work out the food, and I'll send some of the boys around to tell the neighbors.

DELLA: And the music, JG? We want good music.

J.G.: We sure do. You just leave all that to me, Dell. I know a couple of lads just great on the fiddle and banjo. We'll have a whale of a time. Trust me.

(UP MUSIC, WITH BACKGROUND CROWD. HOLD A LITTLE. DOWN FOR FOLLOWING, HOLD UNDER)

CHIP: (*as narrator*) I guess what happened in the middle of that dance just about sealed my fate. I was sitting out a polka, which I was never very good at, when Della Whitmore came right up to me.

DELLA: Chip, I need your help.

CHIP: Sure thing, ma'am. What's the problem?

DELLA: Those blessed Sherman children have got into my office. I can't handle them. There's too many of them.

(MUSIC DOWN, BUT HOLD UNDER)

CHIP: (*as narrator*) I followed her out to her office. The room fairly swarmed with children. About six of them were fighting around the drug cabinet. Its glass door stood wide open. The Little Doctor rushed over, horror-struck. One of the boys had opened a bottle of red pills and handed them out. It turned out that seven of the kids had swallowed some. Luckily they weren't poisonous, but Miss Della Whitmore wasn't taking any chances. The luckless seven were marched out the back door, round the house, and then in again and up to the back bedroom. The Little Doctor tackled them, one by one. She did what she had to do, while I held the wriggling squirming squealing child until the pills were disgorged, along with whatever else was down there. It didn't take long. It was rather like branding calves. When it was all over, and the kids had been escorted back home by the Countess, the Little Doctor sank down on to a chair.

(MUSIC IN BACKGROUND)

DELLA: Go back to the dancing, Chip. And thank you so much.

CHIP: Shucks, it was nothing ma'am.

DELLA: I don't know what I should have done without you. A cow-puncher seems born to deal with emergencies in just the right way.

CHIP: Just pleased to help.

DELLA: I'm really grateful, Chip. If any of those children…
          No, it doesn't bear thinking about.

CHIP: Then don't. All's well that ends well.

DELLA: More Shakespeare!

(UP MUSIC. HOLD A LITTLE. DOWN FOR)

CHIP: (*as narrator*) Later I went over to Silver's stall and
          tangled my fingers in his dimly gleaming mane.

          (*close whisper*) I tell you, Silver, if I ever fall in
          love with a girl – which isn't likely, I grant you
          – but if ever I did, I'll want her to have big,
          grey eyes, and dimples, and a laugh somehow
          like water falling over rocks…You know, Silver
          I think she'd be very much like Miss Della
          Whitmore.

(HORSE WHINNY. UP MUSIC. DOWN FOR)

          Ah, but then she couldn't actually be Miss Della
          Whitmore, Silver, could she? Because there's a Dr
          Cecil Granthum out there, isn't there? A Dr Cecil
          Granthum who writes to her every week. A Dr
          Cecil Granthum she replies to.

**(UP MUSIC. HOLD A LITTLE. CROSSFADE.
INTERIOR OF RANCH HOUSE)**

DELLA: My word, it's gone quiet around here.

J.G.: The same every year, Dell. Most of the boys go off on the round-up, and there's just a few of us left. It'll be like this for a good few weeks. My partner, Duncan Whitaker likes to visit around this time each year. Reckon he'll be arriving before too long.

SLIM: Chip don't see eye to eye with old Dunc sometimes.

J.G.: Oh, they get on right enough, Slim.

SLIM: You know what, JG, I guess the boys lost some horses last night on the way out. They must have turned back by themselves.

J.G.: Why d'you say that?

SLIM: Well, I saw a couple of stallions hanging around the upper fence this morning. And that devil Whizzer's among them. I'd know that one anywhere.

J.G.: Well, maybe you'd best run them into the corral, and hold 'em until Shorty sends someone back for them.

SLIM: Doubt if I could run 'em in alone. Not with Whizzer in the bunch. I certainly don't envy Chip the job of breaking that one in.

DELLA: (*as narrator*) After breakfast I helped the Countess tidy the house, visited Silver armed with the usual lump of sugar, and decided to go up above the grade and sketch the ranch. I climbed the steep bluff, searching for a comfortable place to work. After a while I came upon a great grey boulder, jutting like a giant table from the gravelly soil. I walked out upon it and looked down – a sheer drop to the barren, yellow slope below. The ranch was like a doll's house, and Slim a tiny figure walking towards a group of grazing horses. Then I caught sight of Chip approaching, I saw him single out one of the bunch and leap on his back.

DELLA: (*close*) That must be Whizzer. He's going to try to break him in. Oh, my goodness.

(MIX WILD HORSE'S HOOVES, HORSE SNORTING, WHINNYING, NEIGHING, KICKING. CROSSFADE TO WILD MUSIC. HOLD A LITTLE. DOWN FOR AND FADE BENEATH FOLLOWING)

DELLA: (*as narrator*) Wild with rage at this clinging cowpuncher whom he could not dislodge, who stung his sides and head like the hornets in the meadow, Whizzer gathered himself for a mighty leap. Like a wire spring released he shot into the air, shook himself in one last desperate hope of victory, and failing, came down and turned a somersault. A moment later he struggled to his feet and limped away, beaten in spirit. But Chip lay where he'd fallen and been crushed – a long length of brown chaps, pink-and-white shirt and grey hat. Leaving my sketching things, I went flying down the hill.

Slim got there before me, and JG, who'd also witnessed the accident, came running across from the stable.

(EXTERIOR)

J.G.: (*calling, approaching*) How is he, Slim? Is he dead? Is he?

SLIM: Can't tell, JG. I sure hope not. Hi, Miss Della. What do you say?

DELLA: (***greatly affected, emotional***) Give me a minute. Let me see. Not dead, JG. Thank the good Lord. Not dead. But injured. Badly injured. His collar bone is broken. And he has a scalp wound. And just look at his foot. That ankle is dislocated.

J.G.: Sure is. I reckon he'll be weeks recovering from all that. Dell, you're white as a rag. Doggone it, don't throw up your hands at your first case. Brace up.

DELLA: Look, he's coming round. Thank God. Slim, would you ride back to the house and fetch my medicine bag – the Countess knows where it's kept.

SLIM: (*retreating*) Sure will, ma'am.

DELLA: (*calling*) And bring something to carry him home on.

(FADE OUT. FULL UP. INTERIOR)

CHIP: How long have I got to lie here?

DELLA: A month at least. More likely six weeks.

CHIP: "Tomorrow and tomorrow and tomorrow…"

DELLA: More Shakespeare?

CHIP: Why don't you send me to the hospital? I could stand the trip, I think. You don't want to be bothered with me for six weeks.

DELLA: Quite the opposite. I want you here to practice on. Do you think I'd let such a chance escape? Here you are, and here you stay.

(REMOTE KNOCK ON DOOR. DOOR OPENS)

J.G.: *(remote, advancing)* Hi there, Chip. You OK if I come in?

CHIP: Sure thing, JG. I'm darned sorry, but Miss Whitmore here says I'll be off work for six weeks. Sorry to cost you a man – especially now.

J.G.: Accidents will happen, Chip. Pity Whizzer bucked you off, but these things happen.

CHIP: Bucked me off? Who says Whizzer bucked me off?

J.G.: Well, I thought that's what Slim seems to think.

CHIP:	(*angry*) Doggone it, I'd like to hear Slim stand there and tell me that I got bucked off. I may be pretty badly smashed up, but I'd come pretty near showing him where he stood.
DELLA:	What did happen, Chip?
CHIP:	I did not get bucked off, for a start. Did you see me thrown? You did not. Whizzer leapt and turned a summersault. A fellow can't very well make a pretty ride while his horse is doing gymnastics. JG, did Slim say I got bucked off? Because he knows darned well I wasn't thrown…
J.G.:	Here, young fellow, don't you get to rampaging over nothing. Calm down. Why don't you turn over there, and have a sleep?
DELLA:	Here, let me plump up this pillow.

(BASHING PILLOW)

	There, now. Come on, JG, we'll let him get some rest.
CHIP:	Time for you to write to Dr Cecil Granthum?
DELLA:	Calm down, Chip.
CHIP:	Did Slim say I got bucked off?
DELLA:	No, he didn't. How could he? JG got it wrong. I saw it all from the bluff – I saw Whizzer make

365

that jump, then turn over upon you. It's a wonder you weren't killed outright . Slim thinks the world of you. I wonder if you know how much? I didn't – till I saw how he looked when you were lying flat out… Here, drink this. It'll help you sleep.

(FADE OUT. FULL UP)

DELLA: (*as narrator*) The weeks passed. JG's silent partner, Duncan Whitaker, turned up for his annual visit, but I didn't see much of him. Chip's ankle couldn't be hurried into recovery, so I spent long hours by his bedside – sometimes talking to him, but more often painting while he read, or while he watched me at work

(EDGE OUT. FULL UP)

CHIP: I know that spot. That's what we call the Bad Lands, down the river.

DELLA: That's right. I've captured the spot quite well, I suppose, but the foreground's rather bare. Look, you've seen me using these paints and brushes for long enough. How about you sketch in some Indian tepees and squaws for me, to fill in the picture?

CHIP: I'll do no such thing. For one thing there just ain't no Indians in that country. But I sure wish you'd hurry up and finish the darn thing. It's only half done. Those lonesome hills are getting on my nerves.

DELLA: Well, I certainly can't today. I'm off very soon to see Miss Satterly.

CHIP: And what business have you got with the schoolmarm?

DELLA: My business, Chip. Amy Satterly and I are very good friends. The Countess will bring you your midday meal. You'll be all right for a few hours, won't you?

CHIP: Well, I just can't guarantee that, ma'am. You leave me alone all day, and heaven knows what I could get up to. I might take Whizzer out for a trot.

DELLA: *(laughs)* You'll be OK. See you this evening.

(FADE OUT. FULL UP)

CHIP: *(as narrator)* Truth is, it was most awfully lonesome when she was gone all day. Besides which she'd spent most of the last evening writing to that damn Dr Cecil Granthum.

I lay back in my chair gazing at the unfinished painting. I knew the place so well. Jagged pinnacles, dotted here and there with scrubby pines, hemmed in a tiny basin far beneath – but there the canvas was empty, blank. My mind went back to a scene I'd once witnessed at that very spot. Winter. Dirty grey snow drifts and icy side hills. In the foreground a poor half-starved range cow with her calf which had overlooked by the round-up in the fall, stood at bay. Before them squatted five great gaunt wolves, intent on fresh beef for their supper.

The calf snuggled close to her mother's side, shivering with the cold and the fear of death. The wolves licked their cruel lips and their eyes gleamed hungrily, but the cow stood her ground, her horns long and sharp and threatening. If only it could all be put on canvas just as I'd seen it, with the bitter biting cold of the chinook showing grey and sinister in the sky. If only...

(START MUSIC. HOLD UNDER FOLLOWING)

I shifted myself, chair and all, towards the canvas and the little Doctor's paints and brushes...

(UP MUSIC. HOLD A LITTLE. FADE BENEATH FOLLOWING, AND HOLD UNDER)

DELLA: *(softly, emotional)* Oh Chip. Chip.

CHIP: I told you I'd get into mischief if you went gadding around and left me alone. Now I've spoiled your painting.

DELLA: Oh Chip. That brave creature defending her baby. Doesn't your heart go out to her? And those wolves. Ravenous. You can hear them panting. There's only one ending to this. That calf is doomed. The poor little thing.

(FADE MUSIC)

Why didn't you tell me you could paint like this? Here you've sat day after day and watched me daubing away – and all the while you could do so much better.

CHIP: I'm darned if I'll go around the country claiming skills I don't have. I've never had an art lesson in my life. I dare say you've had heaps. I just drew and coloured what came into my head.

DELLA: Oh for heaven's sake, Chip. Don't you know what you've done? Can't you feel proud? It's wonderful. But where did the idea come from?

CHIP: It so happens I was riding through that country last winter, and I came upon that very cow, just as you see her there, defending her calf against those five wolves. Of course I pulled my six-shooter and opened up on the wolves. I got two – that big feller there, ready to howl, and that one next the cut-bank. The rest broke out down the coulee.

DELLA: So the little calf survived.

CHIP: Sure did. I drove them both up to the ranch. You can see them any time you want.

DELLA: I'm so glad. You know what? After dinner I'm going to get J.G and Mr Whitaker and Slim in here, and see what they think of the painting.

CHIP: Oh no, and specially not Dunk Whitaker. Don't do that. I don't want anyone knowing I had

369

anything to do with it. Do you understand? You're not to say what I got up to. I mean it.

DELLA: Well, we needn't tell them you had a hand in it, if you don't want me to. Oh, I wish Cecil could be here. I always miss Cecil when there's anything in the way of fun going on.

CHIP: Yes? It's a wonder you haven't sent for him if you miss him that bad.

DELLA: I did beg, but Cecil's in a hospital – as a physician, you understand, not as a patient – and can't get off just yet. In a month or two perhaps... Yes, it'll be fun to see what the others think of this painting of ours.

(FADE OUT. FULL UP)

DELLA: Well, say something JG, for goodness sake.

J.G.: I...I don't reckon I've the words. It's kinda knocked me sideways. That cow, there – that's one of ours. Doggone it, Dell, how the dickens did you get that cow and calf in? You must have had a photograph to work from.

SLIM: I know that cow – that's the one I had such a time chasing. I run her and that calf of hers till I was plum sick. Lost them in the end, and had to get on with the round up. I'd have organized a search, but there they both were in the corral next day.

J.G.: Yes, Chip ran across them and brought them in. (*calls*) That's right. Chip, ain't it?

CHIP: (*remote, calls*) That's right.

SLIM: Just look at the old gray sinner with his nose reared straight up in the air. I reckon he's calling his wife's relatives to come and help them out. He's thinking that feisty cow is going to give them a hard time. She sure looks fighty. You know what — I'd like to be behind that old pine with a thirty-thirty and a fistful of shells. I'd sure make a scatteration among them.

DELLA: But Slim, they're nothing but paint.

SLIM: Sorry, ma'am. I kinds forgot it wasn't nothing but a picture.

DUNCAN: And that's the whole point.

DELLA: How do you mean, Mr Whitaker?

DUNCAN: Dunk, please, Miss Whitmore.

DELLA: Then it's Della.

DUNCAN: Della. You couldn't ask for greater praise than that. Slim forgot it was a painting. It's so real, so vivid, that his hand itched for a rifle. It's a wonderful picture, Della. You must let me take it with me to Butte. What do you call it?

DELLA: The Last Stand.

DUNCAN: The Last Stand. That painting will make you famous out here in the West. If you're prepared to sell it, I can guarantee you'd get a really good price for it.

DELLA: Do you mean all that?

DUNCAN: I certainly do. It's the best picture of its kind I've ever seen.

J.G.: You'd best let him take it with him to Bute, Dell.

(EDGE OUT. EDGE IN)

DELLA: You don't mind, Chip, do you? Dunk trying to sell the painting.

CHIP: Why should I mind? It's your picture.

DELLA: It's at least half yours – more, really.

CHIP: It's yours. I put in a little time meddling with your property for want of something else to do. What I painted doesn't cover a quarter of the canvas. I hope Dunk sells it for a good price. Just keep still about my part in it.

(FADE OUT. FADE IN)

DELLA: (*as narrator*) It wasn't till Chip was back up on his feet, even though he still hobbled around on crutches, that my friend Amy Satterly and I decided to take a week off together during the school vacation. We planned a visit to the Rainbow Falls, and then to indulge in a real shopping spree in Giant Spring.

(FULL UP)

CHIP: How long?

DELLA: A week.

CHIP: A week? What on earth am I going to do with myself for a week?

DELLA: I can tell you, Chip. Now listen to me. I'm deadly serious.

CHIP: Seven days.

DELLA: Chip, while I'm gone I want you to paint me another picture. Will you? Please.

CHIP: I don't know. Maybe I can't a second time.

DELLA: And maybe you can. See that 18 by 24 canvas? Over there. Leaning against the wall.

CHIP: Yup.

DELLA: And here are all the paints and brushes. Now I'll expect to see something worthwhile when I return.

CHIP: Well, but if I can't…

DELLA: Look at me. Straight in the eye, if you please. Now, will you try?

CHIP: Oh, I suppose so. Are you going to sell it?

DELLA: Of course I won't sell it. It won't be mine to sell. This will be yours – your own work.

(FADE OUT. FULL UP)

J.G.: Well I'll be doggoned.

CHIP: *(startled)* Darn it, JG. What you doing creeping up on a feller like that? You half scared me to death.

J.G.: I made enough noise coming in to waken the dead. Only you were too deep in that picture. You done all that?

CHIP: Kinda looks that way.

J.G.: Then all I can say is that you must have made that other one. Dell's never painted like that in her life. That was you, wasn't it? Admit it. Why didn't you tell us?

CHIP: Because it wasn't my painting. I took hold of it without permission. And I added in the cow and one or two other things…

J.G.:	Yes – just the parts that make the picture what it is. As for Dell – well I must say I never thought she'd lay claim… I'll give her thunder when she gets back.
CHIP:	You'll do no such thing. It was her picture. She started it, and she meant to finish it. I painted on it one day when she wasn't here. And I made her promise not to tell anyone that I had anything to do with it.
J.G.:	If you say so. Anyway, it's a rattling good picture – but this one's better. So much better.

(FADE OUT. FULL UP. EXTERIOR. BIRDS. HORSES)

DUNCAN:	(*approaching*) Ah, Della. There you are. There's something in this paper may interest you.
DELLA:	The only thing I'm interested in at the moment is drinking in the sun.
DUNCAN:	You'll want to see this.
DELLA:	Really, Dunk? Show me.

(NEWSPAPER)

DUNCAN:	There.
DELLA:	Oh my goodness! My goodness! You've sold "The Last Stand". You've sold the painting

DUNCAN: Not quite, Della. I've had an offer. Quite a good one. I arranged for it to be exhibited in the lobby of the Summit hotel, and there was a lot of interest. I turned down one or two people who didn't meet my asking price. Then came this one, which I accepted subject to your agreement.

DELLA: But. but...*[I can't take the credit for...]*

DUNCAN: (*sweeps on*) I wish you could have seen the old stockmen stand around it and tell wolf stories to one another by the hour. The women came and cried over it – they were so sorry for the cow and her baby calf. No one would believe it was painted by a woman.

DELLA: Who's made the offer, Dunk? Do I know him?

DUNCAN: None other than Senator Blake. He wouldn't haggle – agreed to pay the full price as soon as he clapped eyes on it. There's one condition, though. He insists on the artist's name being attached to it. He wants to come over here to the Flying U to get that signature, once you agree to sell. He'll bring the painting with him. I'm to wire your decision as soon as possible.

DELLA: You can tell Senator Blake to come over. I'd like to see him very much.

(FADE OUT. FADE IN)

BLAKE: My dear young lady, I'm delighted to meet you. I just refused to believe Mr Whitaker here when he insisted that the artist was a young woman – simply refused. But here you are, and he was quite right.

DELLA: Yes, here I am Senator. And there's something I have to tell you.

BLAKE: A remarkable piece of work, Miss Whitmore, if I may say so. Remarkable. My wife just fell in love with it. That little calf, you know, being protected by its mother. But I was taken with the sheer savagery of those ravenous wolves. Never been so moved by a work of art before. Never.

DELLA: Very kind of you to say so, Senator. But I have a confession to make.

BLAKE: A confession?

DUNCAN: What do you mean, Della ?

DELLA: Dunk, I never told you that I painted The Last Stand. And in fact I didn't – not exactly.

DUNCAN: But good heavens, Della, you never said you didn't. You knew darn well that's what I – that's what we all – believed. You handed the painting over to me. Anyway, what do you mean by "not exactly"?

DELLA: I'm sorry for deceiving you, Dunk – for that's what I did. And I'm sorry you've been misled,

Senator. The truth is, unfortunately for myself, I did not paint the ravening wolves that caught your fancy. Nor the cow defending her calf. All that would have been utterly beyond me.

DUNCAN: Then who…? Chip! Your friend Chip!

DELLA: You have it in one, Dunk. Chip painted the best part of The Last Stand.

DUNCAN: Senator Blake, I apologise profusely for insisting that the artist was a young lady. I have misled you – though, as you can see, I am as much a victim of this conspiracy as you.

BLAKE: Good grief, man, do you think I care a hoot who painted it? It's a great work of art.

DUNCAN: If that Chip has been guilty of a deliberate fraud…

CHIP: *(remote, advancing)* Yes, Dunk, you'll do what? There's no fraud involved or intended. The painting was Miss Della's. Without her knowledge I took it and added some figures. Then I made her promise not to let anyone know that I'd dabbled with her work. That's the beginning and the end of it.

BLAKE: Kid Bennett! What are you doing here, you rascal? Aren't you gonna shake hands?

CHIP: How do you do, Blake? I didn't think you'd remember me.

BLAKE: How could I forget you? I can feel the cold water as I speak, and your rope settling over my shoulders. You never gave me a chance to say thank you. Just coiled up your rope, swearing all the time because it was wet, and then rode off, dripping like a muskrat. What was all the rush?

CHIP: I was in a hurry to get back to camp. And you weren't a senator then.

BLAKE: And if I had been? You'd have let me drown?

CHIP: I reckon not.

BLAKE: Well, well. So you're the genius! No offence, Miss Whitmore.

DELLA: None taken, Senator.

BLAKE: Bennett – Chip – do you remember that picture you drew with charcoal on a piece of pineboard?

CHIP: What of it?

BLAKE: It stands on the mantel in my library. I always point it out to my friends as the work of a young man with a future. So you painted "The Last Stand"?

CHIP: Part of it.

DELLA: The best part.

BLAKE: Well, I think I'll have pay a bit more than I agreed, just to get even with you for swearing at me when my lungs were so full of water I couldn't swear back.

DELLA: Senator, I think there's something else you ought to see. Over here – under this cloth. Just a moment. There.

BLAKE: Oh my goodness.

DELLA: I've had no hand in this. This is all Chip's work. He calls it "The Spoils of Victory."

BLAKE: It's… it's… breathtaking. Tell me, Chip, do the two pictures go together?

CHIP: Shucks, I don't know. I painted it for Miss Whitmore.

DELLA: Did you?

CHIP: Reckon so.

DELLA: Well, in that case I'd much rather have you paint me another one. This one makes me want to cry – and that's not good in a doctor.

BLAKE: Excellent. In that case, Mr Whitaker, perhaps we can agree a figure for both paintings. I take it you're acting as agent for young Mr Bennett, here?

DUNCAN:	I reckon, so, Senator. That OK with you Chip?
CHIP:	I've got no head for business.
DUNCAN:	Right, then. I'm your agent, but don't think I'll be taking any commission. This way, Senator.

(FADE OUT. FADE IN. EXTERIOR)

DELLA:	*(approaching, calling)* Chip! Hey, Chip.
CHIP:	Ma'am?
DELLA:	I've got some wonderful news. Absolutely wonderful.
CHIP:	Really?
DELLA:	Well, can't you look even a little bit excited? I've just heard. The Gilroy Hospital – you know, where Cecil is…
CHIP:	I know.
DELLA:	Well they've just had a case of blighted love.
CHIP:	How do you mean?
DELLA:	A doctor there was planning to get married and go away on his honeymoon. You know.
CHIP:	And?

DELLA: Well, now he isn't. His ladylove was faithless, and loves another. So no honeymoon. Do you see now where the good news comes in?

CHIP: Sorry.

DELLA: Well, you *are* dull. Since that fellow isn't going to have any vacation, Cecil can come out here to the Flying U almost at once. Next week! Think of that.

CHIP: I'm thinking.

(FADE IN BENEATH FOLLOWING STEAM TRAIN CHUGGING TOWARDS US. A MIGHTY BLOW ON THE WHISTLE AS IT SCREECHES TO A HALT)

DELLA: Next Wednesday on the midday train. Now you *will* drive me down to the station, won't you? We'll need the buggy because of the luggage, and I can't really manage those creams. You'll like Cecil. Everyone likes Cecil.

(TRAIN DOORS OPENING AND SLAMMING SHUT

CHIP: (*as narrator*) I had no intention of coming further than the station yard. I had no wish to see Della greet Cecil as he came off the train. So I sat behind the creams waiting for them to appear, imagining the scene. He steps down from the carriage. Della comes forward. He flings his arms around her. They kiss. At that moment I came to a firm decision. I wasn't going to stay with the Flying U one day longer than necessary. I'd be off just as soon as possible. Wretched and lost in bitter thoughts, I didn't hear them coming up behind me.

DELLA: (*calls*) Chip! You fallen asleep?

CHIP: (*calls*) I most certainly have not.

DELLA: Then let me introduce you. Chip, this is Dr Cecil Granthum.

CECIL: Hullo, Chip. I'm very pleased to meet you. I've heard so much about you.

CHIP: (*as narrator*) She held out her hand. Too utterly at sea to say anything, I took it. Then I shook it, filled with a mixture of relief and joy. Cecil Granthum was a big, breezy, blue-eyed young woman, and I adored her.

(FADE IN UNDER FOLLOWING TWO HORSES TROTTING, AND CARRIAGE WHEELS)

As we drove back to the ranch I had no idea whether the sun was shining, whether the grass was green and the sky blue – or the other way around. All I knew was that my dark thoughts had vanished into thin air. Della had no beau.

(LOSE HORSES AND CART, CROSSFADE TO EXTERIOR. FADE IN)

DELLA: I did nothing of the sort.

CHIP: You did so. You led me to believe that Dr Cecil Cranthum was a man.

DELLA: I never said that.

CHIP: No, and you didn't say she was your woman friend, either.

DELLA: It makes no odds. Cecil and I are going somewhere to practise medicine together. We're going to be partners. And we aren't either of us going to get married. Ever.

CHIP: Setting up a new practice? You'll need a licence for that.

DELLA: I have my licence.

CHIP: You're ahead of me there. I can soon get one, though.

DELLA: What on earth are you talking about?

CHIP: I'm talking ... *(close, intimate, soft)* ... about this. *(kiss)*

DELLA: *(close, intimate, soft)* Chip. *(kiss. pause)* Well, aren't you going to let me go?

CHIP: Never.

DELLA:	Are you quite sure about that?
CHIP:	Absolutely. Unless, of course, you can't stand me.
DELLA:	I wouldn't say that.
CHIP:	I wasn't sure. After all, you've dealt me misery ever since I first set eyes on you. And on my soul. I believe you liked watching me squirm.
DELLA:	Oh, no, no. *(laughs)* Well, just a little, perhaps.
CHIP:	Della, will you marry me? I haven't the faintest idea how we'll live, but I do know we must be together.
DELLA:	Oh, I've worked it all out. Had it sorted weeks ago.
CHIP:	Weeks?
DELLA:	Yes, Cecil and I will set up a joint medical practice somewhere. We'll be partners. And you, Chip, will turn professional artist. You will paint.
CHIP:	Will I?
DELLA:	Paint and paint and paint. Your canvases will sell – of that I'm certain. You'll become quite famous. And I'll wallow in your fame. I'll say, "I'm his wife, you know." *(sudden thought)* Oh!
CHIP:	What's the matter?

DELLA: Isn't this ridiculous? I know your surname's Bennett. Senator Blake told us that. But what's your Christian name? I've never called you anything but Chip.

CHIP: Names. What's in a name? That which we call a rose by any other name would smell as sweet.

DELLA: Shakespeare again!. You're a mine of quotations. But no Chip, I need to know. Who exactly am I marrying?

CHIP: You won't like it. I certainly don't.

DELLA: Out with it.

CHIP: Heaven knows why, but they landed me with Claude. I'm Claude Bennett.

DELLA: (*deadly serious*) Claude Bennett. Sounds just right to me for a famous artist. On the other hand… Would you mind very much if I remained Dr Della Whitmore for professional purposes?

CHIP: Mind? I'd much prefer it.

CHIP: }   (*both burst out laughing*)
DELLA: }

                  (UP MERRY MUSIC. LOSE CHIP AND DELLA. DOWN MUSIC FOR CLOSING ANNOUNCEMENT. UP MUSIC TO SATISFYING FINAL CHORDS).

THE STRANGE CASE OF DR JEKYLL AND MR HYDE

BY ROBERT LOUIS STEVENSON
DRAMATISED FOR RADIO
BY NEVILLE TELLER

Running Time: 60'

FIRST BROADCAST IN THE UK
IN A PRODUCTION BY LBC IN 1989
BROADCAST ACROSS THE USA IN 2007
IN A PRODUCTION BY SHOESTRING RADIO THEATRE
DIRECTED BY JONATHAN WILD

CAST

MAIN CHARACTERS:

UTTERSON	*50s. Lawyer.*
LARKIN	*50s. Butler*
LANYON	*60s. Doctor*
HYDE	*30s. Embodiment of evil*
MRS POOLE	*50s. Housekeeper*
JEKYLL	*Late-40s.*
GRANT	*Mid-40s. Legal clerk.*

SUBSIDIARY CHARACTERS:

ENFIELD	*20s.*
DOCTOR	
WOMAN 1	

WOMAN 2

WOMAN 3

BUTLER 2

INSPECTOR   *Police officer*

MRS SELLAND   *50s*

(STREET, NIGHT. A YOUNG GIRL, HYSTERICAL WITH FRIGHT. GIVES TWO OR THREE SHORT SCREAMS, THEN A LONG SUSTAINED SHRIEK OF PURE TERROR. A MAN'S FOOTSTEPS RUN ON ECHOING PAVEMENTS. CROSSFADE TO STREET, NIGHT)

ENFIELD: Horrible, Utterson. The most horrible thing I've witnessed.

UTTERSON: And you say it happened here – in this street?

ENFIELD: Do you see that front door?

UTTERSON: With the paintwork peeling off?

(HORSEDRAWN CAB CLATTERS BY UNDER FOLLOWING)

ENFIELD: That's the one. Well, it happened just over there, and that door's part of the story. As a student of the human race, Utterson, this should interest you. Perhaps you can throw some light on it.

UTTERSON: My dear cousin, I'm only a lawyer, you know, not one of these newfangled explorers into the human soul. I'm not sure we ought to venture too far in that direction.

ENFIELD: Cousin Gabriel, you've learned more about the human soul in your dusty legal practice then most of these young doctors will ever do. Now listen to this. A few weeks ago I was walking home through these streets about three o'clock of a black winter morning. They were deserted – empty as a church. All at once I saw two figures. One was

(FADE UP MAN'S FOOTSTEPS WALKING FAST ON PAVEMENT. HOLD UNDER FOLLOWING)

a shortish man, stumping along in one direction. The other was a girl

(FADE UP CHILD'S FOOTSTEPS RUNNING)

of maybe eight or ten, who was running as fast as she could down a street that went at right angles to him. Well, Utterson, naturally enough the two ran into each other at the corner.

(FOOTSTEPS STOP; THE GIRL CRIES OUT; HYDE GROWLS, THEN REPLAY OF OPENING SCREAM SEQUENCE. CROSSFADE)

And then came the horrible part. The child slipped and fell over, and the man, just as if he were stamping on a monstrous spider, trampled all over the girl's body. Then, with her screaming on the ground, he took to his heels.

UTTERSON: What did you do?

ENFIELD: I ran after him, collared the fellow and brought him back. There was already quite a group around the child…

(FADE OUT. FADE IN SOBBING CHILD AND CROWD CHATTER. DOWN FOR)

DOCTOR: There, there, Ellie. You know me, don't you? Doctor MacFarlane. Quiet child. Let me see… There, now. That didn't hurt, did it?

(CHILD'S SOBS FADE)

ENFIELD: How is she, doctor?

DOCTOR: As well as can be expected, given that a grown man has walked all over her. Not this person?

ENFIELD: I'm afraid so.

DOCTOR: Good God, man, are you a human being or a monster?

WOMAN: *(calls)* Let me get at him.

ENFIELD: Back. Keep back

HYDE: Save yourself the trouble. I'm quite able to protect myself.

DOCTOR: I dare say. But you'd do better, sir, protecting the weak and innocent. By Heaven, sir, I'll make such a scandal out of this, your name will stink from one end of London to the other.

WOMAN 2: *(calls)* You devil!

HYDE: If you choose to make capital out of this accident, I'm naturally helpless to stop you. However, any gentlemen wishes to avoid a scene. Name your price.

WOMAN 3: *(calls)* Make him pay up.

ENFIELD: I'd say a hundred pounds for the girl's family would be fair compensation, wouldn't you, doctor?

DOCTOR: Very fair.

(FADE OUT. FADE IN)

ENFIELD: The next thing was to get the money. And where do you think he led us, Utterson? To that door over there.

UTTERSON: Good heavens.

ENFIELD: He whipped out a key, went in, and presently came back with ten pounds in gold and a cheque for the balance drawn payable to bearer. The cheque was signed with a name I can't mention...

UTTERSON: Why?

ENFIELD: It's very well known.

UTTERSON: I see. I take it, then, that it wasn't the name of the man who trampled the child?

ENFIELD: Oh no.

UTTERSON: And the cheque – was it made good?

ENFIELD: Certainly. Next day the doctor, the child's father and I went to the bank and redeemed the cash.

UTTERSON: An odd tale certainly, Enfield, as you promised.

ENFIELD: Yes. The fellow we dealt with was really damnable, while the person who drew the cheque is propriety itself. Celebrated, too. Blackmail, I suppose.

            (UNDER FOLLOWING, TWO PAIRS OF FOOTSTEPS. HORSEDRAWN CAB SOME TIME AFTER)

            Intrigued?

UTTERSON: I admit it, cousin. The name of that fellow – did you discover what It was?

ENFIELD: Yes – his name was Hyde, Edward Hyde.

UTTERSON: What sort of man is he?

ENFIELD: Not easy to describe. There's something … wrong … with his appearance – something downright detestable. I never saw a man I so disliked and yet I scarcely know why. No, I can't describe him – and yet I can see him in my mind as clearly as I see you.

UTTERSON: And you're sure he used a key to open that street door?

ENFIELD: My dear cousin…

UTTERSON: Because, my dear Enfield, the fact is, if I don't ask you the name of the person who wrote that cheque, it's because I know it already. Tell me if I'm wrong – I don't think I can be – but wasn't the name of the other party Jekyll. Dr Henry Jekyll?

ENFIELD: How … how on earth…

UTTERSON: Ah, that's where I exercise my own brand of legal discretion…

(FADE OUT. FADE IN, DRAWING ROOM)

LARKIN: (*approaching*) Your brandy and soda, sir,

UTTERSON: Ah, thank you, Larkin.

LARKIN: Will there be anything else?

UTTERSON: Not tonight, thank you.

LARKIN: Then goodnight Mr Utterson, sir.

(DOOR CLOSES)

(close) Poor Jekyll – poor fellow. How on earth have you become entangled with such a monster? Edward Hyde. I knew that name as soon as I heard it – how could I forget the extraordinary terms of your Will, my dear friend?

Now where are the keys of that strongbox…?

(KEYS, LOCK TURNS. PAPERS RUSTLE)

Here we are… "Last Will and Testament of Henry Jekyll, MD, DCL, FRS."

(PAPER RUSTLES)

As I thought. Extraordinary. "In the event of my decease all my possessions are to pass into the hands of my friend and benefactor, Edward Hyde." Benefactor! I wonder! There's worse. "In case of my disappearance or unexplained absence for any period exceeding three calendar months, the said Edward Hyde is to become sole legal owner of all my wordly possessions." It's all too absurd. I thought it madness at the time. Now I begin to fear it is worse – disgrace, or even danger…

(FADE OUT. DOORBELL RINGS. PAUSE HEAVY DOOR OPENS)

BUTLER 2:   Good evening, sir.

UTTERSON;   Ah, I'm glad the house is still up. Is Dr Lanyon at home?

BUTLER 2:   I believe he is, Mr Utterson. May I take your hat. sir?

(DOOR CLOSES)

UTTERSON: Thank you.

BUTLER 2:   I believe he's still in the dining room. This way, sir.

(INTERIOR DOOR OPENS. DRAWING ROOM)

Mr Utterson.

LANYON: Good grief, Utterson, what are you doing out at this time of night? You'll catch your death.

UTTERSON: Thank you for your professional concern, Lanyon. I might ask what a practising physician is doing lingering over the port at past midnight?

LANYON: Come and join me in a glass.

UTTERSON: I won't say no. It's pretty sharp out tonight.

(CLINK OF GLASS: POURING)

LANYON: Sit yourself down. Now what's this all about?

UTTERSON:	I'm troubled in my mind about an old friend – a friend of both of ours. Lanyon, you and I must be the two oldest friends that Henry Jekyll has.
LANYON:	*(chuckles).* I could wish the friends younger. But I suppose we are. What of it? I see little of him nowadays.
UTTERSON:	Indeed? I thought you had a bond of common interest. Didn't you set up some research together?
LANYON:	At one time. But it's more than ten years since Henry Jekyll became far too fanciful for me. He started lines of enquiry that I refused to pursue with him. And though of course I continue to take an interest in him for old times' sake, I see devilish little of the man. Such unscientific balderdash…
UTTERSON:	Tell me, did you ever come across a protegé of his – one Edward Hyde?
LANYON:	Never heard of him. What's the problem?
UTTERSON:	The details, I fear, I can't divulge – for professional reasons. But this I will say: I've reason to believe that this Hyde has somehow managed to acquire some influence over our poor friend. I believe he's exercising that power for evil – possibly criminal – ends. I've never set eyes on the man myself, but all I've heard leads me to believe that he's casting an ominous shadow over Henry Jekyll's life. I assure you, Lanyon, that I intend to find out all

I can about him. If he is Mr Hyde, Lanyon, I'm going to become a veritable Mr Seek. One day I shall encounter our Mr Edward Hyde. And when I do, my dear Lanyon, I shall not hesitate to challenge him.

(FADE OUT. FADE IN CAB AND HORSE CLATTERING BY. BRING UP MAN'S FOOTSTEPS ON ECHOING PAVEMENT. THEY STOP)

UTTERSON: Mr Hyde?

HYDE: (*hiss of surprise*) That is my name.

UTTERSON: I see you're going in through that door. I happen to know that it's a back entrance to the house of an old friend of mine – Dr Henry Jekyll. My name is Utterson, of Gaunt Street – you must have heard Jekyll speak of me. Meeting you so conveniently, I thought you might admit me.

HYDE: You won't find Dr Jekyll. He's not at home. But it's just as well that we've met. And you ought to have my address. Here is my card. And now, goodnight to you.

(DOOR UNLOCKS, OPENS AND CLOSES)

UTTERSON: (*Close*) What is there about the man that fills me with disgust? No, it's more than that. Loathing. And fear.

(MAN'S SLOW FOOTSTEPS ON PAVEMENT UNDER FOLLOWING)

If only I could find a name for it. Oh, my poor Jekyll. If ever I read Satan's signature on a face, it's wrItten large on that of your new friend.

(FOOTSTEPS STOP. KNOCKER ON FRONT DOOR. DOOR OPENS)

UTTERSON: Good evening, Mrs Poole. I wonder whether Dr Jekyll is at home?

MRS POOLE: I'II see, Mr Utterson. Will you come in?

(DOOR CLOSES)

This way, sir. Will you wait here by the fire? (*retreating*) I'll be back in just a minute.

UTTERSON: (*close*) It's as though the foulness were permanently lodged within the man's body. An evil soul cannot but be reflected in a man's outward form. And if ever a man were evil, that man is Edward Hyde.

MRS POOLE: (*approaching*) I'm sorry, sir, but Dr Jekyll has gone out.

UTTERSON: Mrs Poole, I just saw Mr Hyde go in by the old street door to the dissecting room – into Dr Jekyll's laboratory. Is that right, when Dr Jekyll's away from home?

MRS POOLE: That's perfectly all right, sir. Mr Hyde has a key.

UTTERSON: Your master seems to repose a great deal of trust in that young man, Mrs Poole.

MRS POOLE: Yes sir, he do indeed. We all have orders to obey him.

UTTERSON: And yet I don't think I ever met Mr Hyde in the house.

MRS POOLE: Oh, you won't have done, sir. He never dines here. We don't see him this side of the house. He comes and goes by the side door.

UTTERSON: I see. Then I won't be meeting him here tomorrow night?

MRS POOLE: Oh no, sir. He won't be among the dinner guests. Certainly not.

UTTERSON: H'mm. Pity.   Ah well, I'd best be on my way,

(DOOR OPENS)

Goodnight Mrs Poole. It's 8.30 tomorrow evening, is it not?

MRS POOLE: Quite correct, Mr Utterson. Goodnight sir.

(DOOR CLOSES. FADE IN)

UTTERSON: I do hope you don*t mind my staying behind after your other guests, my dear Jekyll . . .

JEKYLL: On the contrary. A great pleasure.

UTTERSON: The fact is, I've been wanting to speak to you for some time. You know that Will of yours?

JEKYLL: Poor Utterson. What an unsatisfactory client I must be. I never saw anyone so distressed as you are by that Will – unless it's my old friend Lanyon when you get him on the subject of my so–called scientific heresies!

UTTERSON: You know I never approved of it.

JEKYLL: My Will, do you mean? Yes, I certainly do know that. You've told me so, often enough.

UTTERSON: Well, I tell you so again. I've been learning something of your beneficiary, young Hyde.

JEKYLL: Please don't go on. I don't care to hear any more. I thought we'd agreed not to discuss this?

UTTERSON: What l heard was ... abominable.

JEKYLL: It can't alter matters. I'm ... painfully situated, Utterson. The circumstances are very strange. It's one of those affairs that can't be mended by talking.

UTTERSON: Jekyll, my old friend – you know me. I'm a man to be trusted. Make a clean breast of this. In confidence. I've no doubt I can get you out of it.

JEKYLL: Dear Utterson. I'd trust you before any man alive you know that. I can't find the words to thank you. But indeed the affair isn't as bad as you imagine. And just to set your good heart at rest, I'll tell you one thing more. The moment I choose, I can be rid of Mr Hyde. I give you my word on that. Now please take this in good part, but this is a private matter, and I beg you to let it rest.

UTTERSON: Ah well, I've no doubt you're perfectly right.

JEKYLL: Just one last thing. I really do have a very great interest in poor Hyde, and if I do disappear, I want you to promise that you'll get his rights for him. I think you would if you knew all. It would be a great weight off my mind if you would promise.

UTTERSON: I can't pretend I'll ever like him.

JEKYLL: I don*t ask that. I ask you only to help him for my sake were I no longer to be here.

UTTERSON: (*sighs*) Ah, well. I promise. I promise.

(FADE OUT. FADE IN URGENT AND REPEATED KNOCKING WITH KNUCKLES ON WOODEN DOOR)

GRANT: (*muffled, calling*) Mr Utterson! Mr Utterson, sir!

UTTERSON: (*awaking, drowsy*) Eh? What? Who's that?

(KNOCKING)

GRANT: (*muffled, calling*) Mr Utterson! Are you awake, sir?

UTTERSON: Eh? (*calls*) Yes. Yes, I'm awake. What is it? Come in.

(DOOR OPENS)

GRANT: (*advancing*) It's me, sir – Grant. From the office.

UTTERSON: Grant? What on earth are you doing here? I haven*t overslept, have I? What's the time?

GRANT: Oh no, sir. It*s not that. It's just 5 a.m, sir. Oh, Mr Utterson, it's very serious.

UTTERSON: Now calm down, Grant. Sit down – over there. That's right. Now tell me all about it.

GRANT: It's murder, sir – and the police want you.

UTTERSON: Want me? For murder? Don't be absurd.

GRANT: Oh no, sir. it's not that. The police think you'll be able to identify the body.

UTTERSON: Me? But why?

GRANT:	Because the man was carrying an unposted letter addressed to the firm.
UTTERSON:	I see. Well, of course I'll come. Tell me about it while I dress. *(retreating)* I'll leave the door of my dressing room ajar.
GRANT:	*(slightly raised voice)* I don't know the whole story, sir, but it seems a maidservant, who happened to be alone in a house not far from the river, was looking out of a window, and saw two men coming towards each other in the moonlight.
UTTERSON:	*(calls)* When was this?
GRANT:	Late last night, sir – or rather, early this morning. About half–past one. Well, the older man – one with white hair – stopped the other and seemed to ask the way. She says the younger man, who was carrying a heavy walking stick, scarcely let the other one finish what he was saying. He burst out in a fit of temper, stamping and brandishing his stick. The older man took a step back, and at that the younger man's rage broke all bounds, and he clubbed him to the ground. The next moment, in a sort of blind fury, he was trampling the old fellow under his feet. The poor girl says she could actually hear the victim's bones being shattered underfoot.
UTTERSON:	*(approaching)* Dear heaven. Dear heaven.

GRANT: That's not quite all, sir. By a strange chance the maid actually recognised the younger man – he'd once visited her master. I'm afraid, Mr Utterson, it's a name not unknown to the firm.

UTTERSON: (*mutters*) I know it. I know it already.

GRANT: The murderer, sir, is Dr Henry Jekyll's beneficiary – Mr Edward Hyde,

(FADE OUT. FADE IN. ECHO)

INSPECTOR: Are you ready, sir? You'd better prepare yourself. It's not a pleasant sight.

UTTERSON: Quite ready, officer. (*pause*) Oh, my Lord, poor fellow – poor, poor fellow. Yes, Inspector, I can positively identify this man – though I could scarcely say I recognise him. I've never seen anyone so disfigured. It's a very old acquaintance and client of mine. I'm sorry to any that this is Sir Danvers Carew.

INSPECTOR: The Member of Parliament? Good heavens. This is going to cause a great deal of fuss. This way, sir.

(HEAVY DOOR CLOSES. ECHO OFF)

Perhaps you're also acquainted with the other man in the case the one who was recognised by the eyewitness? Mr Edward Hyde? Here's half his walking stick – the murder weapon.

UTTERSON: Only half?

INSPECTOR: It broke during the attack. He must have carried the other half away with hlm.

UTTERSON: If you will come with me in my cab, Inspector, I think I can take you to his house.

INSPECTOR: Indeed? Then don't let's waste another moment, sir. I'm at your service.

(FADE OUT. FADE IN HORSEDRAWN CAB SLOWING AND STOPPING ON COBBLES. CAB DOOR OPENS)

UTTERSON: Thank you,

(CAB DOOR CLOSES)

              (calls) Wait here, please, cabbie. Not a very salubrious neighbourhood, Inspector, is it?

INSPECTOR: Indeed not, sir.

UTTERSON: Now where were we? Number 26. This is it.

(KNOCKER RAPS. PAUSE. DOOR OPENS)

MRS SELLAND: *(suspicious)* Yes?

UTTERSON: Is this the residence or a Mr Hyde – a Mr Edward Hyde?

MRS SELLAND:	Yes. Yes, he lives here. But he's not at home. He's often away. Hadn't seen him for nigh on two month before he turned up yesterday.
UTTERSON:	I see. Well then, Mrs ... er?
MRS SELLAND:	Selland. Mrs Selland.
UTTERSON:	Well then, Mre Selland, we should like to see over his rooms, if you don't mind.
MRS SELLAND:	But I do mind. I never heard anything like it. Certainly not.
UTTERSON:	Perhaps I'd better introduce this gentleman. This is Inspector Newcomen, of Scotland Yard.
INSPECTOR:	Ma'am. My warrant card.
MRS SELLAND:	Ah, then he's in trouble. What's he done?
INSPECTOR:	Not in your good books, then, Mrs Selland?
MRS SELLAND:	He's certainly not that. Oh well, you'd better come in. Mr Hyde has these rooms on the ground floor...

(FRONT DOOR CLOSES)

... I live in the basement, myself.

(DOOR OPENS)

This is his drawing room. The bedroom's beyond, through there.

INSPECTOR: Thank you very much, ma'am. And now if you'd kindly leave us…

MRS SELLAND: *(retreating)* As you wish. You'll find me downstairs.

(DOOR CLOSES)

UTTERSON: Well, at least the fellow has good taste…

INSPECTOR: Very nice.

(CUPBOARD OPENS)

UTTERSON: … and he knows something about wine.

(CUPBOARD CLOSES)

INSPECTOR: He left in something of a hurry. Look at those drawers half open. And the fireplace. He's been burning papers. Ah ha! A cheque book, and only partly consumed. Perhaps we'll catch him through the bank – the fellow will need to draw cash out some time,

UTTERSON: *(calls)* Over here, Inspector. Behind the doors

INSPECTOR: That clinches it. The other half of the walking stick, or I'm a Dutchman. Now I have him!

(FADE OUT. OLDFASHIONED DOORBELL RINGS FROM WITHIN HOUSE. PAUSE. DOOR OPENS)

UTTERSON: Good afternoon Mrs Poole. Is Dr Jekyll at home?

MRS POOLE: I believe he's in the laboratory, sir. If you'll follow me...

(DOOR CLOSES. FOOTSTEPS ON STONE)

UTTERSON: How Is he?

MRS POOLE: Not well, sir. Not at all well. I must say I'm rather worried about him. He spends so much time out there. Through here, Mr Utterson, sir.

UTTERSON: I don't believe I've ever been in the laboratory.

(DOOR OPENS)

MRS POOLE: This is the main part, sir. Not much used now, as you can see. All that dusty glassware it needs a good tidying up. Dr Jekyll's through here, sir, in his cabinet.

(RAP ON DOOR. DOOR OPENS)

Mr Utterson to see you, sir.

JEKYLL: (*remote, calling*) Show him in, show him in.

(DOOR CLOSES)

Ah, Utterson my old friend. Forgive me if I don't rise to receive you. I'm not feeling very well at present. I find I can do no more than sit by this fire. Pray be seated.

UTTERSON: Do not disturb yourself, Jekyll. And now you've heard the news?

JEKYLL: The newsboys were calling it out in the square.

UTTERSON: One word. Carew was my client – but so are you. And I want to know where I stand. Now you haven't been mad enough to conceal this fellow Hyde?

JEKYLL: Utterson, I swear to high heaven I'll never set eyes on him again. I give you my word. I'm done with him. It's all over. And in any case, he doesn't need my help. You don't know him as I do. He's disappeared. Mark my words, no more will be heard of him.

UTTERSONS For your sake I hope you're right though not for his. If it came to a trial, your name might well be involved.

JEKYLL: Oh, I'm quite sure of what I say. I have reasons I can't share with anyone. But there's one thing you can advise me about. I've … I've received a letter. And I don't know whether I ought to show it to the police. I'd like to leave it in your hands, Utterson. You would judge wisely, I'm sure. I trust you implicitly.

UTTERSON: I suppose you fear it might lead to his detection?

JEKYLL: No. I don't care what becomes of Hyde. I'm quite done with him. I was thinking of my own character, which this hateful business has rather exposed.

UTTERSON: Well, let me see this letter.

JEKYLL: Here. I have it here.

(RUSTLE OF PAPER)

UTTERSON: *(reads)* "My dear Jekyll. I write to you as my benefactor, to whom I am so greatly indebted. I fear that if I were to remain here in London, I would repay your past kindness most unworthily. Please have no fears about my safety. I have means of escape which are quite infallible. Edward Hyde." Hm'm. Shall I keep this and sleep on it?

JEKYLL: Please judge for me entirely. I've quite lost confidence In myself.

UTTERSON: Well, I'll think about it. And now, just one question. It *was* Hyde, wasn't it, who dictated the terms in your Will … the ones concerning your disappearance? You don't answer. Well, that's answer enough. I know it. He meant to murder you. You've had a lucky escape.

(FADE OUT. FADE IN CLOCK CHIMING SIX. THE FOLLOWING STARTS OVER CHIMES)

UTTERSON: Sit yourself down, Grant, and take a glass of wine before you set off for home.

GRANT: That's very kind of you, Mr Utterson, sir.

(POURING. CLINK OF GLASS)

UTTERSON: There. That'll keep the fog out of your bones. (*Pause*) You know, Grant, I keep fewer secrets from you than from any man alive.

GRANT: You know how greatly I value your trust, sir.

UTTERSON: This business about Sir Danvers – it's very sad.

GRANT: Yes indeed. That man Hyde – quite mad, of course.

UTTERSON: Well, I'd like your views on that. I have a document here in his own handwriting. Now, this is entirely between ourselves, Grant, because I scarcely know what to do about it. But here it is – a murderer's autograph.

(PAPER RUSTLES)

GRANT: (*pause*) No, sir, not mad. But the writing is very odd.

(KNOCK ON DOOR)

UTTERSON: Enter.

(DOOR OPENS)

LARKIN: A note has just arrived for you, sir. By hand.

UTTERSON: Thank'ee.

(DOOR CLOSES. ENVELOPE SLITS, PAPER RUSTLES)

GRANT: Is that from Dr Jekyll, sir?

UTTERSON: It is.

GRANT: I thought I knew the writing. Anything private, Mr Utterson?

UTTERSON: Only an invitation to dinner. Why? Do you want to see it?

GRANT: Just for a moment, sir. I thank you. Ah, just as I thought. May I ask you to step over here, Mr Utterson, sir? Now, just compare these two documents. See – there? And there…

UTTERSON: Good heavens.

GRANT: That word – and that …

UTTERSON: There's no doubt about it.

GRANT: Not very much, sir. I'd wager anything you care to name that these two papers were written by the same person…

UTTERSON:	… and that person is Dr Jekyll. But *why* would my old friend forge a letter for a murderer? Answer me that!

(FADE IN INTERIOR. JEKYLL, UTTERSON AND LANYON LAUGHING UPROARIOUSLY)

LANYON:	*(still laughing)* And now, my dear Jekyll, I really must be on my way.
JEKYLL:	A nlghtcap, Lanyon. One more glass.
LANYON:	No, no, Jekyll. Really not. I've had more than my fair share.
JEKYLL:	Well, *you* won't refuse another, Utterson.
UTTERSON:	You've twisted my arm. A very small whisky.

(GLASS POURING)

JEKYLL:	There. Now hasn't this been quite Iike old times?
LANYON:	Better better than they ever were. What an evening, Jekyll.
UTTERSON:	It does my heart good to see you so restored, my dear fellow so like your old self.
JEKYLL:	I've never felt better.

LANYON: Nor looked better – and I speak as your medical practitioner. And we all three know the reason, don't we? It's two months since any of us heard or saw anything of that monster, Hyde.

UTTERSON: There's a mystery, if you Ilke. How can a man vanish utterly into thin air Iike that? He never returned to that house in Soho, you know. He's simply ceased to exist.

JEKYLL: What do we care *where* he's gone? Thank heaven he's disappeared – just as I said he would. Let's put him out of our minds.

(EDGE OUT. FADE IN OLD-FASHIONED FRONT DOORBELL RINGING FROM INSIDE HOUSE, FRONT DOOR OPENS)

MRS POOLE: Ah, Mr Utterson, sir. I'm sorry, but Dr Jekyll's unwell today. He's given strict orders not to be disturbed on any account.

UTTERSON: I'm sorry to hear that, Mrs Poole. Will you tell him I called?

(CROSSFADE)

MRS POOLE: My apologies, Mr Utterson. Dr Jekyll's still confined to his room. He's seeing no-one, no-one at all. I'm very sorry, sir.

UTTERSON: That's bad news, Mrs Poole. Please wish him well for me.

(CROSSFADE)

MRS POOLE:	No, sir. Dr Jekyll says he can't receive you, I*m afraid. I've scarcely set eyes on him for the past week. He has all his meals on a tray, and he even sleeps in the laboratory sometimes. He's very out of spirits, sir. Very low.

(FADE OUT. FADE IN)

UTTERSON:	My dear Lanyon you at least don't refuse to see me, even though you are so ill. What on earth has befallen you? You look so unlike yourself.
LANYON:	(*weak*) My dear Utterson. I fear this is the end for me. I don't think I have very much time left.
UTTERSON:	Nonsense!
LANYON:	No – you mark my words. I'm not long for this world.
UTTERSON:	Why, man? What has happened?
LANYON:	A shock I shall never recover from. It has done for me.
UTTERSON:	Jekyll's ill too, you know. Have you seen him?
LANYON:	I wish to see or hear no more of Dr Jekyll. I'm quite done with that person. I beg you to spare me any talk of someone I regard as dead.

UTTERSON: What's all this? Come, come, man. We three are very old friends, Lanyon. We shan't live to make others. Can't I do anything?

LANYON: There's nothing to be done. Ask him for yourself.

UTTERSON: But he won't see me.

LANYON: I'm not surprised. Some day, Utterson, after I'm dead, you may come to know the rights and wrongs of this. I can't tell you.

(FADE OUT. FADE IN STEEL NIB SCRATCHING ON PAPER. HOLD UNDER FOLLOWING BRIEFLY, THEN OUT)

UTTERSON: (*reading*) My dear Jekyll. I write in some bewilderment and no little distress of mind. Every day for the past week I have called to see you, and on each occasion I've been denied your presence. Surely, my dear friend, we have known each other long enough for me to be admitted to comfort you in your illness? I am no less distressed to learn of your break with our tried and trusty friend, Lanyon. He will say nothing, but if you could only see the state he's in, you would do all in your power to mend the breach between you. For I greatly fear that he has not very much time left. Believe me your devoted friend, Gabriel Utterson.

(CROSSFADE)

JEKYLL:	My dear good Utterson. I am as distressed as you by the rift with our old friend, Lanyon, but I share his view that we must never meet. I mean from henceforth to lead a life of extreme seclusion. You must not be surprised, nor must you doubt my friendship, if my door is often shut to you. I have brought on myself a punishment and a danger I cannot name. The one thing you can do, Utterson, is to respect my silence. Ever your true friend, Henry Jekyll.

(CROSSFADE)

UTTERSON:	My dear Jekyll. Three weeks have gone by since your letter was delivered to me, and in all that time I have not set eyes on you. Now I write with a heavy heart to tell you that Lanyon, our old friend is dead. Up to the last he refused to speak of the cause of the quarrel between you – but I truly believe it was this that brought him to the grave. As you have not stirred from your house these three months, I presume you will not be attending the interment, which has been arranged for Friday next at eleven in the morning. Your friend, Gabriel Utterson.

(INTERIOR. KNOCK ON DOOR)

UTTERSON:	Enter.
GRANT:	Dr Lanyon's box, sir, as you requested.
UTTERSON:	Ah yes, thank'ee, Grant. Set it down over there, will you, and open it for me. I seem to recall

a recent package to be preserved against his death.

(CREAK OF METAL LID)

GRANT: Quite correct, Mr Utterson, sir. There *is* an envelope here. "Private – for the hands of G.J. Utterson alone."

UTTERSON: Show me. Ah yes – rather mysterious. Well, let me see…

(ENVELOPE SLIT)

Good grief – quite a Chinese puzzle. Another sealed envelope within. "Not to be opened till the death or disappearance of Dr Henry Jekyll."

GRANT: That form of words, sir, seems very strange. Almost the same terms as Dr Jekyll's Will.

UTTERSON: Very, very strange. When I thought that monster Hyde was blackmailing our client, I could make some sense of it. But now? In Dr Lanyon's hand? What can it all mean? I'm very tempted… But no! We'll keep our professional faith. Open the safe, Grant, and deposit the envelope inside. Unless Dr Jekyll does indeed die or disappear, we'll not unseal it.

(FADE OUT. FADE IN VICTORIAN STREET SOUNDS – HORSES, CABS)

ENFIELD: Remember the last time we stopped outside this door, Utterson?

UTTERSON: I do indeed, my dear Enfield.

ENFIELD: Well, that story's at an end, at least. We shall see nothing more of Mr Edward Hyde.

UTTERSON: I devoutly hope not.

ENFIELD: By the way, what an ass you must have thought me, not to know that this was a back way to Dr Jekyll's.

UTTERSON: So you found it out, did you? Might we step into the court and take a look at the windows? To tell the truth, I'm uneasy about poor Jekyll. Through here... And there he is, by George! *(calls)* Hullo there, Jekyll! I trust you're better?

JEKYLL: *(calls)* Utterson! No, I'm very low, very low. But it won't last long, thank heaven.

UTTERSON: *(calls)* You stay indoors too much. You should he out, whipping up the circulation Iike Enfield and me (my cousin, Mr Enfield – Dr Jekyll). Come now get your hat and take a quick turn with us.

JEKYLL: *(calls)* I should like to very much. But no – no. It's quite impossible. Impossible... (*the words choke in his mouth. A drawn–out half–strangulated cry*)

UTTERSON: *(calls)* Jekyll! Jekyll! *(to Enfield)* Heaven help us! What do you make of that?

(FADE OUT. FADE IN INTERIOR. DISCREET RAP ON DOOR. DOOR OPENS)

LARKIN: Excuse me, Mr Utterson.

UTTERSON: Yes, Larkin, what is it?

LARKIN: Mrs Poole has called to see you, sir.

UTTERSON: Mrs Poole? Who's Mrs Poole?

LARKIN: I believe she's Dr Jekyll's housekeeper, sir.

UTTERSON: Oh, Mrs *Poole*. Good heavens. Show her in. Quickly.

LARKIN: Sir.

UTTERSON: *(to himself)* What on earth can have happened?

MRS POOLE: *(advancing)* Oh, Mr Utterson…

(DOOR CLOSES)

UTTERSON: Bless me, Mrs Poole, what brings you here? Is the doctor ill?

MRS POOLE: Mr Utterson, something's wrong. The doctor's shut himself up again in that cabinet in the laboratory. And I'm afraid, sir…

UTTERSON: What of? What do you fear, Mrs Poole?

MRS POOLE; I think there's been foul play.

UTTERSON: Foul play? What foul play? What do you mean?

MRS POOLE: I daren't say, sir. But Mr Utterson, come along with me and see for yourself. Will you come, Mr Utterson? Please come, I beg you.

(FADE IN INTERIOR. RAP ON DOOR)

MRS POOLE: *(calls)* Dr Jekyll, sir. It's Mrs Poole. There's Mr Utterson asking to see you.

HYDE: *(muffled, calls)* Tell him I can see noone.

MRS POOLE: *(calls)* Thank you, sir. *(whispers)* Now come with me, Mr Utterson. Mind... watch that crate ... that's right ...

(DOOR CLOSES)

Sir, I ask you. Was that my master's voice?

UTTERSON: It seems much changed ...

MRS POOLE: Changed? Indeed it is. Have I been twenty years in Dr Jekyll's house to be deceived about his voice? No, sir – the master's dead. He was killed eight days ago, when we heard him cry out in the name of the Almighty. And *who's* in that room instead of him, and *why* he stays there – well, that reeks to high heaven.

UTTERSON: This is all very strange, Mrs Poole. Suppose it's as you think. Suppose Dr Jekyll has been – well, murdered. What could possibly induce the murderer to stay? It doesn't make sense.

MRS POOLE: Mr Utterson, you're a hard man to satisfy – but I'll try. All this last week, whatever it is that lives in that room has been calling night and day for some sort of medicine. It was sometimes the master's way to write his orders on a sheet of paper and throw it on the stairs. Well, we've had nothing this week but papers and a closed door, and the very meals left there to be smuggled in when nobody was looking. Every day I've been sent flying to all the pharmacies in town. Every time I brought the stuff, there'd be another paper telling me to return it because it wasn't pure, and another order to a different firm. This drug is wanted bitter bad, sir, whatever it's for.

UTTERSON: Do you have any of those papers?

MRS POOLE: I must have... Here, sir. Here's one.

UTTERSON: *(reads)* "Dr Jekyll presents his compliments to Messrs Maw. He assures them that their last sample is impure and quite useless for his present purpose. Three years ago he purchased a large quantity from them, and now begs them to search most carefully and, should any of the same quality be left, to forward it to him at once. Expense is no consideration. The importance of this to Dr Jekyll can hardly be exaggerated." Well, that seems composed enough.

MRS POOLE: There's more writing, sir. Turn over the paper.

(RUSTLE OF PAPER)

UTTERSON: Good heavens. "For God's sake find me some of the old." This is a strange note. *(sharply)* How do you come to have it open?

MRS POOLE: The man at Maw's was very angry, sir, and he threw it back at me.

UTTERSON: But this is unquestionably the doctor's hand, isn't it?

MRS POOLE: It *looks* like it. But what does that matter? I've seen him.

UTTERSON: Seen him? Seen whom?

MRS POOLE: I came into the laboratory suddenly from the garden. It seems he'd slipped out of his room at the far end to look for this drug, or whatever it is, and he was digging among the crates. He looked up when I came in. He gave a kind of cry...

HYDE: *(drawn-out shriek)* No-oo...

MRS POOLE; …and whipped back into the room. I saw him for only a second, but the hair stood up on my head. Sir, if that was my master, why did he have a mask on his face? Yes, he was masked. Why did he cry out and run from me? I've served him long enough…

UTTERSON: I think I begin to see daylight. Mrs Poole, your master has one of those maladies that deform and torture the sufferer. That would explain the alteration In his voice, the mask and the avoidance of his friends – and his eagerness to find this drug, through which the poor soul hopes to cure himself. Heaven grant that he may! There's my explanation, Mrs Poole. It's appalling enough, in all conscience, but it hangs together, and it's plain and natural.

MRS POOLE: Mr Utterson, that thing was not my master. Dr Jekyll is tall and well-built. That thing was more like a monkey than a man. No, sir, heaven alone knows what it was, but it was never Dr Jekyll. It's my certain belief that murder has been done.

UTTERSON: If you say that, Mrs Poole, I shall have to make certain. I'll have to break down that door.

MRS POOLE: Ah, Mr Utterson that's talking! There's an axe in the laboratory.

UTTERSON: Mrs Poole, you and I are about to put ourselves in the way of some danger, so we should be frank with each other. We both think more than we've said. Let's be honest. This masked figure you saw did you recognise it?

MRS POOLE: Well, sir, it went so quick, I could hardly swear to that. But if you mean was it Mr Hyde – why, yes, I think it was.

UTTERSON: That's good enough for me. Let's get moving.

MRS POOLE: This way, sir. *(whispers)* Be careful, now – especially inside the laboratory...

(CAREFUL OPENING OF DOOR)

... you will mind those crates and bottles, sir, won't you?

UTTERSON: I'm all right. Look! No, over there. That shadow crossing and recrossing the glass partition.

MRS POOLE: So it will walk all day, sir – aye, and the better part of the night. Only when a new sample comes from the chemist is there a bit of a break. But go a bit closer, sir, and listen.

(LIGHT FOOTSTEPS TO AND FRO)

Tell me, Mr Utterson, is that the doctor's step?

UTTERSON: Where's the axe you spoke of?

MRS POOLE: Here, sir. Under this packing straw.

UTTERSON: Right. (*calls*) Jekyll, I demand to see you. (*pause*) I give you fair warnIng. Our suspicions are aroused. I must and shall see you – with your consent, or by force.

HYDE: (*muffled; calls*) Utterson! For heaven's sake have mercy.

UTTERSON: That's not Jekyll's voice – it's Hyde's. Down with the door!

(AXE CRASHES AGAINST TIMBER DOOR. A HOWL, LIKE AN ANIMAL IN AGONY MINGLES WITH THE CRASHING AND THE SPLINTERING OF WOOD. CRASH OF FALLING DOOR)

UTTERSON: Dear heaven! On the floor there by the fire! Edward Hyde, as I live and breathe.

MRS POOLE: I knew it, sir. I knew it. He's done away with Dr Jekyll.

UTTERSON: One minute, Mrs Poole. (*pause*) We've come too late – to save *or* to punish. Hyde's taken his own life. Now it only remains for us to find the body of your master.

MRS POOLE: Look, sir. How strange. He's wearing the master's clothes.

UTTERSON: Where can he have hidden poor Jekyll? Do you think he buried the body?

MRS POOLE: But he never left this room or the laboratory. I'll vouch for that, sir, with my life.

UTTERSON: Then where is Dr Jekyll? This is beyond me, Mrs Poole.

MRS POOLE: *(remote – calls)* Over here, Mr Utterson.

UTTERSON: What is it?

MRS POOLE: This envelope, sir, on the table. It's addressed to you.

UTTERSON: So it is, by George.

(ENVELOPE SLITS)

A Will – and not the one drawn by me. Good grief, the man's made me his beneficiary … "In the event of my death or disappearance … " Those words again.

MRS POOLE: I pray my master's not dead, sir – though I greatly fear he is. He's most certainly disappeared.

UTTERSON: Quite right, Mrs Poole. He seems in some strange way to have foreseen all this. My head's spinning, Mrs Poole I admit it. Here lies Edward Hyde. He's been living in this room all these days. He has no cause to like me – no, he must have raged to see himself displaced in the Will. And yet he hasn't destroyed the document. Why not? *(pause)* Look this other paper. A note in Dr Jekyll's hand dated today. He can't have been disposed of so quickly. He must still be alive. He must have fled.

MRS POOLE: Why don't you read it, sir?

UTTERSON: I fear what I shall see. Pray heaven, I've no cause. (*reads*)

(FADE UP JEKYLL IN PARALLEL: FADE OUT UTTERSON)

My dear Utterson. When you read this I shall have disappeared…

JEKYLL: My dear Utterson. When you read this I shall have disappeared – how exactly I'm not farsighted enough to foresee. Go then, and first read the document which Lanyon warned me he'd he placing in your hands. If you care to hear more, then turn to the enclosed confession of … Your unworthy and unhappy friend, Henry Jekyll.

(FADE IN UTTERSON IN PARALLEL. FADE OUT JEKYLL)

UTTERSON: … your unworthy and unhappy friend, Henry Jekyll." I must go home and read these documents in peace. It's now ten. I shall be back before midnight, Mrs Poole, and we'll send for the police then. Meanwhile, lock the outer laboratory door. And say nothing of all this, Mrs Poole, to anyone.

(FADE OUT. FADE IN. INTERIOR)

LARKIN: Will that be all sir?

UTTERSON: Thank you, Larkin. (*pause*) Oh, Larkin – I shall be going out again tonight just before midnight. Don't wait up. I'll see myself out, and back in again.

LARKIN: Very good, Mr Utterson. Are you sure there's nothing more I can get you?

UTTERSON: Thank you, no. This brandy and soda will serve admirably to see me through. I have these two lengthy documents to read in the next hour or so. Goodnight, Larkin.

LARKIN: Goodnight, sir.

(DOOR CLOSES)

UTTERSON: (*close*) I may as well start with Lanyon's paper, as Jekyll suggested. "Not to be opened till the death or disappearance of Dr Henry Jekyll." Well, the time has come …

(SLITTING OF ENVELOPE; PAPER RUSTLES)

Now, my dear Lanyon, what is it you have to tell me?

(CROSSFADE)

LANYON: On the 9th day of January, now four days ago, I received a registered envelope addressed in the hand of my colleague and old friend, Henry Jekyll. I was a good deal surprised by this, for I had dined with the man only the night before. The contents increased my wonder.

(FADE IN)

JEKYLL: The 10th of December. Dear Lanyon. You are one of my oldest friends, and although we may have differed at times on scientific questions, I cannot recall any break in our affection. There never was a time when I would not have sacrificed anything to preserve your life, your honour or your reason. Lanyon, *my* life, *my* honour and *my* reason are at your mercy. I want you to postpone all other engagements for tonight, and with this letter as reference, to drive straight to my house. Mrs Poole, my housekeeper, has her orders. You will find her waiting your arrival with a locksmith. The door of my room in the laboratory is to be forced. You are to go in alone, to open the glassfronted chest of drawers – breaking the lock, if necessary – and to take out, with all its contents, the fourth drawer from the top. This drawer contains some powders, a glass tube and a paper book. Take the drawer back with you to your house exactly as it stands. That is the first part of what I ask. Now for the second. At midnight please be alone in your consulting room, and admit with your own hand into the house a man who will present himself in my name, and give him the drawer.

Five minutes afterwards you will have understood why these arrangements are of the utmost importance, and that the neglect of any could cause my death or the loss of my reason. Confident as I am that you will not trifle with my appeal, my heart sinks at the bare thought of such a possibility. Do what I ask, my dear Lanyon and serve… Your friend, Henry Jekyll.

(FADE OUT. FULL UP)

LANYON: (*as narrator*) On reading this letter I was sure my colleague was insane, but till this was proved I felt bound to do as he asked. Accordingly, I drove to Jekyll's house. The housekeeper was awaiting my arrival, and she had sent for a locksmith and carpenter. They managed with some difficulty to remove the lock from the door of the inner room. I found the drawer with all its contents, as Jekyll had described, and returned home.

Midnight had scarce rung out over London before the knocker sounded very gently at the front door. I found a small man crouching against the pillar of the portico.

"Are you from Dr Jekyll?" I said.

He indicated he was, and I bade him enter. In the light of my consulting room I saw him clearly, and was struck by the sheer depravity of his expression. The man's clothes were not the least unusual thing about him they were of excellent quality, but enormously too large for him.

(FADE IN)

HYDE: Have you got it? The drawer – have you got it?

LANYON: A moment's patience, sir. It's there, on the table.

HYDE: Thank heaven! Thank heaven!

LANYON: Compose yourself, sir.

HYDE: All there – it's all there. (*to Lanyon*) Have you a
                 graduated glass?

LANYON: Of course. Here, sir.
                 (*as narrator*) He measured out a few minims of
                 a red tincture, and added one of the powders.
                 The mixture, which was at first of a reddish
                 hue, began as the crystals melted to brighten, to
                 effervesce and to throw off a vapour. Suddenly the
                 compound became still, changed to a dark purple
                 which faded slowly to a watery green. My visitor
                 turned towards me...

                 (FADE IN)

HYDE: And now to settle what remains. Will you
                 allow me to take this glass and go? Or are you
                 determined to discover what lies at the bottom
                 of these events? Think before you answer. If
                 you choose to learn the truth, a new province of
                 knowledge and new avenues to fame and power
                 will be laid open to you – here in this room, and
                 your eyes will be blasted by a sight to stagger the
                 unbelief of Satan.

LANYON: Sir, you speak enigmas. But I've gone too far in the way of inexplicable events to pause before I see the end.

HYDE: It is well. Lanyon, what follows is under the seal of our profession. But now, you who have so long been bound to the most material views – behold!

LANYON: (*as narrator*) He put the glass to his lips and drank at one gulp. A cry followed; he reeled, staggered, clutched at the table. And as I looked, there came a change. He seemed to swell; his features seemed to melt and alter ... And the next moment, I'd sprung to my feet and leaped back against the wall, my arm raised to shield me from what I was seeing, my mind submerged in terror. I cried out: "Oh, heaven; oh, heaven", again and again. For there, before my eyes, pale and shaken and half-fainting, groping before him like a man restored from death – there stood ... Henry Jekyll.

(BURST OF MUSIC. MUSIC DOWN – AND OUT UNDER FOLLOWING)

LANYON: My dear Utterson, when you read these words I shall be beyond all terror, all pain. Yet what Henry Jekyll told me in the next hour, I cannot bring myself to set on paper. My life is shaken to its roots. I cannot, even in memory, dwell on the moral turpitude that man unveiled to me – even though tears or penitence ran down his face. I will say but one thing, Utterson – and that, if you can bring your mind to credit it, will be more than enough. The creature who crept into my house that night was, on Jekyll's own confession, the man hunted for in every corner of the land as the murderer of Carew the man known as Edward Hyde. May the Almighty help me through my last days. Your friend, Hastie Lanyon.

(FADE OUT, FADE UP FOLLOWING IN PARALLEL)

UTTERSON: May the Almighty help me through my last days. Your friend. Hastie Lanyon.

(RUSTLE OF PAPER)

(*close*) Dear heaven! It defies belief. He must have been mistaken in some way. He has been deceived. There's still Jekyll's own account to read. That will put matters straight. He will surely provide a rational explanation of all this.

(RUSTLE OF PAPER)

Now, let me see...

(FADE UP)

JEKYLL: I was born to a large fortune, and as a young man indulged in all the pleasures that my wealth permitted. But I also cherished the respect of my fellowmen, and so I concealed my pleasures. Thus, when I reached years of discretion, I was already committed to a profound duplicity of life. Please understand that I was in no sense a hypocrite. Both sides of me were in dead earnest. I was as much myself when I laid aside restraint and plunged in shame, as when I laboured at the furtherance of knowledge or the relief of suffering. Thus with every day I drew steadily nearer to the truth which has doomed me – that man is not truly one, but truly two. I saw that of the two natures that contended in me, I could not rightly be said to be either, because I was truly both.

From an early date, then, I learned to dwell with pleasure on the thought of the separation of these elements. If each, I told myself, could but he housed In separate identities, life would be relieved of all that was unbearable. The unjust might go his way, delivered from the aspirations and remorse of his more upright twin; and the just could walk steadfastly on his upward path, no longer exposed to disgrace at the hands of this extraneous evil.

I was so far in my reflections, when a light began to shine upon the subject from the laboratory table. I hesitated long before I put my theories to the test. I knew well that I risked death. But the temptation of a discovery so singular and profound at last overcame my fears. I had long since prepared my tincture. I now purchased from a firm of wholesale chemists a large quantity of a particular chemical which I knew, from my experiments, to be the last ingredient required. And late one accursed night I compounded the elements and drank off the potion.

The most racking pang succeeded a grinding in the bones, deadly nausea. Then these agonies began to subside, and I came to myself as if out of a great sickness. There was something strange in my sensations, something indescribably sweet. I felt younger, lighter. Within, I was conscious of a heady recklessness – a current of disordered sensual images running like a mill-race In my fancy. I knew myself to be tenfold more wicked – and the thought braced and delighted me like wine.

There was no mirror in my room, so I stole through the corridors, a stranger in my own home – and coming to my room, I saw for the first time, the appearance of Edward Hyde – the embodiment of pure evil.

I lingered but a moment at the mirror. The second and conclusive experiment had yet to be attempted. It yet remained to be seen if I had lost my identity beyond redemption.

Hurrying back to my cabinet, I once more prepared and drank the cup, once more suffered the pangs of dissolution – and came to myself once more with the character, the stature and the face of Henry Jekyll.

My new power tempted me. I had but to drink the cup to doff at once the body of the noted professor, and to assume, like a thick cloak, that of Edward Hyde. I made my preparations with the utmost care.

I took and furnished that house in Soho. I announced to my servants that a Mr Hyde (whom I described) was to have full liberty about my house in the square. And I drew up that Will, to which you so much objected, so that if anything befell me in the person or Dr Jekyll, I could enter on that of Edward Hyde without pecuniary loss.

Thus fortified, I began to profit by the strange immunity of my position. The pleasures which I made haste to seek in my disguise were undignified – but in the hands of Edward Hyde they soon began to turn towards the monstrous. Henry Jekyll stood at times aghast before the acts of Edward Hyde. But finally it was Hyde alone who was guilty. When woke his good qualities were unimpaired. He'd even make try, where possible, to undo the evil done by Hyde. And thus his conscience slumbered.

Some two months before the murder of Sir Danvers, I had been out for one of my adventures, had returned at a late hour, resumed my character, and gone to bed. I awoke the next day with somewhat odd sensations. Suddenly I caught sight of my hand. Now the hand of Henry Jekyll was large and firm. But the hand which I now saw lying half-shut on the bedclothes was lean, corded, hairy. It was the hand of Edward Hyde.

At the sight my blood was changed to ice. I had gone to bed Henry Jekyll; I had awakened Edward Hyde. I slipped back to the laboratory, and ten minutes later Dr Jekyll was sitting down to breakfast.

Slowly, I was losing hold of my original and better self, and becoming incorporated with my second and worse. Between the two I now felt I had to choose, and I preferred the older and discontented doctor, surrounded by friends. So I bade a resolute farewell to the liberty, the comparative youth, the leaping pulses and secret pleasures that I had enjoyed in the disguise of Hyde.

For two months I was true to my determination. But time began to obliterate my alarm. I began to be tortured with longings, as of Hyde struggling after freedom. And at last, in an hour of moral weakness, I once again compounded and swallowed the transforming draught.

My devil had been long caged; he came out roarlng. That was the night I struck down that wretched old man, Sir Danvers Carew. But the deed done, I saw my life forfeit. I fled from the scene, my lust of evil gratified. I ran to the house in Soho and destroyed my papers. Then I ran out through the lamplit streets back to my laboratory.

The pangs of transformation had not done tearing him before, Henry Jekyll, streaming tears of gratitude and remorse, had fallen on his knees. The problem of my conduct was solved. Hyde was thenceforth impossible.

Shortly afterwards I was stepping across the court after breakfast, when I was seized with those indescribable sensations that heralded the change. I scarcely had time to gain the shelter of my cabinet before I was once again raging and freezing with the passions of Hyde. It took a double dose to recall me to myself. Alas, six hours after, as I sat looking sadly in the fire, the pangs returned, and the drug had to be readministered.

From that day forth only under the immediate stimulation of the drug was I able to wear the countenance of Jekyll. If I slept, or even dozed for a moment in my chair, it was always as Hyde that I awakened. Under the strain I became a creature eaten up by fever. No one has ever suffered such torment.

My punishment might have gone on for years, but for the last calamity which has now fallen. The chemical began to run low. I sent out for a fresh supply and mixed the draught. I drank it – and it was without effect. You will learn from Mrs Poole how I have had London ransacked. It was in vain, and I am now convinced that my first supply was impure, and that it was that unknown impurity which lent efficacy to the draught.

(CREEP MUSIC UNDER FOLLOWING)

About a week has passed, and I am now finishing this statement under the influence of the last of the old powder. This, then, is the last time, short of a miracle, that Henry Jekyll can think his own thoughts or see his own face in the glass. This is the true hour of my death, and what is to follow concerns another than myself.

Here, then, as I lay down the pen and proceed to seal up my confession, I bring the life of that unhappy Henry Jekyll to an end.

(UP MUSIC. DOWN FOR CLOSING ANNOUNCEMENT)

AFTERWARD

BY EDITH WHARTON
DRAMATISED FOR RADIO
BY NEVILLE TELLER

Running time: 30'

FIRST BROADCAST ACROSS THE
USA ON 18 APRIL 2018
IN A PRODUCTION BY SHOESTRING
RADIO THEATRE, SAN FRANCISCO
DIRECTED BY JONATHAN WIND

CHARACTERS IN
ORDER OF APPEARANCE

MARY   East coast American, about 40. Henry James
                  type woman of the 1900 period. Intelligent,
                  imaginative, sensitive.

NED   East coast American, about 40. Rather insensitive.
                  Surface charm hides somewhat ruthless
                  indifference to others.

ALIDA   East coast American, about 50. Pleasant, good
                  natured.

POLLY   English, aged about 25. A well-trained maid.
                  Polite and willing.

ELWELL   Mid-West American, about 30. Well educated,
                  well-spoken young businessman.

PARVIS   Mid-West American lawyer, about 60.

NEWSMAN   American newspaper journalist, mid-30s. Urgent,
                  newsy.

(MUSIC. DOWN FOR OPENING ANNOUNCEMENT. UP MUSIC. FADE SLOWLY BENEATH FIRST SPEECH)

MARY: (*as narrator*) As the nineteenth century drifted to its close, Ned and I were enduring the soul-deadening ugliness of the Middle West. For fourteen years we lived in Wisconsin because that was where Ned's engineering firm was based, and we had no expectation of ever leaving till he retired. We dreamed, of course…

NED: The exact opposite of this post-colonial bungalow, Mary – that's what I'd go for.

MARY: And what is the exact opposite?

NED: An ancient manor house.

MARY: Oh yes, Ned. In the English countryside.

NED: Obviously. Built in the sixteenth century.

MARY: Set in its own grounds.

NED: And Mary – no central heating, uncertain drains, and no electricity. Oil lamps – that would be the thing.

MARY:	And a ghost!
NED:	Oh, of course. A ghost.
MARY:	(*as narrator*) Dreams. And then, out of the blue, with a suddenness that left me breathless and bewildered, the prodigious windfall of the Blue Star Mine bestowed on us, at a stroke, the life and leisure we had dreamed of.
NED:	It's unbelievable, Mary, but it's true. I just couldn't tell you about it before – it was a gamble, a speculation. I had to get in front of the field to pull it off.
MARY:	Of course I knew something was going on. You haven't been yourself for weeks. I wondered… [*whether you might have found someone…*]
NED:	Well, all that's over and done with. I managed it. I got in ahead and bought the whole stock of the Blue Star Mine while it was still struggling. And now – now I've disposed of it at a prodigious profit. We're rich, Mary. Really rich. I need never do a day's work again in my life. We can live our dream.
MARY:	But how did you know that the mine would become productive again?
NED:	A tip-off, Mary. That's what business is all about. Inside knowledge. I had it on excellent authority. And I acted on it. It's made our fortune. We'll

sell up here as soon as possible, and take ship to Merrie England.

MARY: Why not? I'll write to my cousin Alida at once. She took herself off years ago to what the English call the Home Counties – somewhere called Pangbourne, I think. She'll surely put us up while we find our manor house.

(CROSSFADE TO MUSIC. HOLD A LITTLE. FADE UNDER FOLLOWING)

NED: No, Alida, nothing has caught our fancy so far.

MARY: But we *have* settled on the location.

ALIDA: Well, that's something. And where do you wish to set up home?

MARY: Down in the south west. Not Cornwall – too remote – but Devon perhaps, or better still Dorset.

NED: Yes, Dorset attracted us from the moment we stepped foot in it.

MARY: It has a sort of feeling of remoteness – although, of course, it's plumb in the middle of the south coast.

NED: That's one of the wonders of this incredibly compressed island, you know – this nest of counties. Just a few miles becomes a real distance…

MARY: …and quite a short distance makes an enormous difference. We got that feeling more in Dorset than anywhere else.

ALIDA: Dorset? Good heavens. Why didn't I think of it before? Here you've spent days viewing all sorts of old ruins, while the ideal answer was staring me in the face.

NED: What ideal answer?

MARY: Do you know of somewhere, Alida?

ALIDA: Lyng, in Dorset. It belongs to Hugo's cousins, and you can get it for a song. Hugo tells me they're itching to sell, but they can't find a buyer.

NED: Why?

ALIDA: Well it's so remote. Miles from the nearest station. I don't think it's been connected to the electricity supply. Or to the drains, come to that – you'd have to cope with a cesspit. And you can forget about central heating.

NED: My God – our ideal. I'd never believe I was living in an old house unless I was thoroughly uncomfortable.

MARY: We agreed years ago that what we wanted was an absence of modern conveniences. How old is Lyng?

ALIDA:	I believe it was built during Henry the Eighth's reign – around 1540.
NED:	It's too perfect. Now Alida, there's something you're hiding from us.
MARY:	I know – there's no ghost. Without a ghost, I'm afraid...[*we wouldn't be able to take the place...*]
ALIDA:	But Dorset's full of ghosts.
NED:	Yes, yes, but that won't do. I don't want to have to drive ten miles to see someone else's ghost. I want one on my own premises. Now, is there a ghost at Lyng?
ALIDA:	Of course there is – but you'll never know it. That's the local legend. You don't recognise the Lyng ghost until afterward.
MARY:	Afterward?
ALIDA:	Long, long afterward. At the time you don't know you're encountering a ghost. It's only afterward that you suddenly realize what it was you saw.
NED:	Well, that's a poor sort of ghost. How has it managed to preserve its incognito all these years?
ALIDA:	Don't ask me. But it has. Hugo's cousins say the locals know all about the ghostly visitations at Lyng.

MARY:	You mean that suddenly ... long afterward ... you say to yourself: "That person we saw – that person we spoke to...That was it! That was a ghostly visitation. Now, at last, I understand!"
ALIDA:	I suppose that's the way it goes – a sudden realization. All I know is that the impact of ghostly encounters at Lynge are...well, delayed. It happens – afterward.

(EDGE OUT. FULL UP)

MARY:	(*as narrator*) Three months later we were established at Lynge, and the life we'd yearned for had actually begun. We'd always envisaged a life filled with enjoyable activities. I thought I'd take up painting and gardening; Ned really yearned to write his long-planned book on "The Economic Basis of Culture". Lynge provided us with the ideal background. Lynge – the old grey house hidden under a shoulder of the Dorset downs, not far from ancient Bulbarrow and the River Stour [Note: *rhyme with tower*]. It exuded a sense of having been for centuries a deep, dim reservoir of life. From time to time I seemed to catch an echo of this intense memory of the past. It came to me late one December afternoon as I stood in the library, waiting for the oil lamps to be brought in. I was alone in the house, except for the servants.

(CROSSFADE)

NED: I'm off for my walk, Mary.

MARY: Would you like me to come with you today?

NED: No, no. I prefer to be alone.

MARY: So I've noticed recently. I've actually been quite concerned. You haven't seemed yourself these past weeks. It's as though you're worried about something?

NED: Nonsense! It's only that, out there on the downs, I can think.

MARY: Is it the book, Ned? Isn't it working out as you hoped?

NED: It's coming along very well.

MARY: Well, that's what I thought, judging by the pages you've read to me so far. You have the whole thing planned out, and the synopsis was most impressive. Well, it impressed me, anyway. So what is it that's worrying you so much?

NED: You're quite mistaken, Mary dear. I'm not in the slightest bit worried. But tramping out there on the downs, all alone, I can certainly order my thoughts. So when I sit down to write, it all flows.

MARY: Off you go, then. But don't forget, it gets dark quite early, these December evenings. We don't want you getting lost. Be back by four-thirty – in time for tea.

NED: I hear – and will obey. Goodbye.

(CROSSFADE)

MARY: (*as narrator*) So he pulled on his overcoat and went out, leaving me with an indefinable sense that somehow a secret had taken root between us. Standing alone in the dim, long room, lit intermittently by the flickering of the log fire, I suddenly wondered if the house itself could be the source of undiscovered secrets – or perhaps the very room I was in, with its dusky walls of books, its hooded hearth surrounded by smoke-blurred sculpture.

MARY: (*to herself*) That's it, of course – it's the house itself that's haunted. It's communing with its own past all the time, three hundred and fifty years of it. If only I could get close enough to discover its secret. Is it something to do with Lynge's ghost? Perhaps Ned has discovered something. Perhaps that's what's been affecting him these past few weeks – some terrible secret he's stumbled on, something to do with Lynge's ghost. And of course, the ghost being what it is, he won't have realized until long afterward what he'd seen. Is that it? Is that why he hasn't seemed to be himself?

MARY: (*as narrator*) "Not till long afterward," my cousin Alida had said. Well, supposing Ned had experienced some ghostly visitation when we first came, and only in the past week or so had realized what had happened to him? So I began searching back through the six months since we'd come to Lynge. Was there some occurrence, some happening, that now – looking back, after the event, "afterward" – seemed out of the ordinary? I sent my memory back to the first days of our tenancy, to the happy confusion of unpacking, to discovering odd features of the house...

(CROSSFADE)

MARY: *(calls)* Ned, look what I've found. You'll never believe it.

NED: *(remote, calls)* What won't I believe?

MARY: *(calls)* A secret panel.

NED: *(remote, approaching)* A secret panel? This house is beginning to live up to expectations. Show me.

MARY: Look. I pressed it by chance ... just here. It swung open to reveal – a flight of stairs.

NED: They must lead up to the roof.

MARY: I wonder if it was some way of escape, should the house ever be invaded? Perhaps during the Civil War? What a deal of stories Lynge could tell, if only it could speak. Come on, Ned, *(retreating)* Let's explore.

(FEET ON WOODEN STAIRS)

(*retreating*) Follow me. Come on.

NED: Yes, ma'am. Right behind you. (***pause as feet continue***) Good grief, how much further?

MARY: (*calls*) I've hit daylight. And yes, it *is* the roof.

NED: (*puffed*) Oh, Mary. What a view!

MARY: Isn't it magnificent? Look, the downs stretch right to the horizon. See the river?

NED: And down below. Our fish pond. And the yew hedges.

MARY: See the shadow of the cedar on the lawn? It's magical.

NED: Turn around. Let's see the other way. Ah, the lime avenue, the gates, the two lions either side. Hullo! Who's that on the drive?

MARY: We've a visitor. Someone's calling on us.

NED: (*retreating*) I'll see. You stay here.

MARY: (*calls*) No. Ned! Wait for me!

(FADE OUT. FADE IN)

MARY: Who was it, Ned?

NED: Who do you mean?

MARY: The man we saw coming toward the house.

NED: Oh, I thought it was Peters. I dashed down to say a word about the stable drains, but by the time I reached the front door he'd disappeared.

MARY: Disappeared? He seemed to be walking very slowly when we saw him.

NED: That's what I thought, but he must have got up steam in the interval. What do you say to trying a scramble up Meldon Steep before sunset?

MARY: Oh, yes. We've been thinking about that since we set foot in Lynge. This is just the day for it. Let's get changed at once.

MARY: (*as narrator*) That was all. At the time it seemed perfectly natural for Ned to dash down to tackle the tradesman working on our stables. But now, afterward, it seemed to me that Ned's explanation had been …well, negated, by the look of anxiety on his face.

(DOOR OPENS)

NED: Good grief, Mary, what are you doing standing here all alone in the dark?

MARY: Oh hullo, Ned. I was thinking about the Lyng ghost, if you must know.

457

NED: Good heavens, I wouldn't bother my head about that. According to your cousin, you never know when you see it, anyway. Oh come in, Polly, there's a good girl. A light in the darkness.

POLLY: Where would you like the lamp set this evening, sir?

NED: Over there, I think. That side table by the fire. And the tea?

POLLY: I'll bring it at once, sir. *(retreating)* The tray's all ready.

NED: I could do with my tea. It's freezing out there.

MARY: Have you stopped bothering your head about it, then?

NED: About what?

MARY: The Lyng ghost.

NED: I never started. It seemed to me a waste of time from the beginning.

POLLY: *(remote, approaching)* Here we are, madam. Cook's made some scones [*pronounced SCONS*]. They're hot from the oven. The butter will simply melt into them.

NED: I can't wait.

POLLY: Oh, and I have your newspaper here, sir. And some letters.

NED: Thank you, Polly.

(DOOR CLOSES. FALL INTO EASY CHAIR)

Ah! That's better. Tea by the fire – what could be more English?

MARY: I'll pour.

(CROCKERY, POURING. ENVELOPE OPENED, PAPER RUSTLES)

NED: (*eating, drinking*) The morning mail and the London paper at four o'clock in the afternoon. That's one inconvenience I didn't count on. (*pause*) Talking of ghosts, this apparition of ours – any idea how long it is before people become aware they've seen it?

MARY: (*eating, drinking*) Not a notion. Have you?

NED: Lord, no. I just wondered if you'd heard any local tales about it. Oh look, here's a letter for you.

MARY: Thank you.

(TEARING ENVELOPE. PAPER)

Oh, my goodness! Ned! Look at this. What does it mean?

NED: What it is? What have you there?

MARY: It's from my aunt. A newspaper cutting. From the Waukusha Sentinel. Look It says a man named Elwell has filed a suit against you. That there was something wrong about the Blue Star Mine. You read it.

NED: I don't have to. And I thought you'd received bad news.

MARY: You knew about this, then? It's all right?

NED: Certainly I knew all about it. And yes, Mary, it's all right.

MARY: But I don't understand. What does this man Elwell accuse you of?

NED: It's just a squabble over the Blue Star – rather technical and complicated. I thought that kind of thing bored you.

MARY: Well, yes, it does.

NED: That's why I never talked about it. It's all ancient history now. Your aunt must have got hold of a back number of the Sentinel. Let's see. Yes, months old.

MARY: You mean it's over? He's lost his case?

NED: The suit's been withdrawn. I've just learned about it in one of my letters. By chance our attorney wrote at the same time as your aunt. I've been expecting this for a long time.

MARY: So everything's all right?

NED: I give you my word, Mary. It was never righter.

(GENTLE SOFT MUSIC. HOLD A LITTLE. DOWN FOR FOLLOWING AND HOLD THROUGHOUT FIRST PARAGRAPH. THEN LOSE)

MARY: (*as narrator*) The next morning I awoke to a day as clear and bright as my mood. After weeks of worry, doubt and uncertainty, I felt carefree, just as in our first days at Lynge. After breakfast I left Ned working at his desk, and went out for my daily round of the gardens. On this particular morning my recovered sense of safety made my progress through the grounds a special delight. Finally I reached the far grass terrace. From here I could see, over the fish-pond and the yew hedges, the long house-front laid out before me. Seen like this, with its smoking chimneys and its open windows, Lynge seemed almost a human presence. I felt a sudden intimacy with it – a fancy that I could trust it to gather up our lives, mine and Ned's, into the harmonious pattern of its own long, long story.

I sensed rather than heard footsteps behind me, and turned, expecting to see the gardener. But the youngish, slightly built man walking toward me was a stranger, his pale face partially obscured by his wide-brimmed hat.

(EDGE OUT. FULL UP OPEN AIR, BIRDS)

MARY:	Good morning. Is there someone you wish to see?
ELWELL:	I came to see Mr Boyne.
MARY:	He's very busy this morning. Do you have an appointment?
ELWELL:	Not exactly an appointment.
MARY:	I'm afraid this is his working time. He's immersed in his writing. He won't be able to see you right now. I'll take a message, if you like. Or perhaps you can come back later?
ELWELL:	I'll come back later. *(retreating)* Good morning.

(FADE IN. INTERIOR)

MARY:	I see Mr Boyne isn't in the library, Polly. He must have gone upstairs. Would you please tell him that luncheon is ready.
POLLY:	If you please, madam, Mr Boyne's not upstairs.
MARY:	Not in his room? Are you sure?
POLLY:	Oh yes, madam. Quite sure.

MARY: Then where is he?

POLLY: He's gone out.

MARY: Then he must have come into the gardens to meet me. We must have missed each other. I'll just go out *[and meet up with him…]*

POLLY: He didn't go into the gardens, madam.

MARY: Then where did he go? And when?

POLLY: He went out of the front door, madam. Up the drive.

MARY: Up the drive? At this hour? Did Mr Boyne leave no message?

POLLY: No, madam. He just went out with the gentleman.

MARY: The gentleman? What gentleman?

POLLY: The gentleman who called, madam.

MARY: Now, Polly, I need to get this straight. When did the gentleman call?

POLLY: It was about one o'clock. He asked to see Mr Boyne.

MARY: What was his name?

POLLY: He didn't say, madam. He handed me a folded piece of paper and asked me to give it to Mr Boyne. I showed him into the library, and a few minutes later they went out together.

MARY: And Mr Boyne left no message?

POLLY: No, madam.

MARY: (*as narrator*) I ate luncheon alone, wondering why Ned had acted as he did, and when Polly brought me coffee in the drawing-room, my wonder had acquired a first tinge of disquiet. The whole episode was so ... unusual. Out of the ordinary. In the end I convinced myself that Ned had cut short a tiresome visit by walking with his caller to the station. Having calmed my unease, I decided to have a discussion with the gardener about plans for the spring and summer, and then I walked down to the village post office. Early twilight was setting in as I started back home, utterly convinced that I would find Ned had beaten me back to the house.

(FADE IN)

POLLY: No, madam. He's not returned.

MARY: He hasn't been back at all? Not since he left with the gentleman?

POLLY: No, madam.

MARY: But who was he – this caller?

POLLY: I couldn't say, madam. He handed me a folded piece of paper.

MARY: Then perhaps it's still here. On Mr Boyne's desk. Is it? Could it be? He seems to have been writing a letter when the gentleman called. "My dear Parvis?" Who's Parvis?

NED: My dear Parvis. I have just received your letter with the news of Elwell's death. While I suppose there is no further risk of trouble, it might be safer…

(PAPERS SHUFFLED)

MARY: (*cuts in*) No, nothing. But you saw him, Polly. What did he look like?

POLLY: Look like? Well, he wasn't very old – not even middle-aged.

MARY: Young? He was young?

POLLY: I'd say so. He seemed a little pale.

MARY: His hat – did you see his hat?

POLLY: Oh yes, madam. It was a bit unusual. It had a very wide brim.

(MUSIC. HOLD A LITTLE. FADE OUT BENEATH FOLLOWING)

MARY: (*as narrator*) The next two weeks were a nightmare. The police set the official search procedure into operation. Soon Ned's name was blazing down from the walls of every town and village, his picture hawked up and down the country like a hunted criminal's. But no word came back about him, no trace of his movements. Since Polly saw him leave the house that afternoon, not a single person came forward claiming to have seen him, or his mysterious caller. The sunny English noon had swallowed him up.

Again and again I scrutinised the letter he had been writing, trying to extract even the smallest evidence of his frame of mind. "My dear Parvis. I have just heard of Elwell's death. While I suppose there is now no further risk of trouble, it might be safer…" But Ned had told me that the suit Elwell had brought against him had been dropped. Why was he was still apprehensive about it?

At the end of the second week, I learned that the Parvis he was writing to was a Waukesha lawyer who had been marginally involved in the Elwell affair, but no idea why Ned might have been seeking his professional help.

Several more weeks passed, life moved on, and the urgency of the original enquiries slackened. I felt the same lowering of velocity myself. Gradually I began to feel that the horror had taken up permanent residence inside me, that I must accept its perpetual presence for the rest of my life.

(CREEP MUSIC UNDER FOLLOWING AND HOLD UNDER)

This deepening apathy held me fast at Lynge. My friends supposed I stayed because I believed Ned would one day return. I had no such expectation. I had slowly come to believe that I would never see Ned again, that he had left me as surely as if Death had claimed him, that I would never know what had become of him.

Oh, but the house knew. The library knew. After all, this was where that last scene had been enacted. This was where Ned had put down his pen, stood up and followed the stranger out of Lynge, out of life.

(UP MUSIC. HOLD A LITTLE. CROSSFADE)

POLLY: Excuse me, madam. There's a gentleman to see you.

MARY: A gentleman? What gentleman? Not... not...the man who called... *[for Mr Boyne.]*

POLLY: Oh, no, madam. Here's his card.

MARY: Parvis? Oh, show him in, Polly. Show him in.

POLLY: *(retreating)* Certainly madam. *(remote)* This way, sir.

PARVIS: *(remote, advancing)* Thank you for seeing me, Mrs Boyne. I'm sorry for not giving you more notice.

MARY: That's quite all right, Mr Parvis. Do sit down.

PARVIS: Thank you. I had to come to England on business, London mostly, but I thought that I'd try to get down to Dorset if at all possible.

MARY: I'm very pleased that you did. Do you have something special you wish to tell me?

PARVIS: Well, to ask you, really. I wondered what you intended to do about Bob Elwell's family.

MARY: I'm sorry, Mr Parvis. I don't understand. I really have no idea what you're referring to.

PARVIS: Did your husband not tell you about the Blue Star Mine?

MARY: He said it had been something of a speculation, and that his gamble had paid off.

PARVIS: Nothing more than that?

MARY: I think he said something about getting in front of the field in order to pull off his coup.

PARVIS: Indeed. The person he beat to the finishing post was young Robert Elwell. Bob Elwell wasn't smart enough – that's all. If he had been, he might have turned round and served Mr Boyne the same way. It's the kind of thing that happens every day in business. I guess it's what scientists call the survival of the fittest.

MARY: So you're saying my husband did something ... dishonourable? Illegal, perhaps?

PARVIS: No, no, I don't say it wasn't straight. And yet, I can hardly say it was. It was business.

MARY: But Mr Elwell's lawyers withdrew the case.

PARVIS: Because technically he hadn't a leg to stand on. And it was when they advised him to withdraw that he got desperate. You see, he'd borrowed most of the money he lost in the Blue Star. He was not only penniless, but he owed vast sums of money that he knew he could never repay. He had nowhere to turn. That's why he shot himself.

MARY: Shot himself? He killed himself because of the Blue Star Mine?

PARVIS: Well, he didn't kill himself, exactly. The wound he inflicted on himself never healed. He dragged on two months before he died.

MARY: But I wrote to you when my husband disappeared. I explained about the letter he was writing to you. Why didn't you tell me all this?

PARVIS: I didn't understand his letter – and nothing I knew could have helped find your husband.

MARY: Then why are you telling me now?

PARVIS: Because the whole affair is being raked up again, back in Waukusha. It's only just come out what a bad state Elwell's affairs were in. His wife tried to keep it all quiet. She went out to work, took in sewing at home. But she had his bedridden mother to look after, and the children, of course. Finally she broke under the strain – heart trouble, I think – and simply had to ask for help. The whole affair came to light again, the papers took it up, and a subscription was started. Everyone liked Bob Elwell. And then people began to ask why he'd fallen on such bad times. Here... I've got the account from the Sentinel. A bit sensational of course. Here you are.

NEWSMAN: *Widow of Boyne's Victim Forced to Appeal for Aid*

MARY: Oh, no!

MARY: *(as narrator)* The story was illustrated by two photographs. One was of Ned, taken just before we left Wisconsin for England. The other was of a youngish man, slightly built, with features somewhat blurred by the shadow of a wide-brimmed hat.

MARY: *(near hysterical)* But this is the man! This is the man who came for my husband. I'd know him anywhere. It's the man, I tell you.

PARVIS: Mrs Boyne, you're not very well. Shall I call someone?

MARY: No, no, no! This is the man who called on my husband. I spoke to him in the garden. I know him.

PARVIS: It can't be, Mrs Boyne. This is a picture of Robert Elwell.

MARY: Then it was Robert Elwell who came for him.

PARVIS: But Mrs Boyne, when your husband disappeared Elwell was already dead. Don't you remember? The letter Mr Boyne was writing to me – he was writing just after he'd heard of Elwell's death. Surely you remember.

MARY: (*as narrator*) Oh yes, I remembered. That was the deep horror of it. Robert Elwell had died. My husband knew it the day before he disappeared. I knew it. And this, this picture I held in my hand, this photograph of Robert Elwell – this was without a shadow of doubt the man who had spoken to me in the garden…

(EDGE OUT. FULL UP OPEN AIR, BIRDS. *REPEATED SEQUENCE*)

MARY: Good morning. Is there someone you wish to see?

ELWELL: I came to see Mr Boyne.

MARY: He's very busy this morning. Do you have an appointment?

ELWELL: Not exactly an appointment.

MARY: I'm afraid this is his working time. He's immersed in his writing. He won't be able to see you right now. I'll take a message, if you like. Or perhaps you can come back later?

ELWELL: I'll come back later. *(retreating)* Good morning.

(FULL UP)

MARY: *(as narrator)* I looked around the library, that long, dim room buried in the middle of the house. A room that kept its secrets within a house filled with mystery. Yes, the library could have borne witness that the photograph in my hand was the picture of the man who'd entered that day to call Ned from his unfinished letter.

(HALF-ECHO FOR FOLLOWING. *REPEATED SEQUENCE*)

ALIDA: Dorset's full of ghosts.

NED: Yes, yes, but that won't do. I don't want to have to drive ten miles to see someone else's ghost. I want one on my own premises. Now, is there a ghost at Lyng?

ALIDA: Of course there is — but you'll never know it. That's the local legend. You don't recognise the Lyng ghost until afterward.

MARY:	Afterward?
ALIDA:	Long, long afterward. At the time you don't know you're encountering a ghost. It's only afterward that you suddenly realize what it was you saw.
NED:	Well, that's a poor sort of ghost. How has it managed to preserve its incognito all these years?
ALIDA:	Don't ask me. But it has. Hugo's cousins say the locals know all about the ghostly visitations at Lyng.
MARY:	You mean that suddenly … long afterward … you say to yourself: "That person we saw – that person we spoke to…That was it! That was a ghostly visitation. Now, at last, I understand!"
ALIDA:	I suppose that's the way it goes – a sudden realization. All I know is that the impact of ghostly encounters at Lynge are…well, delayed. It happens – afterward.

(EDGE OUT. ECHO OFF. FULL UP)

MARY:	All I can say, Mr Parvis, is that this was the man who spoke to me out there in the garden, the day that my husband disappeared.
MARY:	(*very close*) He thinks me mad. See the way he's looking at me. He thinks I've lost my mind. But I haven't.

MARY: Mr Parvis, will you answer me one question please?

PARVIS: Certainly. How can I help you?

MARY: When was it that Robert Elwell tried to kill himself?

PARVIS: *(nervous)* When? How do you mean, exactly?

MARY: The date. The date he shot himself. Please try to remember.

PARVIS: Oh, I really... I haven't... Perhaps I ought to... *[be thinking of leaving]*

MARY: I have a reason, Mr Parvis.

PARVIS: Yes, yes. I'm sure you do, Mrs Boyne. Only I can't really remember. Let me think. He lingered for about two months. Yes, it must be seven or eight weeks before he died.

MARY: But the date. I need the date.

PARVIS: It might be in this cutting. Would you let me see? Thank you.

NEWSMAN: Widow of Boyne's Victim Forced to Appeal for Aid.

Christina Elwell, wife of Robert Elwell who died of self-inflicted wounds four weeks ago, has been reduced to seeking help from the Charity Organization Society. Left widowed, with a bedridden mother-in-law and four children to care for, Mrs Elwell struggled to provide for them in the weeks following her husband's death. The strain proved too much for her, and her health gave way. She could no longer earn sufficient money to feed her family. The Sentinel has ample evidence of the open-hearted nature of its readers. Today we open a subscription to provide Mrs Elwell with the resources to cope with the tragedy that has overtaken her.

Robert Elwell was ruined financially when he trusted the man he believed to be his friend, Edward Boyne, with certain information regarding the future of the Blue Star Mine. Boyne used that knowledge to make a personal fortune, indifferent to the fate of the man he had ruined. Robert Elwell, burdened by debts he could never repay, tried to take his own life. On October the 20th police found him with a gunshot wound close to this heart…

PARVIS: *(breaks in)* Here it is! The very date. October the 20th.

MARY: Sunday October the 20th. Yes, of course.

PARVIS: What do you mean?

MARY: Sunday October the 20th – that was the day he came first.

PARVIS: Came here first? Do you mean to say that he came here twice? You saw him twice?

MARY: Yes, twice. He came first on the 20th of October. I remember the date because it was the day that Ned and I went up Meldon Steep for the first time. We saw him from the roof…

                           (CROSSFADE. HALF-ECHO. *REPEATED SEQUENCE*)

NED: (*puffed*) Oh, Mary. What a view!

MARY: Isn't it magnificent? Look, the downs stretch right to the horizon. See the river?

NED: And down there. Our fish pond. And the yew hedges.

MARY: And the shadow of the cedar on the lawn. Enchanting.

NED: Let's turn round. Ah, the lime avenue, the gates, the two lions either side. Hullo! Who's that on the drive?

MARY: We've a visitor. Someone's calling on us.

NED: (*retreating*) I'll see. You stay here.

MARY: (*calls*) Ned! Wait for me!

                           (FADE OUT. FADE IN)

MARY: Who was it, Ned?

NED: Who do you mean?

MARY: The man we saw coming toward the house.

NED: Oh, I thought it was Peters. I dashed after him to say a word about the stable drains, but he'd disappeared before I could get down.

MARY: Disappeared? He seemed to be walking very slowly when we saw him.

NED: That's what I thought, but he must have got up steam in the interval. What do you say to trying a scramble up Meldon Steep before sunset?

(FADE OUT. ECHO OFF. FULL UP)

MARY: We saw him from the roof. He came down the lime avenue toward the house. He was dressed just as he is in that picture. My husband saw him first. He was frightened and ran down ahead of me.

PARVIS: Did they meet? Did your husband talk to him?

MARY: I don't know. That's the thing. All he told me was that when he got to the front door, the stranger had vanished.

PARVIS: But did Mr Boyne recognize him?

MARY: He pretended that it was some local tradesman we'd employed to renew the drains in the stable.

But oh yes. Ned recognized our visitor all right. Of course he had no idea at the time that it wasn't Robert Elwell in person. I don't think they exchanged words. What Ned told me was that by the time he'd stepped out into the grounds, there was no one there. The visitor had vanished.

PARVIS: Vanished?

MARY: Yes. At the time I couldn't think what had happened. But I believe him. I see it all now. Robert Elwell had tried to come then. He'd just shot himself. He was close to death. But not close enough. He made a brief appearance, but he couldn't reach us. He was pulled back. He had to wait for two months – and then he came back again. This time Ned went with him.

PARVIS: Mrs Boyne...

MARY: *(rising hysteria)* Oh, my God! It's my fault. I told him Ned was in the house. I told him Ned was immersed in his writing. I sent him to this room. I did. Oh God, can I ever forgive myself? It's all my fault.

PARVIS: No, no, Mrs Boyne. Really, you can't blame yourself.

(CREEP MUSIC BENEATH FOLLOWING)

MARY: This house. This house. It's a horrible place. A place full of past secrets. A place that allows

— no not allows, encourages — spirits, ghosts, visitations. But it's cunning — oh, it's cunning. It doesn't let you know what it is you're seeing. If only I'd known at the time. If only...

(KEEP MUSIC BENEATH, BUT HALF-ECHO FOR FOLLOWING. *REPEATED SEQUENCE*)

NED: Now, is there a ghost at Lyng?

ALIDA: Of course there is — but you'll never know it. That's the local legend. You don't recognise the Lyng ghost until afterward.

MARY: Afterward?

ALIDA: Long, long afterward. At the time you don't know you're encountering a ghost. It's only afterward that you suddenly realize what it was you saw.

MARY: (*as narrator*) Afterward...when it's too late to do anything about it. Afterward...

(UP MUSIC. DOWN FOR CLOSING ANNOUNCEMENT. UP MUSIC TO END)

THE FALL OF THE HOUSE OF USHER

BY EDGAR ALLAN POE
DRAMATISED FOR RADIO
BY NEVILLE TELLER

Running time: 30'

FIRST BROADCAST ACROSS THE
USA ON 25 MARCH 2020
IN A PRODUCTION BY SHOESTRING
RADIO THEATRE, SAN FRANCISCO
DIRECTED BY MELISSA FLOWER

CHARACTERS IN ORDER OF APPEARANCE

NARRATOR   *One speech*

POE   *Edgar Allan Poe in person. Aged about 30. A lively imagination. Needs to be able to send shivers down listeners' spines when recounting dramatic and horrific events.*

USHER   *About 30. Quite clearly mentally disturbed – probably both depression and anxiety. Beset by internal fears and terrors.*

VENUS   *About 30, Venus is a half plantation slave and half white American. She is probably the child of Roderick Usher's father, and thus Roderick's half-sister. She is a sort of housekeeper , or a superior servant.*

JEFFERSON   *60. The family doctor. Starchy, professional.*

MADELINE   *About 30. Weak, ill, actually at death's door. But we must hear every word she utters – frail, yes, but not faint!*

NOTE ON MUSIC

POE SPECIFIES IN THE STORY THAT USHER PLAYS "THE LAST WALTZ OF VON WEBER" ON THE GUITAR. I FOUND ONE EXAMPLE ON-LINE: HTTPS://WWW.YOUTUBE.COM/ WATCH?V=PTCPQJHIRDQ

(FULL UP "THE LAST WALTZ OF VON WEBER", PLAYED ON THE GUITAR: DOWN FOR OPENING ANNOUNCEMENT. UP MUSIC. DOWN FOR FOLLOWING. REPEAT TRACK PERHAPS TWICE TO MAINTAIN MUSIC BENEATH)

NARRATOR : *In the greenest of our valleys,*
By good angels tenanted
Once a fair and stately palace –
Radiant palace – reared its head.

Travellers now within that valley
Through the red-lit windows see
Vast forms that move fantastically
To a discordant melody.

(UP MUSIC. HOLD TO END OF MELODY. CROSSFADE TO HORSE AMBLING ON ROADWAY. FULL UP)

POE: *(as narrator)* A dull November day in Virginia. Evening was drawing on and I had been on horseback for many hours. The road had been following the contours of a hillside, but suddenly it twisted to one side, and below me in the valley I saw the House of Usher for the first time.

(HORSE STOPS)

At my first glimpse of the building – how can I explain this? – a cold shiver ran through me, a sense of unutterable foreboding. Throughout my two-day journey I had been borne up by the feeling that I was on a mission of mercy. But looking at those bleak walls, I experienced an iciness, a sinking – a sickening – of the heart. So this was the mansion of the ancient Usher family.

(FADE IN)

USHER: My dear, dear friend, nothing can excuse my long silence. I failed to respond to your early letters, and so the falling away of our friendship is entirely my fault. Please excuse me, but I have been ill, so very ill, and ill I remain. And I fear I am growing worse. It is a malady of the mind that I suffer from and, my dear friend, suffering is too mild a word to describe the agonies I live with. I beg you, for the sake of those happy times we spent together in our boyhood, oh I beg you to come and stay with me for a while. I am convinced that nothing is more likely to relieve my symptoms and restore me to health than a visit from you. Do please come to the House of Usher as soon as possible. I await your positive response with hope. I need your presence so badly. The friend of your youth. Roderick Usher.

(FADE OUT. FULL UP)

POE: My good intentions seemed to shrivel within me as I gazed at the windswept walls of the mansion, and especially at the vacant eye-like windows set across them at intervals. Close to the house, amid tufts of grasses and rushes, rose the white trunks of decaying trees, while a little further from the building stretched the dark waters of an extensive lake.

(EXTERIOR. HORSE STARTS MOVING SLOWLY. KEEP HOOVES BENEATH FOLLOWING TILL "FRONT DOOR". THEN MAN DISMOUNTING)

I picked my way down the steep road, which skirted the lake to the eastern side, and slowly approached the building. There was only a glimmer of light left in the sky as I came to the front door, a massive piece of black timber adorned with iron studs. I dismounted, and released my bulging saddle bag. There was a large bell-pull to one side of the entrance, and I tugged on it.

(BELL SOUNDS FROM INTERIOR. PAUSE. HEAVY METAL LATCH, DOOR OPENS, THEN CREAKS AS IT OPENS FURTHER. EXTERIOR)

VENUS: Yes?

POE: My name is Poe. I believe Mr Usher is expecting me.

VENUS: Ah, Mr Poe. He sure is, sir. Mr Usher said you're staying with him for a while. Please come in, sir.

I'll send the stable boy round to take care of your horse.

POE:	(*moving*) Thank you.

(INTERIOR. DOOR CREAKS AS IT SHUTS WITH A BANG)

VENUS:	Leave your bag here, sir. The housemaid will take it up. Now, follow me if you please.

(TWO WALKING, THEN CLIMBING WOODEN STAIRS, BENEATH FOLLOWING)

Mr Usher's studio is on the next floor and at the back of the house. It's a little way. Mr Usher prefers the view of the grounds from the rear of the building.

POE:	This is a magnificent staircase.

VENUS:	It sure is, sir. The old master was very proud of it. As you see, at the top it sweeps round in two directions so that you can reach whichever part of the building you choose.

(STAIR CLIMBING STOPS)

JEFFERSON:	(*approaching*) Ah, Venus. Good evening. I see you have a visitor

VENUS:	Ah, Dr Jefferson, sir. Good evening. May I introduce Mr Poe, sir? He's visiting with Mr Usher for a few weeks.

JEFFERSON	How do you do, Mr Poe? And I am very pleased to hear it. Mr Usher is in great need of company. He has been somewhat low of late.
POE:	You've been attending him, Dr Jefferson?
JEFFERSON	Not on this occasion. His sister has been rather unwell recently. She was my patient today. I must be on my way. *(retreating)* Pleasant to have met you, Mr Poe.

(FEET DESCENDING STAIRS, AND FADING)

POE:	*(calling)* Perhaps we may meet again.
JEFFERSON:	*(retreating, calling)* Perhaps. Good evening.

(UNDER FOLLOWING TWO FEET CLIMB STAIRS BRIEFLY. THEN WALK ON WOOD)

VENUS:	This way, Mr Poe.
POE:	I knew Miss Madeline Usher years ago, Venus – that *is* your name?
VENUS:	It sure is, sir. Has been all my life *(hearty laugh)*. In fact, it was old Mr Usher christened me.
POE:	I didn't know Miss Madeline was living here.
VENUS:	Oh, she's Mrs Selden now. She came a few months ago, after her husband passed away.

POE: Poor Madeline. How did he die?

VENUS: It's a strange story, sir. Like all the white gentlemen, he was always much too free with the slave girls on the plantation, but once he went too far. The girl ran screaming to her mother. Now that old woman is well known among the slaves as a medicine woman – she practises what they call Conjure. And she knows all about African black magic – too much. She put a curse on him. Three weeks later he was dead.

POE: Dead? From what?

VENUS: The doctors couldn't say. So no-one can charge the old witch with anything. But as soon as he was told of the curse, Mr Selden started to have fits of shivering. After a while he couldn't stop. It weakened him so much that he took to his bed. And there he lay, shivering and shaking. Miss Madeline was distraught. She loved him dearly. She nursed him – she tried to restore his strength, but she could do nothing for him. He grew weaker by the day. One morning she went to wake him, and she found him dead.

(FOOTSTEPS STOP)

Here we are, sir.

(KNOCK ON DOOR)

USHER: *(distant, muffled)* Is that you, Venus? Come in, woman, come in.

(DOOR OPENS)

VENUS: *(moving)* I've brought you your guest, Mr Usher. Here's Mr Poe, sir.

USHER: *(distant)* My dear Poe, my dear friend. Do come in. Here, I must stand up. Venus, give me a hand. *(advancing)* Poe, how very good of you to come. Was the journey very tiring? Venus, bring Mr Poe a chair. There. Sit yourself down. That's better. Poe, you look just as I remember you.

POE: Now, that's certainly not the case. The years take their toll. I fear they have not treated you kindly, Usher.

USHER: No, indeed. And this illness of mine certainly hasn't assisted. Venus, pour Mr Poe a cider. You'll have a hard cider, Poe?

POE: I won't say no. It's been a long and dusty ride. Two days on the road, Usher. I spent last night at an inn.

(POURING INTO TALL GLASS)

VENUS: There we are, sir. Will you partake, Mr Usher?

USHER: Just a very little, Venus, a mere taste – and then

you must escort our guest to his room. You'll need time to recuperate, my dear Poe.

(POURING)

VENUS: Mr Poe, sir.

(POURING)

USHER: And the water, Venus. You must dilute it for me. More. Thank you. We take supper at 8 o'clock, Poe. That will give you plenty of time to rest a little and spruce up. Meanwhile, may I offer you a toast? To our renewed friendship. I hope you will be very happy here.

(CLINK OF GLASSES. PAUSE. SLOW FADE IN OF GUITAR "THE LAST WALTZ OF VON WEBER". HOLD A LITTLE. FADE IN POE, BUT KEEP MUSIC UNDER FOLLOWING TILL END OF TUNE)

POE: You play the guitar extremely well, Usher. What is that melody?

USHER: I play the guitar, Poe, because I simply I cannot bear to hear any other instrument. Every other musical instrument – even the piano – is an agony to me. I have become hypersensitive to every sort of intrusion on my senses.

POE: Is this the malady you spoke of in your letter?

USHER:	It is. And I'm not alone in suffering from it. It's a constitutional – a family – evil. There is no remedy. Once it strikes a member of the Usher family, they have to endure its ill effects until the episode passes.
POE:	So it does pass off?
USHER:	In time. And then I live in dread, waiting for it to strike again. There's no determining when. Out of the blue it comes.
POE:	And you're suffering at the moment?
USHER:	I have been for a month.
POE:	What are the symptoms?
USHER:	When the disease is at its worst, it's as if all my senses were stretched tight. I can endure no food that has taste or texture. I live on insipid milky slops. See these garments? Pure silk, Poe – the only fabric I can bear near my skin. I cannot venture forth into the garden. My senses are immediately overwhelmed by the sound of the birds, the scent of the flowers. They are unendurable – ten times more intense than they would be to you.
POE:	I see you wear darkened lenses – even indoors with the curtains drawn.
USHER:	My eyes become unbelievably sensitive to light. Expose them to ordinary daylight, and it's as if they were besieged by ten thousand candles.

POE: My poor friend.

USHER: When I'm enduring the agony of these episodes, I am sure that one day I shall succumb – I'll simply pass away.

POE: Oh, no…

USHER: Yes, Poe. It will overpower me in the end. I am certain of it. You ask what this melody is that I play on the guitar.

> **(FULL UP "THE LAST WALTZ OF VON WEBER" ON GUITAR. HOLD A LITTLE AND STOP ABRUPTLY)**

POE: Yes, it's not familiar to me.

USHER: It's "The Last Waltz of Von Weber". It appeals to me greatly. It expresses exactly how I feel.

> **(FULL UP "THE LAST WALTZ OF VON WEBER" ON GUITAR. HOLD A LITTLE. FADE OUT. FULL UP)**

MADELINE: *(remote, advancing)* I trust I am not intruding?

USHER: My dear Madeline, of course not.

POE: I hope you remember me, Miss Madeline?

MADELINE: Of course, Mr Poe. But I am Miss Madeline no longer. I am the widowed Mrs Selden.

POE: So I understand. I am so sorry for your tragic loss.

MADELINE: Tragedy has overcome the House of Usher, Mr Poe. You see before you its last surviving members. When we die, the family dies with us.

POE: There is no other branch, however remote?

USHER: There is not. With us, the Usher family comes to an end. I never could marry – my malady prevented it...

MADELINE: ...and nothing would induce me to wed again. In any event, I too am far from well. Ever since my dear Thomas passed away, I've been overcome by melancholy.

POE: Entirely understandable, surely?

MADELINE: Perhaps. But it has weakened me. My strength has faded. I have so little left. My life seems to be ebbing away.

USHER: Madeline. Please. Do not talk like that.

MADELINE: But it is true, Roderick. It is true.

USHER: I shall send for Dr Jefferson. You must see him, Madeline. He may be able to help.

MADELINE: As you wish, Roderick. Just as you wish.

(FADE OUT. FADE IN)

USHER: You know what, Poe, I've come to believe that the curse that old slave woman put on Madeline's husband – it's spread to the whole House of Usher. I thought I was emerging from my latest episode, but I find it's not so. I am as afflicted as ever. And Madeline – she's simply fading away. Before our eyes.

POE: I don't believe in curses, Usher – and neither should you. Black magic, Conjure – all that is so much mumbo-jumbo. Superstition.

USHER: I was once of your mind, Poe. But look about you. What do you see? Two frail invalids in a mansion that is itself crumbling away. The House of Usher is finished, Poe. Dead. You're witnessing its last days. And the curse placed on Thomas – that's playing its part. Believe me, my friend. I am right.

POE: I cannot think it so, Usher.

USHER: These thoughts assail me, especially in the long watches of the night. I have tried to express them in verse.

POE: You write poetry?

USHER: From time to time. Would you care to hear what I have written?

POE: Very much so. Please do read your verses to me.

USHER: In the greenest of our valleys,
By good angels tenanted

Once a fair and stately palace –
Radiant palace – reared its head.

But evil things, in robes of sorrow,
Assailed the monarch's high estate;
(Ah, let us mourn, for never morrow
Shall dawn upon him, desolate!)

Travellers now within that valley
Through the red-lit windows see
Vast forms that move fantastically
To a discordant melody.

POE: This is pure depression, melancholy. It is itself an illness, Usher – an illness of the mind, as real as the malady that afflicts your body. I hope, I pray, that my presence here may go some way towards alleviating the symptoms and effecting a cure.

USHER: Things *are* better since you came, Poe. The malady is stlll on me, but I feel very much improved. Your company lifts my spirits.

(URGENT KNOCKING ON THE DOOR)

(*calling*) Yes? Who is it? Come in.

(DOOR OPENS)

VENUS: (*remote, distraught, sobbing*) Oh, Mr Usher! Oh, Mr Usher, sir!

USHER: What is it, Venus? What has happened? (*beat*) Dr Jefferson?

JEFFERSON (*remote, advancing*) I'm very sorry to tell you, Mr Usher, that your sister has just passed away.

POE: Oh, Usher. I'm so very, very sorry.

USHER: The tragedy plays itself out. All is as I told you, Poe. But I will not give way. Matters will be arranged to suit me.

VENUS: What about the funeral, Mr Usher? Shall I send for the parson?

USHER: Most certainly not, Venus. You may send to the undertaker, and order a coffin to be delivered. I shall require it here tomorrow morning.

VENUS: Yes, Mr Usher.

USHER: You will gather the staff, and tell them to prepare my sister for a temporary entombment in one of the vaults beneath the house. Tomorrow, Mr Poe and I will convey her body down there.

POE: Oh, Usher, do you really think…[*this is a sensible course…*]

VENUS: Oh, Mr Usher.

USHER: Venus, you'll carry out my orders to the letter. Is that understood?

VENUS: (*retreating*) Yes, Mr Usher, sir. I'll get about it.

(DOOR CLOSES)

JEFFERSON   Mr Usher is this necessary?

USHER: It is to me, Dr Jefferson. And it should be to you.

JEFFERSON   How do you mean, sir?

USHER: You have on several occasions expressed some uncertainty about the cause and nature of my sister's illness. Why should a young woman sicken and die in this fashion? Can you give me a cause of death?

JEFFERSON   You have me there, Mr Usher.

USHER: Then I shall afford you two weeks in which to discover it. Her body will remain in the vaults, here in the House of Usher, for 14 days. At the end of that time, she will be accorded a full funeral in the family church, and be laid to rest in the family tomb.

JEFFERSON   Very well, Mr Usher. I shall inform the county coroner of your wishes. Meanwhile I'll undertake some forensic investigations. I wish you good day, sir, *(retreating)* and please accept my condolences in your loss.

(DOOR OPENS)

Mr Poe.

POE: Good day, doctor.

(DOOR CLOSES. FULL UP VAULTS. ECHO FULL ON. POE AND USHER NEED TO SPEAK MORE SLOWLY THAN USUAL TO BE UNDERSTANDABLE OVER THE ECHO. SHUFFLING FEET ON STONE)

USHER: (*struggling*) Careful, Poe – take care.

POE: (*struggling*) This coffin's damned heavy.

USHER: That's exactly what it is – the coffin. Madeline was skin and bone. As light as a feather. Look at all these brass trimmings. That rogue has sent along the most expensive item in his shop. Careful... careful.

POE: How much further, for heaven's sake?

USHER: Just round this corner. Here. Let's lay it down here.

(HEAVY LOAD SET DOWN ON STONE)

POE: I'm indulging your fancy in all this, Usher. I do hope you know what you're about.

USHER: She'll be entombed soon enough – and for long enough. Let her rest here in the House of Usher for a few days. Now I must look at her again – perhaps for the last time. The lid's not screwed down. It's only laid on the top. Help me lift it off. Come on, Poe.

POE: I'm not sure… I'm really not sure…

USHER: Squeamish, are you?

POE: No, no. All right. (*effort*)

(HEAVY WOOD SLIDING ON WOOD – *devise a really distinctive sound. We're going to need it again just a little further on***)**

USHER: (*effort*) There.

(CREEP MUSIC IN BENEATH FOLLOWING)

POE: (*as narrator*) We gazed down at the body of Usher's sister, Madeline. The disease which had robbed the young woman of her life – whatever that disease may have been – had left the mockery of a faint blush on her cheeks. Also present was that suspiciously lingering smile upon the lips which is so terrible in death. All anxiety, all worry, all fear had been wiped from her face. In short, we seemed to have before us a beautiful young woman in perfect health, who had drifted off into untroubled slumber. Saying nothing to each other we looked down on her for a long moment. Then we replaced the coffin lid, and made our way up into the scarcely less gloomy apartments of the upper portion of the house.

(UP MUSIC. HOLD. FADE OUT. FULL UP)

POE: You cannot continue like this, Usher. I never know

where to find you. You're continually roaming from room to room as if you were searching for something. What are you looking for, Usher? Tell me, and perhaps I can help you.

USHER: No, no, my dear friend. I'm not looking for anything in particular. And yet there *is* something I seem to be lacking. Do you think it's simply the loss of Madeline that is haunting me? Did you know that we were twins, born within minutes of each other?

POE: No, indeed. That is something I did not know. I never seem to have been with you when you celebrated your birthday.

USHER: So Madeline and I always felt a special bond between us.

POE: Understandably.

USHER: Her passing has left me feeling as though a part of myself has been torn away. But there is something even deeper in my mind. With Madeline dead, the House of Usher rests only on my fragile existence. When I die, so does the House of Usher.

POE: But there is nothing new in all this, Usher. You have always known it – and so has Madeline.

USHER: No, no. While there was life, there was hope. When Madeline married, she believed she would have children through whom the name of Usher might be carried forward. And as for me, it is only in the past few years that I have abandoned the idea of finding a wife. Slowly, slowly, all hope has been extinguished, and the House of Usher has been brought to face its inevitable demise.

(REMOTE KNOCK ON DOOR. DOOR OPENS)

VENUS: *(remote)* Mr Usher, sir. Dr Jefferson is here to see you.

POE: In that case, I'll leave you Usher.

USHER: No, no. Please stay. *(calls)* Show him in, Venus.

JEFFERSON: *(remote, advancing)* Mr Usher. Mr Poe. Good afternoon, gentlemen. I trust this is not inconvenient?

USHER: Not at all, doctor. Do you bring any news?

JEFFERSON: Only of a somewhat negative character, I fear.

POE: I take it you have not established the cause of Madeline's death.

JEFFERSON: You anticipate me, Mr Poe. I have been undertaking a series of forensic examinations, all of which, I'm sorry to report, have proved inconclusive. I'm afraid that neither I, nor my medical colleagues, have been able to identify the malady which overtook her, and which eventually led to her death.

503

USHER: One thought does strike me, doctor. Were you not in precisely the same quandary over the death of my sister's husband? In that case, too, you were unable to provide a rational explanation for his rapid decline, and eventual demise.

JEFFERSON: That is so, Mr Usher.

POE: Might it be reasonable to assume that if her husband had been infected with some little known disease, she might have harboured the same malady? In short, that they both died from the same cause?

JEFFERSON: That is a very possible explanation, Mr Poe. Medical science has made great strides in recent years, but there is a long way to go.

USHER: Dr Jefferson, I know you have heard of the curse that was said to have been laid on my brother-in-law.

JEFFERSON: Yes, yes, Mr Usher. But we don't want to place too much credence on that.

USHER: All the same, if there is something in it, and if Madeline's husband was struck down by some form of black magic, might she not also be a victim?

POE: (*as narrator*) Following Dr Jefferson's visit there were times when I thought my friend's unceasingly agitated mind was labouring with some oppressive secret – that he was struggling for the necessary courage to divulge it. At other times it seemed to me that he was on the verge of madness, for I would see him gazing on nothing at all for long hours in an attitude of profound attention, as if listening to some imaginary sound. As the days passed his condition infected me. I felt creeping upon me, by slow yet certain degrees, a feeling of impending doom.

(FULL UP CRASH OF THUNDER. THEN HEAVY WIND AND RAIN. MAINTAIN STORM AND THUNDER THROUGHOUT FOLLOWING, SO LOUD THAT POE AND USHER WILL HAVE TO KEEP THEIR VOICES RAISED)

POE: What are you doing, Usher? Close that casement. Close the window, for heaven's sake. We're both soaked to the skin .

USHER: But you haven't seen it. Look. Look, Poe. Look.

(CUT STORM. SILENCE)

POE: (*as narrator*) I looked, and what I saw filled me with horror. The whole mansion was enshrouded in a thick reddish vapour, which seemed to glow from within. It was as if the House of Usher was being consumed by hell fire, while every now and then the pitch blackness of the night was pierced by jagged flashes of lightning.

(BURST OF THUNDER. RESUME STORM BACKGROUND)

USHER: It's a sign. It's what I told you. The House of Usher is marked out for destruction.

POE: What utter nonsense. Here let me close the window.

> **(WINDOW CLOSED. SOUNDS OF STORM LESSEN, BUT CONTINUE AT LOW LEVEL)**

Now, listen to me, Usher. What we see is simply an electrical phenomenon brought on by the storm. The mist comes from that lake that fronts the mansion. There is nothing supernatural about it at all.

USHER: If you say so, Poe. It's an unnerving sight, nevertheless.

POE: With that, I can agree with you.

> **(REMOTE – HEAVY WOOD SLIDING ON WOOD – *as above*)**

USHER: What was that?

POE: It's the storm. It's rattling those widows.

USHER: No, no. That was no window. Listen. Listen, Poe.

> **(REMOTE – HEAVY WOOD SLIDING ON WOOD. REMOTE – WOMAN'S SCREAM)**

POE: Yes. Yes, I certainly heard that. Is it the servants? Are they frightened by the storm?

USHER: It is not the servants.

POE: Then who is it? Could it be Venus?

USHER: It is not Venus.

(REMOTE – HEAVY WOODEN COFFIN LID FALLING TO STONE FLOOR)

POE: Oh, my good Lord! What was that? Do you know what that was, Usher?

USHER: Only too well. I have been hearing sounds for long, long minutes, for hours, for days. Many days I've been hearing them. But I did not dare – oh, coward that I am – I did not have the courage to tell you. If only I'd told you. But I could not. Poe, I couldn't.

POE: What on earth are you trying to tell me, Usher? What have you heard? What do you think you've heard?

USHER: I've been hearing the sound of my sister, Madeline, trying to escape from her coffin.

POE: What?

USHER: I told you my senses have grown acute. They're so sharp that I hear the slightest sound anywhere in this house. Yes, Poe, the noises we've been hearing come from the vault. I heard the first feeble movements a week ago. Pity me, wretch that I am, but I didn't dare speak out. The sounds grew stronger day by day, and still I could say nothing. Nothing. Tonight we heard the coffin lid slide back and fall to the floor. Oh Poe, may the good Lord forgive me. We put Madeline into her coffin while she was still alive.

POE: No, no. That is certainly not so. Dr Jefferson pronounced her dead, and I'm as completely sure that there was no life in her when we looked on her for the last time. You're mistaken, my friend, completely mistaken.

USHER: No, no. She is coming up from her tomb at this moment. At any second she will be at that door. She is coming to demand why I was so hasty. Listen! Isn't that her on the stairs? Listen.

POE: Enough of this foolishness. Usher. This is all your fevered imagination. You're not well, my friend. Your mind is playing tricks. Come now, let me take you to your bed. Come along, Usher.

USHER: Get off me. Let me be. Listen to me, Poe. I'm utterly certain. My sister Madeline is standing just outside that door.

(CUT STORM BACKGROUND)

POE: (*as narrator*) As if he had uttered a spell, the huge antique double doors to which he pointed swung inwards. It was surely the gusts of wind blowing down the corridors that did it, for the curtains were billowing out in all directions. At first I could see nothing, but a second later I could distinguish, to my ineffable horror, the figure of Madeline – Madeline wrapped in the shroud we had last seen as we laid her to rest in the vault. There was one difference. The white purity of the cloth was besmirched with blood. She gazed wildly from side to side, evidence of some bitter struggle clear in her emaciated frame. For a moment, as she remained trembling and reeling to and fro upon the threshold, Usher took an uncertain step toward her.

USHER: Madeline!

POE: (*as narrator*) Then with a low moaning cry, she fell heavily inward upon her brother. He clasped her in his arms as they fell together to the floor, united in death.

(CRASH OF THUNDER. WIND, RAIN. ENTRANCE HALL)

POE: Not another second, Venus. Not one second.

VENUS: Has something happened, sir? Have you fallen out with Mr Usher?

POE: The moment I've gone, please go up to Mr Usher's room. I am leaving now. This very minute.

VENUS: But in this storm sir?

POE: I want my horse, Venus. Now, if you please

VENUS: If you insist, Mr Poe. (*retreating*) I'll see to it right away.

(CUT STORM BACKGROUND)

POE: (*as narrator*) From that house of horror I fled aghast, despite the storm which persisted in all its fury, As I was crossing the old causeway, a wild light suddenly shot along the path ahead of me. It was a steady light, not a bolt of lightning, and I turned to see where it could possibly have come from. The sight that met my eyes is forever imprinted on my memory. The House of Usher had split asunder, and what I could see was the full blood-red moon shining between the two halves of the mansion.

(FADE IN "THE LAST WALTZ OF VON WEBER", PLAYED ON THE GUITAR BENEATH THE FOLLOWING)

As I gazed, the fissure rapidly widened. The moon shone full in my face as I saw the mighty walls rushing asunder. There was a long, tumultuous shouting sound, like the voice of a thousand waters – and the deep and dank lake closed silently over the fragments of the House of Usher.

(UP MUSIC TO END. CLOSING ANNOUNCEMENT OVER SILENCE)

SOME WORDS WITH A MUMMY

A PLAY FOR RADIO
BY NEVILLE TELLER
INSPIRED BY THE SHORT STORY
BY EDGAR ALLAN POE

Running time: 30'

FIRST BROADCAST ACROSS
THE USA IN MAY 2021
IN A PRODUCTION BY SHOESTRING
RADIO THEATRE, SAN FRANCISCO
DIRECTED BY STEVE RUBENSTEIN

CHARACTERS IN ORDER OF APPEARANCE

WINTHROP: *Male 40s. A bit precise and scholarly.*

PONNONNER: *Male 60s. Professor, and true to type.*

MRS BUCKINGHAM: *Female – 50s. Enthusiastic amateur in Egyptology.*

GLIDDON: *Male 40s. Rather cynical and disbelieving*

MRS ROBERTS: *Female 50s. Winthrop's housekeeper. Motherly and caring. Full of commonsense. . Sharp as a needle*

ALAMIS-TAK-AYO: *The 5000-year old Egyptian Mummy come back to life. I envisage a creaky sort of voice, with slow delivery in some indeterminate accent. He needs to be strange and rather mesmerising*

(FULL UP GRANDFATHER CLOCK TICKING: FOUR TICKS ONLY. THEN CLOCK CHIMING. FULL SET OF WESTMINSTER CHIMES. AFTER FIRST HOUR CHIME CLOCK DOWN FOR START OF OPENING ANNOUNCEMENT THEN CLOCK OUT. AFTER ANNOUNCEMENT BRING UP LAST THREE HOUR CHIMES)

WINTHROP: (*as narrator*) Lewisburg Square, Boston. Wednesday, October the 15th 1845. The time is precisely 7 a.m. After a highly disturbed, not to say disturbing, night, I am sitting at my desk in order to record the astounding events that I have witnessed in the past 24 hours.

Where on earth shall I begin?

Let me go back half a century, to the discovery in 1799 of the Rosetta Stone. I suppose the current craze for everything Egyptian started then. What a discovery that was! Until then Egyptian hieroglyphics had been a closed book. Over the many centuries since the collapse of the ancient Egyptian civilization. nobody had been able to decipher those strange pictures found on the walls of tombs, and convert them into words.

Then some French soldiers, rebuilding a fort in a small village called Rosetta in the Egyptian Delta. unearthed the Stone. On it was carved three versions of the same text – one in the old hieroglyphics, one in an early form of script, and one in Greek. That was the key that unlocked the whole of ancient Egypt's civilization.

Suddenly all things Egyptian became the fashion. Expeditions were mounted to excavate ancient tombs. There were no rules, and Europeans took whatever they fancied and carried them back home. In other words, they looted them.

(FADE IN)

PONNONNER: My dear friends, thank you for coming. I know you are all as fascinated by ancient Egypt as I am, and I have some amazing news.

MRS BUCKINGHAM: News about ancient Egypt, Dr Ponnonner?

PONNONNER: In a way, Mrs Buckingham. In a way.

GLIDDON: You're deliberately keeping us in suspense, Ponnonner.

WINTHROP: I agree, Gliddon. Get on with it.

PONNONNER: Patience. Patience. Well you all know that last year my cousin, Captain Arthur Sabertash, was excavating a tomb in the Lybian mountains.

WINTHROP: Not far from Thebes, wasn't it?

PONNONNER: That's right, Winthrop. Thebes that was, of course. It's called Luxor today.

GLIDDON: For heaven's sake, Ponnonner.

PONNONNER: Yes, yes – Thebes, Luxor. That's not the point. The point is that he dug up a mummy, and has shipped it back here to the States.

MRS BUCKINGHAM: Good heavens above. You mean your cousin has an original Egyptian mummy in his possession?

PONNONNER: Yes. And no, Mrs Buckingham.

GLIDDON: What do you mean? He hasn't disturbed it in any way, has he? I mean, it's still in its original sarcophogus?

PONNONNER: It's still precisely as he found it, Gliddon. I can testify to that, because I have here photographs that he took of the interior of the tomb. Gather round.

MRS BUCKINGHAM: The sarcophagus is huge, isn't it? But the decorations! Pity we can't see the colours.

PONNONNER: My cousin described them, Mrs Buckingham. All that is gold.

GLIDDON: Look at those frescos and bas-reliefs on the walls. I've never seen anything like it.

WINTHROP: And the statues. The vases. This is the tomb of a very wealthy individual.

PONNONNER: Wealthy and powerful. A trusted official, close to the Pharoah, I'd say.

WINTHROP: It's a treasure trove, Ponnonner. How much of all that did your cousin cart away?

PONNONNER: I'm not exactly sure. But what interests me is the mummy.

WINTHROP: Yes, what's happened to it?

PONNONNER: Well, Winthrop, obviously he couldn't simply take it home with him. Not burdened with all his luggage and the other artifacts. So he deposited it in the Boston Museum of Science for safe-keeping.

GLIDDON: But I know Walter Channing – he's in charge of the place. Used to practise medicine at one time. Now he runs the museum. Director, I think he's called.

PONNONNER: Excellent, Gliddon. I'm very pleased he's a friend of yours. Perhaps you could talk a little sense into him.

GLIDDON: How do you mean?

PONNONNER: Well, having taken the mummy into his collection, he's refusing to part with it.

WINTHROP: You mean…?

PONNONNER: Precisely. He has put the sarcophagus on prominent display, on the ground floor of the museum, and he says that's where it will stay.

MRS BUCKINGHAM: But it's your cousin's property. He can't do that.

PONNONNER: I'm afraid we're on rather delicate ground there, Mrs Buckingham. To be strictly accurate, that mummy is the property of the Egyptian government. So Dr Channing has dared my cousin to contact the police. And Captain Sabertash has decided not to risk it. So, much as I would have liked you to witness the opening of the sarcophagus, and the extraction of the mummy...

MRS BUCKINGHAM: Oh, Dr Ponnonner. What a thrill that would have been.

PONNONNER: Indeed. But I'm afraid we shall have to postpone that pleasure until such time as Dr Channing can be persuaded to change his mind. Such a very great pity [*don't you all think...*]

(FADE OUT. FULL UP)

WINTHROP: (*as narrator*) All this took place five years ago, back in 1840. For five long years Andrew Gliddon begged and cajoled and beseeched his friend, Dr Channing, to release the sarcophagus so that we could open it. And for five long years Walter Channing steadfastly refused to allow it to leave his museum. Truth to tell, our little group of amateur Egyptologists had quite given up hope.

And so we come to the events of last night, Tuesday October the 14th, 1845. Now I wish to be scrupulously accurate, so I will include in this account every detail that I can recall. I remember that I dined quite late, and that at the end of the meal I sent for my cook, Mrs Roberts, not something I often did…

(CROSSFADE)

MRS ROBERTS: You wanted to see me, sir?

WINTHROP: Indeed I did, Mrs Roberts.

MRS ROBERTS: Oh, I do hope there was nothing wrong with the meal, sir.

WINTHROP: Wrong? Wrong, Mrs Roberts? Quite the reverse. It was magnificent. You don't often serve up Welsh rabbit. But that was the tastiest dish I've sampled in many a long day.

MRS ROBERTS: Oh, Mr Winthrop. I'm so pleased. What can I say? But I have to put you right, sir. The dish isn't Welsh rabbit. That's a mistake people often make. There's no meat in it at all. It's Welsh RAREBIT. And the secret lies in how the cheese is prepared. That's a secret recipe my grandma taught me when I was a very little girl. Long before the family came over to the States.

WINTHROP: I stand corrected, Mrs Roberts. Welsh Rarebit. And that's what it certainly is. That cheese – so creamy, so tasty, yet with a kick you can feel right down in your tummy.

MRS ROBERTS: That's the mustard powder, sir. That much I *can* tell you.

WINTHROP: 'Mmmm. I could almost do with another portion, as I speak.

MRS ROBERTS: I do have some extra in the kitchen, Mr Winthrop. Shall I bring it to table?

WINTHROP: I really can't say no, Mrs Roberts.

MRS ROBERTS: *(retreating)* Just give me a moment, sir.

WINTHROP: *(as narrator)* I recount this episode in order to explain how very deeply asleep I was in the small hours of this morning,

(FADE IN BANGING ON FRONT DOOR AND OLD-FASHIONED DOORBELL RINGING. DOORBELL SHOULD BE VERY DISTINCTIVE – IT NEEDS TO BE RECOGNIZED IN THE FINAL SCENE)

and how much noise was needed in order to rouse me from my slumbers. But eventually I did become aware that there was someone at my front door who was demanding to be admitted. I forced myself out of bed. In my nightshirt, I descended the stairs.

(PONNONER OUTSIDE THE HOUSE)

PONNONNER: *(calling)* Winthrop! Winthrop! Wake up for heaven's sake.

(FRONT DOOR OPENS)

WINTHROP:	Ponnonner. What on earth are you doing here at this time of night? What time is it?
PONNONNER:	One-thirty. But don't worry about that, Winthrop. May I come in? I have some wonderful news.
WINTHROP:	Yes, of course, old chap. Come along.

(FRONT DOOR CLOSES. THEY MOVE INTO DRAWING ROOM)

	Can I offer you something?
PONNONNER:	No, no, nothing for me. Winthrop, the most amazing thing has happened. Earlier this evening Gliddon and I were summoned to the Boston Museum of Science. Dr Channing sent a lad round to say he had something very important to tell us.
WINTHROP:	Yes? Do go on.
PONNONNER:	We arrived at about nine o'clock. He could scarcely contain his excitement. He took us straight to the main museum on the ground floor, and there, to our astonishment, we saw not one, but two Egyptian sarcophagi.
WINTHROP:	Two?
PONNONNER:	Two. Standing side by side. Then he explained.

There has been an American expedition at work in Egypt for the past three years. In the course of their excavations they unearthed an undisturbed tomb, and found a wonderfully decorated sarcophagus, which they shipped back to the States and bequeathed to our museum. Dr Channing said that he had no need for two Egyptian mummies. One example sufficed for visitors to appreciate the beauty and craftsmanship that the ancient Egyptians lavished on these homes of the dead. And so…

WINTHROP: Yes? Yes?

PONNONNER: And so, he was happy to accede to the many requests he had received over the years to return my cousin's sarcophagus to me.

WINTHROP: No.

PONNONNER: Indeed. Gliddon and I immediately sent for a carter, and we transported the sarcophagus to my residence, where it now awaits us.

WINTHROP: Good heavens, Ponnoner. At last. At long last. And what do you intend?

PONNONNER: I intend that our little group proceeds at once, this very night, to open the sarcophagus, extract the mummy, unwind the bandages in which it is undoubtedly wrapped, and see what degree of preservation it has retained over these many centuries. Are you ready?

WINTHROP: Wild horses couldn't restrain me. But what of Mrs Buckingham?

PONNONNER: Gliddon is with her now. She will undoubtedly be joining us.

WINTHROP: I must put some clothes on. *(retreating)* Give me a few minutes, Ponnonner. I'll be with you in no time.

(FADE IN MUSIC. HOLD BRIEFLY. FADE UNDER FOLLOWING, AND OUT. INTERIOR)

MRS BUCKINGHAM: Oh, Dr Ponnonner, this is all too wonderful for words. I've visited the museum so often, I've stood beside this sarcophagus, I've touched it. But to be present as it is opened – this is the thrill of a lifetime. This is a moment I shall treasure to my dying day.

PONNONNER: Mrs Buckingham I really must ask you to restrain your enthusiasm just a little. It is indeed a moment we have all waited – indeed prayed – for, but that is all the more reason for us to proceed scientifically, with caution. I shall myself write up the events we are about to experience, and offer them to the leading research journal on Egyptology. So I shall note down carefully every step we take and what we perceive.

GLIDDON: Very wise, Ponnoner. We really do not want to be seen as a bunch of bungling amateurs.

WINTHROP: Amateurs is what we are, Gliddon, but knowledgeable and dedicated amateurs, who know precisely what they are about.

PONNONNER: Well said, Winthrop. Now my friends, what we see lying before us on this table is a sarcophagus, beautifully and intricately decorated. This is likely to be the first of three separate containers before we reach the Mummy itself.

GLIDDON: The sarcophagus, then the coffin, then the Mummy case?

PONNONNER: Absolutely correct, Gliddon.

WINTHROP: (*as narrator*) And so it proved to be. It took us half an hour, all of us bending to the task. to prise open the sarcophagus and remove the inner coffin. It was no light weight. The space between the two containers was filled with resin, which took a deal of effort to remove. We then opened the coffin and lifted out the case that actually contained the Mummy. This we laid carefully on the cleared table top, and opened – and there lay the Mummy.

MRS BUCKINGHAM: No bandages! There are no bandages, Dr Ponnoner.

PONNONNER: So I observe, Mrs Buckingham. And I am as surprised as you. I have noted the fact down.

GLIDDON: What *is* around the body?

WINTHROP: Looks to me like a sort of sheath. Made of papyrus, isn't it?

PONNONNER: Indeed, all welded together – and just look at those pictures and hieroglyphics. This must have been a very senior member of the royal household. Gliddon, I need your help. As I slit down this sheath, would you please ensure that it is preserved, whole and entire?

GLIDDON: Indeed I will, Ponnoner. I'm ready. Please proceed.

WINTHROP: (*as narrator*) Stripping off the papyrus, we found the flesh in an excellent state of preservation. The teeth and hair were in good condition. The fingers and nails were brilliantly gilded.

GLIDDON: There's something curious here, Pononner.

PONNONNER: Curious? What do you mean?

GLIDDON: Well, I've searched the body thoroughly, but I can't find where the entrails were extracted from. There's no opening.

WINTHROP: Gliddon's right, you know.

MRS BUCKINGHAM: What can it mean, Dr Ponnonner?

PONNONNER: Goodness me there's no mystery about that. There are several known examples of entire or unopened mummies. There's one in the British museum in London, England.

MRS BUCKINGHAM: Do you mean this man was embalmed whole and entire, brain and all?

PONNONNER: I think he must have been. It's getting late, or I'd suggest starting the dissection at once to find out.

WINTHROP: Well, what else can we do with the mummy right now?

PONNONNER: We could try applying the new electricity – the Voltaic machine. I wonder what the galvanic effect might be. Are nerves and muscles sufficiently preserved after four thousand years to respond to an electric shock? A fascinating question. Would you be prepared to write up the experiment, Winthrop?

WINTHROP: Of course,

PONNONNER: The machine is just over here. It's already attached to its battery, which has been fully charged in my laboratory. I think we'll attach one end of the wiring to the temporal region – just here, I think. And the other... about here... Right. Gliddon, would you switch on the machine?

(SWITCH. LOW HUM QUICKLY GETS LOUDER. LOUD SIZZLE AS WHEN TWO LIVE WIRES TOUCH).

PONNONNER: Off. Off.

(SWITCH. HUM OFF)

WINTHROP: I didn't observe any contraction of the lower limb.

PONNONNER: No, neither did I. Rather a disappointment, don't you think?

MRS BUCKINGHAM: Look! Look! His eyes! They're open.

WINTHROP: Weren't they open before?

GLIDDON: They were not, Winthrop. They certainly were not. It must be that electric shock.

MRS BUCKINGHAM: Oh dear Lord! His mouth! It's opening as well.

ALAMIS-TAKO: *(strangulated sounds)*

PONNONNER: I do believe he's trying to speak. Here, Gliddon, help me raise him. Grab hold of his other arm. Now … lift

ALAMIS-TAKO: *(starting slow, speeding up)* How very kind. I'm afraid my muscles aren't in very good shape. After all, I haven't used them for several thousand years.

PONNONNER: You're talking…

ALAMIS-TAKO: Pretty self evident, I'd say. Is there nothing more perceptive you have on your mind?

GLIDDON: But in American? Why aren't you speaking in ancient Egyptian? Where did you learn English?

WINTHROP: Modern English at that.

ALAMIS-TAKO: My dear fellow, if you had stood in a museum for five long years – even in a closed box – with nothing to do but listen to hordes of Americans chattering away, you would have picked up the language, just as I did.

PONNONNER: Do you mean you've been conscious for thousands of years?

ALAMIS-TAKO: Well, I do doze off for a couple of hundred years from time to time.

GLIDDON: Excuse my asking, but who was the Pharoah at the time of your – er – unfortunate demise?

ALAMIS-TAKO: I had the honor of being Vizier to his majesty King Thutmose the Fourth. I passed away shortly after his tragically short reign.

PONNONNER: Ah, the New Kingdom. Around 1400 BC. Something more than three thousand years ago, I believe.

WINTHROP: Thank you, professor. And your name, if I may be so bold as to ask?

ALAMIS-TAKO: You may call me Alamis–Takeo. *[Note: Don't get anywhere near All A Mistake-o. That revelation has to be held till later].* Alamis, for short. On second thoughts, I think I would prefer to be accorded the dignity that my status merits. I was, after all, Vizier to his Majesty throughout his short reign. Would you please address me as Count Alamis.

PONNONNER: Erm... if that is your wish. Certainly. Mrs Buckingham, gentlemen – may I present Count Alamis. He comes to us from 1400 BC. Or thereabouts.

MRS BUCKINGHAM: } Pleased to meet you.
WINTHROP: } How do you do?
GLIDDON: } Hullo, there.

ALAMIS-TAKO: Yes, well let's dispense with the formalities. I should be grateful for some sort of garment before I venture forth from this sarcophagus. I should not like to embarrass the lady.

MRS BUCKINGHAM: My name is Clara. Clara Buckingham.

ALAMIS-TAKO: May I call you Clara?

MRS BUCKINGHAM: Delighted, Count.

PONNONNER: Just give me a moment. I'll fetch a dressing gown from next door. *(retreating)* A moment. Just a moment.

ALAMIS-TAKO: Well, what has modern America to offer that's any better than Egypt in the time of His Majesty Thutmose the Fourth?

WINTHROP: Good heavens, Count, the world has advanced in every sort of direction in the past three thousand years. I mean, you should see our architecture. The New York City Hall is a wonder to behold.

ALAMIS-TAKO: Don't talk to me of architecture. I trust the pyramids that we constructed have stood the test of time. To say nothing of our palaces and sculpture. They still exist, I hope?

GLIDDON: Indeed some do, Count. And very magnificent they are.

ALAMIS-TAKO: Precisely.

PONNONNER: (*advancing*) Here we are, Count. Here we are. My best dressing gown. Allow me to assist you.

WINTHROP: And me. Just slip your arm in here, Count. And the other one. There.

ALAMIS-TAKO: Now a hand, gentlemen if you please, to get me off this table. (*effort*) I'm afraid I'll be rather unsteady on my feet for a while.

(MOVEMENT. CHAIR SCRAPES ON FLOOR)

MRS BUCKINGHAM: This chair, Count Alamis. Here.

ALAMIS-TAKO: Thank you, Clara. You're very kind. I must say this robe is very splendid, Professor... er. I'm sorry. Did you give me your name?

PONNONNER: Ponnonner. It's Ponnonner.

ALAMIS-TAKO: Professor Ponsonner. I feel very regal.

PONNONNER: It's a dressing gown made from Chinese silk. I'm

afraid I rather indulged myself when I made the purchase.

ALAMIS-TAKO: Silk from China. Yes, we had started using silk in my time.

GLIDDON: Now, Count, you won't try to maintain that the world hasn't moved forward in the past three thousand years?

ALAMIS-TAKO: I have no doubt there have been inventions of all sorts. But have human beings themselves improved? Are they any better now than they were three thousand years ago?

WINTHROP: Good question.

ALAMIS-TAKO: Tell me, what is your year, using your reckoning?

GLIDDON: It's 1845.

ALAMIS-TAKO: So you date your civilization from something that happened 18-hundred and forty-five years ago. I don't care what that was. It doesn't matter.

MRS BUCKINGHAM: It does to us.

ALAMIS-TAKO: And then you count backwards from that event. How far back do you count to reach my time?

GLIDDON: Fourteen hundred years. We all wonder what ordinary daily life was like, then?

ALAMIS-TAKO: For those of rank, very pleasant indeed. In fact we thought life so perfect, that we imagined the afterlife would be an eternal continuation of life on earth. Our life consisted of sports and games of all types, reading – oh, we read a great deal – spending time with our friends and family. And our festivals, of course

PONNONNER: Very pleasant.

ALAMIS-TAKO: Horses played a great part in our life. Every noble household had large stables. We tamed thousands of horses and used them to move our carts and chariots. Our armies were conveyed from place to place by them. Is America in 1845 any different?

PONNONNER: You have a point there, Count. We haven't advanced very much in the past three thousand years. We, too, use horses to draw our many vehicles. But we also use steam to pull some vehicles along on rails.

ALAMIS-TAKO: You use steam? We used slaves. Our world was made delightful for us by the huge number of slaves we used. They attended to our every need – and they built those pyramids that you tell me still exist. Does your world use slaves?

MRS BUCKINGHAM: Count, to our eternal shame it does. You're right. We have advanced not an inch, in that respect. Slavery is denounced across the civilized world – and yet it persists right here, in America.

WINTHROP: But rest assured, Count Alamis, we shall get rid of it before many more years have passed. That is certain.

ALAMIS-TAKO: I trust you have other systems of manpower to put in their place.

WINTHROP: The steam engine is our future, Count. Even some of our ships are driven by steam. It's just like magic.

ALAMIS-TAKO: Spare me the details, I beg. But since you mention the word magic, there is one aspect of our life I failed to mention. Our magicians. They were very highly regarded, our magicians. Magic proved that the gods existed. The god Heka endowed certain favoured acolytes with some of his powers, and we mere mortals were able to watch and marvel.

MRS BUCKINGHAM: What wonders did they perform. Count? Do tell us.

ALAMIS-TAKO: You mustn't imagine conjuring tricks, Clara. No, Heka magic filled every part of our lives. From the ancient books of magic our priests learned how to bring wax animals to life, or even roll back the waters of a lake. It was their magic rituals that protected the Pharaoh. The followers of Sekhment, the fearsome goddess of plague, were experts in the magic of healing.

PONNONNER: What about curses, Count? What about the use of magic to wreak death and destruction on your enemies?

ALAMIS-TAKO: Oh yes, professor. We high-ranking officers of the state certainly practised destructive magic. The names of foreign enemies and Egyptian traitors were inscribed on clay pots, or tablets, or figurines, and these objects were then burned, broken, or buried in cemeteries. We knew that this would weaken or destroy the enemy.

GLIDDON: So you yourself practised magic?

ALAMIS-TAKO: Indeed we did. As soon as any of us attained high office, we were instructed in the ancient art by our priests and priestesses. It was one way in which we protected our divine ruler.

GLIDDON: Do you still retain those powers?

ALAMIS-TAKO: I see no reason why not.

GLIDDON: Could you give us a demonstration?

MRS BUCKINGHAM: A small demonstration, Count Alamis, if you don't mind. Nothing too dramatic.

ALAMIS-TAKO: I would not alarm you for the world, Clara. Let me see... Professor Ponnoner, would you mind seating yourself here. Opposite me.

PONNONNER: Certainly. Like this?

ALAMIS-TAKO: Relax, professor. Lean back a little. Excellent. Now everybody, please don't be alarmed by the incantation I'm about to utter. The language in which it is spoken is quite immaterial, so I will render it in the English tongue. Now silence please, while I bend my mind... bend my mind... *(low and mysterious)* Oh you Soul, behold I have come so that I may see you. I have opened up every path in the sky and on earth. Drive away darkness, for I am the well-beloved son of my father Osiris. Oh all you gods and all you spirits, prepare a path for me. And lift ... lift...

(MUSIC - SLOWLY RISING SCALES FROM LOW START)

PONNONNER: Hang on! What's happening?

WINTHROP: You're rising. You're off the floor.

GLIDDON: You and the chair.

PONNONNER: Be careful, Count. I'm likely to slip and hurt myself.

MRS BUCKINGHAM: Professor – professor. Watch out. Your head's about to hit the ceiling.

(STOP MUSIC)

PONNONNER: *(remote)* Let me down. Let me down, I say.

ALAMIS-TAKO: Of course. Hold tight. I'll be as gentle as I can.

(MUSIC. QUICK GLISSANDO OF SCALES FROM HIGH TO LOW. CRASH OF CHAIR ON THE FLOOR)

536

PONNONNER: Ow! You call that gentle?

WINTHROP: What were those words you uttered?

ALAMIS-TAKO: The incantation? Spell, I suppose you'd call it. Those words are very ancient. They are inscribed in the Book of the Dead.

GLIDDON: Levitation. Not so very uncommon, I believe. The Hindus specialise in it.

ALAMIS-TAKO: How do they achieve it?

GLIDDON: I don't know.

ALAMIS-TAKO: Can you do it?

GLIDDON: Certainly not. I don't say that I'm not impressed, Count. I merely observe that others claim to achieve the same effect. So it is not magic exclusive to ancient Egypt.

ALAMIS-TAKO: What if I were to make you all disappear?

MRS BUCKINGHAM: Disappear? But where to, Count? Where would you send us?

ALAMIS-TAKO: Don't be alarmed, Clara. I'd merely despatch you all back to your homes. I'd simply empty this room and send you back to where you were a few hours ago.

WINTHROP: You could do that?

ALAMIS-TAKO:	Certainly. And I gather from your reaction that this art has not survived the centuries. No group or religion possesses it?
GLIDDON:	No, Count. Some claim to possess the art of transportation, but it has never been convincingly demonstrated.
ALAMIS-TAKO:	Then would you like me to manifest this aspect of our magic?
MRS BUCKINGHAM:	I'm … I'm not too sure. Will we be in any danger?
ALAMIS-TAKO:	Not in the least, Clara, I do assure you. One minute you will be here, the next you will find yourself in the comfort of your home.
WINTHROP:	This is too kind an offer for us to refuse, Count Alamis. It would be a privilege to see at first hand this aspect of the ancient Egyptian world.
PONNONNER:	Oh, I do agree, Winthrop. How about you, Gliddon?
GLIDDON:	Yes, I suppose so.
PONNONNER:	Mrs Buckingham?
MRS BUCKINGHAM:	I have Count Alamis's word that no harm will befall us. That is good enough for me.
WINTHROP:	We are of one mind, Count. We would be honoured to have a demonstration of these magic powers.

ALAMIS-TAKO: Very well. May I ask you all to take a seat. That's right. Now relax – and look at me. But no interruptions, please. Ready? *(low, mysterious)* May I have power in my heart, may I have power in my arms, my legs, my mouth. May I have power over water … air … men who would harm me … women who would harm me… those who would give orders to harm me upon earth. Isis, Osiris, seed of eternity. Ra – fill me with the power. The power.

(ELECTRONIC EFFECT TO INDICATE MAGIC TAKING PLACE. WHOOSHING MAYBE MIXED WITH TINKLING? CUT EFFECT AND FADE UP MUSIC. HOLD A LITTLE. FADE DOWN, MIX WITH OPENING OF NEXT SPEECH, THEN OUT)

WINTHROP: And there I was, back in bed, just as Count Alamis had told us. I glanced at my bedside clock. It was a few minutes short of seven. I decided that I must commit to paper the astounding events of the night, and as soon as possible, while they were still fresh in in my mind. I slipped into my dressing gown and hurried downstairs. I sat at my desk and began to write the account to which you have been listening.

(TAPPING AT DOOR. REPEATED)

MRS ROBERTS: *(remote, calling)* Mr Winthrop. Mr Winthrop, sir.

WINTHROP: *(calling)* Oh, do go away, Mrs Roberts. That's the third time I've told you. You're interrupting my train of thought.

539

MRS ROBERTS: But Mr Winthrop, it's half after nine.

(DOOR OPENS)

(*closer*) It's way past breakfast time. Good grief, Mr Winthrop, you're in your dressing gown. Have you not bathed, sir?

WINTHROP: I have not, Mrs Roberts. Nor do I intend to until I have finished this task. And I want no breakfast

MRS ROBERTS: Are you unwell, sir?

WINTHROP: I am perfectly well, Mrs Roberts. It's just that I have had a most disturbing night, and I wish to record what occurred.

MRS ROBERTS: I knew it. I just knew it.

WINTHROP: You knew what, Mrs Roberts? Pray explain yourself.

MRS ROBERTS: It was that second portion of Welsh Rarebit. I had a feeling in my bones that that was a mistake. All that cheese, sir. It was too much for your poor stomach. It was my cooking that kept you up all night. You probably had terrible dreams.

WINTHROP: Nothing of the sort, Mrs Roberts. I was woken up by Professor Ponnonner in the early hours, and went round to his house. That's where I spent most of the night – with him and some friends.

MRS ROBERTS: I didn't hear you go out, sir. Nor your return.

WINTHROP: No. There's a reason for that.

(HALF CHIME ON CLOCK)

Well, I'd best leave writing my account for the moment, and get washed and dressed.

MRS ROBERTS: I really think it would be best, sir. And for breakfast, Mr Winthrop. Would you fancy some pancakes?

WINTHROP: I surely would. After breakfast I must go round to Professor Ponnoner to discuss the events of last night. I wonder what's become of the Count?

MRS ROBERTS: The Count? Why, did you meet a member of the aristocracy last night?

WINTHROP: A very ancient aristocracy, Mrs Roberts. Very ancient indeed.

MRS ROBERTS: How thrilling, sir. What is his name?

WINTHROP: It's very long and complicated. We called him Count Alamis for short. Come over here, Mrs Roberts. I'll write it out for you. Here… A.L.L.A.M.I.S.T.A.K.E.O. Alamis –Takeo.

MRS ROBERTS: But sir.

WINTHROP: Yes?

MRS ROBERTS: Can you not see what you've spelled out?

WINTHROP: The Count's name, Mrs Roberts. Alamis-Takeo. It's not English.

MRS ROBERTS: Oh, but it is, sir. Can't you see? What you've written is "All A Mistake O"

WINTHROP: All a mistake? Oh! Oh dear! Have we all been the subject of some practical joke? Some prank? All of us – Ponnonner, Gliddon, Mrs Buckingham and I? I was with them for most of the night – and that Egyptian Mummy. He wanted us to call him Count. "All a mistake"? I must get to Professor Ponnoner as soon as possible. Out of my way, Mrs Roberts.

MRS ROBERTS: Oh sir, sir, please wait a moment. Do think. Are you quite certain that you left the house last night?

WINTHROP: Of course I did. I remember every detail. It's all here – I've written a complete account.

MRS ROBERTS: Mr Winthrop, I beg you. Everything you remember – did it really happen? Or might it have been a particularly vivid dream? All that Welsh Rarebit you took – all that cheese. Cheese last thing at night – it's well known for bringing on that sort of thing.

WINTHROP: But it's all so clear, Mrs Roberts, Such detail. And you're telling me that I came up with this name in my dream?

MRS ROBERTS: It must have been your own mind telling you that it was all a fantasy. Please think, Mr Winthrop. Suppose you visit Professor Ponnonner and start talking about what you think happened last night, and he denies ever coming to the house and meeting this Count, especially with that name. Would it not be a little … embarrassing?

WINTHROP: Er… Aah. I think you may have a point, Mrs Roberts. Yes, I'll go about things in a more circumspect way. I'll go round to the museum and see if their Mummy is the one they've always had. I'm beginning to suspect that it is. Meanwhile, I think I'll just lock this manuscript

(DESK DRAWER OPENS, THEN CLOSES AND KEY TURNED IN LOCK)

safely away, in here. One day, Mrs Roberts, I will allow you to read it.

(FADE MERRY MUSIC BENEATH FOLLOWING, PRE-TIMED TO END AFTER CLOSING ANNOUNCEMENT)

And the next time you decide to indulge me with your wonderful Welsh Rarebit, please make sure that it's not on the supper menu.

MRS ROBERTS:　　What's more, sir, I'll serve you one portion, and not a mouthful more.

WINTHROP:　　　} *(both burst out laughing)*
MRS ROBERTS:　　}

(UP MUSIC. FADE LAUGHTER. CLOSING ANNOUNCEMENT. UP MUSIC TO END)

RIDERS OF THE
PURPLE SAGE

A PLAY FOR RADIO
BY NEVILLE TELLER
INSPIRED BY THE NOVEL
BY ZANE GRAY

Running time 60'

SCHEDULED FOR BROADCAST
ACROSS THE USA DURING 2021
IN A PRODUCTION BY SHOESTRING
RADIO THEATRE, SAN FRANCISCO

MAIN CHARACTERS

MINOR PARTS WITH JUST ONE SCENE OR ONE SPEECH
ARE EASILY DUPLICATED OR TRIPLICATED

MALE

ZANE	Zane Gray the author. Acts as occasional narrator
TULL	The villain. Corrupt, self-serving
DYER	Tull's side kick. Becoming Judge changes him for the better
VENTERS	Early-30s. Good-natured, but Tull's victim
LASSITER	40s. Tough seasoned gunman, with generous instincts
ZEB	Jane's ranch hand and rider. Loyal to the core

FEMALE

JANE	Early 30s. Sweet natured, but strongly principled
BESS	Aged 19. Tough, but loving nature

MINOR CHARACTERS

MALE

CASEY   Cowhand. 2 speeches. Part 1 only.

OLDRING   Rustler. I scene. Part 1 only

MARSHAL   Clerk of the court. I scene. Part 2 only

BLAKE   Prosecuting attorney. I scene. Part 2 only

PREACHER   Clergyman. 1 scene. Part 2 only

FEMALE

MARTHA   Jane's aunt. 1 scene. Part 1 only

MARYLOU   Bess's "Ma". 2 speeches. Part 2 only.

(FULL UP LOLLOPING COWBOY MELODY. DOWN FOR OPENING ANNOUNCEMENT. UP MUSIC. DOWN FOR FOLLOWING. LOSE BENEATH)

ZANE: (*as narrator*); Gather round, folks. I guess you all know there was a time, way back around the 1880s, when the West was just a vast cattle rearing empire, and life was a whole lot rougher and tougher than it is today. Ordinary decent folk were often the victims of ruthless types – men out to make themselves rich, no matter what – who rode roughshod over law and order, and often over their womenfolk as well. Sometimes, through a mixture of bribery and fear, they managed to manoeuvre themselves into a position of power. One such was Jacob Tull – Sheriff Tull of Cottonwood, Utah – who suddenly found himself the undisputed boss of the whole county. This is how it all began...

(EDGE OUT. EDGE IN)

TULL: OK Dyer, with old man Withersteen in his coffin, that leaves me the big bug in this county. And don't you forget it.

DYER: But that's some act you have to follow, Sheriff. Admit it. The old man ran Cottonwood for nigh on thirty years. He *was* Cottonwood.

TULL: And now he's history.

DYER: But not forgotten. He was well liked.

TULL: Too well liked, Dyer. I don't aim to get myself liked.

DYER: What do you aim to do, Tull?

TULL: Get myself rich. And I reckon you and the rest of the boys won't do too badly neither.

DYER: Sounds all right to me.

TULL: First thing is to get you elected Judge.

DYER: What – take over from Withersteen? Me? Never.

TULL: It'll be a walkover. We'll hold the election next week. Monday, I think. No one's going to run against you. We'll get the boys to make sure of that. You'll get in unopposed.

DYER: But what's that in aid of, Sheriff?

TULL: It's so we'll have the law on our side. You up there playing Your Honour, and some of the boys acting as the jury, I reckon there's nobody going to have a leg to stand on. We'll be the law. We won't be looking over our shoulder all the time wondering what old man Withersteen might do. He's dead and gone – and good riddance.

DYER: So what you going to do about that great ranch of his and those thousands of heads of cattle? To say nothing of his daughter. She owns it all now.

TULL: Oh that's simple, Dyer. I'm going to marry Miss Jane Withersteen and take over the lot. Once she's my wife, her property becomes mine.

DYER: But ain't she sweet on that young feller Venters? After we rustled that herd of his and burned down his ranch-house, she took him in – made him foreman

TULL: Too soft-hearted by half, that girl. Well, since that little operation of ours didn't run Venters out of town, let's finish the job. Gather six of the boys. Meantime I need some youngster to ride out to Withersteen House with a message. Come on, Dyer. Get a wiggle on.

DYER: (*retreating*) Right away, Tull. I'm on to it.

(UP URGENT MUSIC SUGGESTING HORSE'S HOOVES AT A GALLOP. HOLD A LITTLE. DOWN FOR FOLLOWING, AND THEN OUT. OPEN AIR)

JANE: (*calling*) Venters! Just a minute. Over here!

VENTERS:	*(calling, approaching)* Sure thing, Miss Withersteen. What's the problem?
JANE:	This note, Venters. It's from Sheriff Tull. He says he'll be here with a posse directly. He's aiming to arrest you.
VENTERS:	Arrest me? What for?
JANE:	He doesn't say. But I reckon it's some sort of mistake. You can't have done anything – you haven't left the ranch this past week. I'll tell him as much. Mr Tull's a reasonable man.
	(APPROACHING HORSES. THEY PULL UP BENEATH FOLLOWING. KEEP HORSES SNORTING, STAMPING, BENEATH FOLLOWING SCENE)
VENTERS:	You think so, Miss Jane? Never struck me that way.
TULL:	*(calling)* Good afternoon, ma'am. Did you get my message?
JANE:	I sure did, Sheriff. You want to arrest Mr Venters here?
TULL:	That's why I'm here, ma'am. Thought it only courtesy to give you fair warning. *(calls)* Casey, lasso him.
JANE:	Hang fire, Mr Tull. What's he accused of?

TULL: He knows darn well. There was a shooting fray in the town last night, and he was right in the middle of it. I have eye witnesses saw him smash his way through the hardware store. Not sure he didn't lift a good few tools as well.

JANE: Sheriff, whoever they saw, they certainly did not see Mr Venters. He was here in Withersteen House all evening.

TULL: Here in the house? With you? *(suggestive)* Oh, was he?

JANE: Together with my aunt Martha, the servants, and a couple of boys from the ranch-house. He certainly was.

TULL: Why on earth are you defending him, Miss Withersteen?

JANE: Because he's innocent. And neither is he a roughneck. I gave him shelter a few weeks back, after his herd was rustled and his house burned down. Since then he's been acting foreman for me. I couldn't have a better man.

TULL: You talk as if you're in love with the feller.

JANE: My feelings are my business, Sheriff.

TULL: And my business is catching criminals. *(calls)* Casey, rope him.

VENTERS:	*(shouts)* Hey! Stop that. Let me go.
TULL:	In deference to you, Miss Withersteen, I'll give this deadbeat one chance. Venters, will you leave Utah at once and forever?
VENTERS:	Dammit, why should I?
TULL:	Because if you don't, I wouldn't give much for your chances here in Cottonwood.
VENTERS:	I'm pretty much ruined already. A year ago I had horses and cattle. I had land and a ranch-house. Look at me now.
TULL:	Will you leave Utah?
VENTERS:	I know what it is. It galls you, the idea of beautiful, wealthy Miss Jane Withersteen offering a little kindness to someone down on his luck. I reckon you have other plans for her. And Withersteen House. And seven thousand head of cattle.
TULL:	Shut your mouth! One last time – will you leave Utah?
VENTERS:	I will not.
TULL:	Then I'll have you whipped to within an inch of your life. Here and now. *(calls)* Drag him over here, boys.

JANE: Oh, Mr Tull. You won't do that. You couldn't.

TULL: Only doing my duty, ma'am. Miss Jane, your father left you wealth and power. It's turned your head. You and Venters – it's all over. He's going to be whipped – and then he's leaving Utah. For good. Over here, boys.

VENTERS: *(struggles, protests)*

CASEY: *(shouts).* Look, Sherriff. Over there. A rider. Coming out of the sage.

TULL: *(calls)* Who is it? Do you know him, Casey? Does anyone know him?

CASEY: *(approaching)* He's come from far, that's certain. Look at the dust and grime on that black leather. *(whispers)* Watch out, Sheriff – he packs two black-butted guns – low down. Look. They're hard to see akin them black chaps.

(HORSE APPROACHES. STOPS. SOUNDS OF DESCENDING)

TULL: Fellers, careful now about movin' your hands. *(calls)* Hello, stranger.

LASSITER: Evening, ma'am. You Miss Jane Withersteen?

JANE: I am.

LASSITER: May I water my horse?

JANE:	Most certainly. There's the trough. And you're welcome to come into the house for something to eat and drink yourself.
LASSITER:	That's mighty generous of you ma'am, but I've no need.

(SOUNDS OF DISMOUNTING)

JANE:	Here – I'll take him to the water. *(retreating)* Come on, boy.

(HORSE MOVING)

LASSITER:	I seem to have kind of hindered something. Why's that young feller all bound up? What's he done?
JANE:	*(remote, calling)* Nothing. He's innocent. He's an honest man.
LASSITER:	Then why's he tied up like that?
JANE:	*(remote, calling)* Why not ask him?
TULL:	*(calls)* Stranger, this is none of your mix. Water your horse and be on your way.
LASSITER:	Easy, easy Sheriff. I ain't interfering – yet. But I seem to have stumbled into a queer deal. Seven of you packing guns, a young feller roped up, and a woman who swears by his honesty. Odd, ain't it?

TULL: Odd or not, it's none of your business.

LASSITER: Where I was raised, a woman's word was law. I ain't quite outgrowed that yet. Speak up, young man. What you done to be roped that way?

VENTERS: I've done no wrong. It's not long since my cattle were rustled and my ranch house burned to the ground. Miss Withersteen gave me shelter. I reckon that's not to Sheriff Tull's liking. So he's cooked up some false charge against me.

LASSITER: *(calls)* Ma'am, is it true – what he says?

JANE: *(approaching)* Perfectly true. These men intend to whip him – and you know what that means, here in Utah. Can you do nothing to save him?

TULL: *(calls)* Come on men, let's get on with it.

LASSITER: Sheriff, unrope him. There'll be no whipping here today.

TULL: What? He's my prisoner.

LASSITER: Unrope him.

TULL: Men, get him up on a horse. I'm taking him into town.

LASSITER: The young man stays here.

TULL: Who says so. We're seven here. Who are you?

VENTERS: *(calls)* Sheriff, I know who he is! It's just come to me. That's Lassiter. You're the gunman Lassiter, ain't you?

LASSITER: Lassiter's my name.

TULL: *(whispers, fearful)* Lassiter? My good Lord. *(calls)* Casey ... men ... On our way. *(calls, retreating)* I'm sheriff in this here county. You ain't heard the last of this.

> **(HORSES HOOVES MOVE OFF, THEN SPEED UP. FADE. FULL UP. DINING ROOM. CROCKERY, CUTLERY)**

LASSITER: *(eating)* Well, I reckon that's the best meal I've swallowed in many a day.

JANE: *(eating)* I saw you were hungry from the start.

VENTERS: *(eating)* Have you come a long way today, Lassiter?

LASSITER: I reckon I have.

JANE: And how come you ended up at Withersteen House?

LASSITER: Here's the truth, ma'am. I've been hunting all over southern Utah and Nevada for... Well, for something. And through your name I learned where to find it. It's right here in Cottonwood.

VENTERS: Yes, you did know Miss Withersteen's name when you first spoke. How come?

LASSITER: Some folks in a village about fifty miles from here – Glaze, I think it's called...

JANE: Yes, Glaze.

LASSITER: They said you'd be able to tell me where to find it.

JANE: Find what, Lassiter? What are you looking for?

LASSITER: Well, I'll tell you. Milly Erne's grave.

JANE: Milly Erne? What do you know of Milly Erne? She was my best-beloved friend.

LASSITER: That's what they said.

JANE: She died in my arms. What were you to her?

LASSITER: Did I claim to be anything? I just happen to know relatives who've long wanted to know where she's buried.

JANE: Relatives? She never spoke of relatives to me. Parents dead. A brother dead, shot in Texas. But yes, Milly Erne's grave is on my property – in a secret burying ground.

LASSITER: Will you take me there? I've been searching for it a fair while.

JANE: I reckon there's no harm in that. We'll go tomorrow.

(CHAIR SCRAPES ON WOODEN FLOOR. LASSITER STANDS)

LASSITER: In that case, I'll be saying goodnight. I'll be back in the morning.

JANE: Will you not stay – sleep under my roof?

LASSITER: No, ma'am, and thanks again. I never sleep indoors. *(retreating)* No, I'll go to the sage.

(DOOR OPENS)

(remote) Goodnight, ma'am.

(DOOR CLOSES)

VENTERS: Jane, I can't stay here. Who knows what Tull will do next? You'll be much safer with me out of the house. Give me my guns. I need them.

JANE: You're too fierce-blooded by half, Bern. You can't go round killing people.

VENTERS: That's a lesson you need to teach Sheriff Tull. What state do you think I'd be in now, if Lassiter hadn't come by? I need my guns. Jane. I was quite content to give them to you for safe keeping. But now I really need them.

JANE: OK, OK. I'll fetch them.

VENTERS: Don't worry – I'm not going out to murder Tull and his men. I'll try to avoid them. But I can't stay here.

JANE: Bern.

VENTERS: I can't. Tull is out to get me – he wants me out of Cottonwood, alive or dead. Don't reckon he cares which. If it weren't for Lassiter…

JANE: Bern, who is Lassiter? He's only a name to me – a terrible name. Too quick to shoot. Heaven knows how many he's gunned down.

VENTERS: I don't know that much about him – where he came from, all that. Nobody does. Folks know what you know. He's a gunman unmatched anywhere with a Colt for fast shooting and plumb on the target every time. As soon as I realized who he was, I yelled his name. I honestly believe that saved Tull's life. Perhaps his men as well. He could have downed all seven in as many seconds. Did you note he talks a bit like a Texan – like Milly Erne?

JANE: I did. And how strange he knows of her. She lived here twelve full years, and been dead for two. Well, I'll get your guns. I've kept them safe – and you with them, I reckon. Where will you sleep?

VENTERS:	Out in the sage, like Lassiter. I'll be back tomorrow. Perhaps I'll come with you and Lassiter to visit Milly Erne's grave.
	(EDGE OUT. MIX TO MUSIC. HOLD A LITTLE. DOWN AND OUT UNDER FOLLOWING. OPEN AIR)
VENTERS:	(*remote – shouting*) Hi. Hi there. That you, Lassiter?
LASSITER:	(*calling*) Sure thing. You sleep under the stars, last night?
VENTERS:	(*approaching*) That I did. Reckoned it'd be safer for Miss Jane if I were out of the house.
LASSITER:	Did anything come off after I left you?
VENTERS:	Well I snuck back into town and took a look around. You won't know about this, but there's a known rustler hanging about these parts. Name of Oldring.
LASSITER:	Oldring? Oh, his name's well known all over Utah.
VENTERS:	Well, no-one's found out what he does with the cattle him and his men steal. The herds simply vanish.
LASSITER:	That's what he's known for – holing in canyons, him and his troop, and leaving no trace. How big's his crowd, Venters?

VENTERS: About a dozen. One of them's always masked. I saw the lot of them ride through Cottonwood last night with muffled hooves. Reckon they were on some secret mission. Didn't want folks to know they were in town.

LASSITER: That don't bode no good. Oldring's got a high hand here, I reckon. Me and Oldring weren't exactly strangers some years back, when he drove cattle at the head of the Rio Virgin. He got harassed there, so now he's moved to Cottonwood.

VENTERS: Can't help wondering what he and his troop were doing in town last night.

(FADE OUT. FULL UP. INTERIOR)

TULL: Come in, Oldring. Make yourself at home. What you done with your boys?

OLDRING: They're round the back, in your stables. They'll be fine. They're not short of beer.

DYER: And what'll you take, Oldring? We're on fire water here.

OLDRING: Whiskey'll suit me fine.

(GLASS CHINKING. POURING)

Thanks, Dyer. (*sips*). Now, what am I here for?

TULL: Your special skills, Oldring.

OLDRING: Ha. They don't come cheap, Sheriff.

TULL: You'll get your price. On top of what you'll make from the cattle.

OLDRING: OK. So what are you after?

TULL: That red herd of Jane Withersteen's. She's a mite too independent minded, at the moment. She needs a lesson,

OLDRING: That's twenty-five hundred head of cattle, Tull – and they're pretty heavily guarded. I had my eye on that herd some months ago. Couldn't get past her posse.

DYER: Oh, we know all about her troop of cowboys. There's only ten of them – five on in the day, five at night.

TULL: And every man has his price, Oldring.

OLDRING: Ain't that the truth. Right, so when do you want this deal to go through?

TULL: Dawn tomorrow. Now you *will* whisk those cattle away, like you always do?

OLDRING: Sure thing, Sheriff. They'll vanish off the face of the earth.

DYER: Where the devil do you stash them? You must tell us your secret one day.

OLDRING: Wouldn't you like to know.

TULL: }
DYER: } *(laugh)*
OLDRING: }

(FADE OUT. FULL UP. EXTERIOR)

LASSITER: Come on, Venters. Let's get down to the House and pick up Miss Withersteen. . I'm mighty anxious to see Milly Erne's grave. Why don't you tell me Milly Erne's story as we go?

(MOVEMENT, WALKING ON PEBBLE STONES BENEATH THE FOLLOWING)

VENTERS: I'll tell you what I know – and most of it happened long before I arrived in Cottonwood. By the time I showed up, Milly Erne had been here three years or so. She was a slip of a thing, but she came with a baby girl. She adored that child. For a time Millie took over the schoolroom, but I reckon word got out what it was she was teaching – and it wasn't to the liking of Sheriff Tull. She was hot on law and order, and freedom and justice, and the American constitution and such like. She reckoned some of the big boys in Cottonwood had things too much their own way. One or two of them tackled her about it, but that didn't stop her. And there was also some talk that one of them took more than a passing interest in her. It remained a rumour, for not a word of that ever passed her lips. Then one day her little girl disappeared.

LASSITER: What? You don't say.

VENTERS: She was only four. Old man Withersteen ordered a search and an enquiry. No trace of the child was found – certainly no body. All they came up with was that the little girl was lost. Most of the folks I know reckoned she'd been stolen. But that was the end of Milly – it wrecked her. She kept hoping, but her life drained away. I can see her now. A frail thing, and ashen looking, but those eyes of hers. They still haunt me. She had one real friend – Jane Withersteen. But Miss Jane could do nothing to stop Milly fading away. She died, still a young woman.

(EDGE OUT. FADE IN. INTERIOR)

JANE: Yes, Aunt Martha, I took both of them there. I showed them Millie's grave.

MARTHA: But I thought that was your special place, Jane dear. *I've* never seen it.

JANE: I'm sorry, Auntie. It always has been very special. I loved Milly so dearly.

MARTHA: And so did I, my dear.

JANE: To see her sink like that. She died slowly, day by day, before my eyes

MARTHA: That child was all Milly had in this world. I don't know what her real story was, but she came here like a waif or stray. She lived for that little girl. And then to have her snatched away like that… It was too cruel. How did you choose her burial place?

JANE: The day she died I went way up into the sage, and found just the right spot. One of my ranch hands dug the grave. As to the internment, I paid the mortician down in Cottonwood – old Abe Tyler. He passed on five years since. He arranged everything.

MARTHA: And the parson?

JANE: Oh, there was no service.

MARTHA: Jane!

JANE: It was impossible, Aunt Martha. There was just me and old Abe. He brought the coffin over to the House in a donkey cart, and then we strapped up a horse and led him up to the spot.

MARTHA: But your father? How could you do all that without him knowing?

JANE: Oh he knew all about it. I had to ask for his help with the death certificate and all the documents. He fixed everything. After all, he was Cottonwood's judge. Nobody asked too many questions. You see, it was no surprise, her death. Most folks had seen the way Milly was going. As for Sheriff Tull, he was delighted. She'd been a thorn in his flesh for years.

MARTHA: So now she lies up there, in the sage.

JANE: I *will* take you up there, Aunt Martha, if you really want to see it. It's the most peaceful place on earth. There's no sign of the cottonwoods or the alfalfa fields. It's just gray slopes tinged with purple stretching away to the horizon, with the sage waving in the wind.

MARTHA: And Lassiter scoured two states just to find it.

JANE: Which is why I took him up there. He stayed a long time. That grave seemed to mean a great deal to him.

MARTHA: Did it? Now I wonder why.

(MUSIC. HOLD A LITTLE. CROSSFADE TO GALLOPING HORSE'S HOOVES. THEY STOP. MUSIC OUT UNDER FOLLOWING. EXTERIOR)

ZEB: (*calling*) Miss Withersteen! Miss Withersteen!

JANE: What is it, Zeb? What's happened? Good grief, you're bleeding. You've been shot.

ZEB: (*approaching*) Nothing much, ma'am. I got a nick on the shoulder. This ain't all blood. The horse has been throwing lather.

JANE: What's happened, Zeb?

ZEB: The worst. Rustlers have sloped off with the red herd.

JANE: What – all of them?

ZEB: All twenty-five hundred.

JANE: But where were my riders? Weren't they out there, guarding them?

ZEB: That's just it, ma'am. There was no sign of them. I was alone all night with the herd. At daylight the rustlers rode down. As soon as they saw me they began shooting. Then they chased me hard and far, burning powder all the time. But I got away.

JANE: Thank heaven for that. Come back to the house. That wound needs attending to.

(FADE OUT. FADE IN. INTERIOR)

VENTERS: It's Oldring, Jane. It has to be. There's no-one else could make off with a herd that large.

JANE: But what I can't understand is what happened to my riders? Do you think they've been set upon by Oldring's men? Killed?

ZEB: Can't say, ma'am. All I know is they was nowhere to be seen.

JANE: Now, this will sting. Hold tight, Zeb.

ZEB: Ouch!

VENTERS: It's for your own good. That'll stop it becoming infected.

ZEB: (*in pain*) Yes, sir, Mr Venters.

VENTERS: There's an unseen hand behind all this, Jane. You remember what I said. Someone doesn't like you taking me in. Someone wants to give you a warning.

JANE: Tull? Oh, no. Impossible.

VENTERS: I hope so. But we're not going to take this lying down. Doggone it, those cattle can't be all that far away. Jane, I'm going to find out where Oldring drives the herd.

JANE: For years my riders have trailed the tracks of stolen cattle. They get as far as Deception Pass, but Odring drives them down into the network of deceiving canyons, and then somewhere far to the north or east. But don't go now, Bern. Don't risk it now – not with his men in such a shooting mood.

VENTERS: I'm going. I know Deception Pass of old. I'll get through it. I'll find that herd.

ZEB: Then you'll need a hoss that can run, Mr Venters. Miss Withersteen, make him take a fast hoss, or don't let him go.

JANE: You're right. He must have a horse that can't be caught. Which one Zeb?

VENTERS: My own mare will do. I'm not having you risk losing one of your favorites.

JANE: What about Wrangle? What do you think, Zeb?

ZEB: That's the one, Miss Jane. He can certainly outrun Night, and I saw him beat Black Star by a head over a mile run.

JANE: Then if you must go, Bern, you take Wrangle. Ask Jerd for anything you need. And be watchful. Be careful. And Bern...

VENTERS: What, Jane?

JANE: God speed you.

(COWBOY MUSIC. HOLD A LITTLE. DOWN FOR, AND OUT UNDER THE FOLLOWING. TWO SHEEP DOGS BARKING)

ZANE: (*as narrator*) Now I haven't made mention of Venters's two dogs before, but as he turned Wrangle toward the sage, there they were, trotting beside him. He called them Ring and Whitie. They were sheep dogs – half collie, half deerhounds – superb in build, perfectly trained. After a bit, Ring loped into the lead and Whitie loped in the rear, while Wrangle settled into an easy swinging canter. Venters, knowing that long miles stretched ahead, tried to make sense of everything.

VENTERS: (*close up*) What can Oldring do with twenty-five hundred head of cattle? He'd have to drive them out of Utah before selling them. Did he meet up with Tull last night? Are they in cahoots? It certainly looks like a plot to me. But Jane always gives Tull the benefit of any doubt. She so soft-hearted.

ZANE: (*as narrator*) Wrangle did the 25 miles to Deception Pass in three hours. The afternoon was well advanced when Venters struck the trail of the red herd. The crushed sage looked like the path of a monster snake. The cattle trail led to a concealed entrance into the pass, but Venters made for its head.

Now, folks, that opening into Deception Pass was one of the most remarkable sights in a country noted for vast slopes of sage, uplands insulated by gigantic red walls, and deep canyons. As you stood at the head, you looked down five hundred feet of sheer depth, and way below was the flat bottom of the valley. To reach it you had to make your way down the sheer drop of the trail. The steep slope meant nothing to the dogs, who bounded down. Wrangle snorted defiance rather than fear. Led by Venters, dislodging gravel, then stones, then boulders, sliding a bit here and there, finally Wrangle was down at the level floor of the pass.

By then dusk was upon them. Venters knew the way through a thicket of slender oaks to a spring, and there he made camp. Next morning he rode up the canyon for some five miles, with Ring and Whitie trotting behind.

(INTERIOR)

VENTERS: And that, Jane, was the furthest point I'd ever reached before. This was the real door to the mysteries of Deception Pass.

JANE: What did you find?

VENTERS: Well, the canyon walls seemed to grow higher and higher the further I traveled. In the end they towered hundreds of feet above me. Meanwhile, as I went forward sometimes the trail widened, sometimes it narrowed – and sometimes the canyon closed in so much I could almost touch both sides as I rode through.

JANE: Goodness. Lassiter told me that's just the kinda place Oldring used to favor back in the Rio Virgin. I reckon he's found some way through into somewhere hidden, but big enough for a herd. Did you find it, Bern?

VENTERS: All in good time. First the passageway began to grow very narrow indeed. I twisted and turned through it for more than a mile. Then, to my amazement, it suddenly opened out into a vast valley, miles long, all clothed in purple sage and enclosed in unscalable walls. But I saw that the canyon walls were pierced here and there by cracks and caves, so we followed them round. After a mile or two skirting the open valley we came upon an entrance much wider than the others. In we went, and it opened into a great oval area covered by plants of green and gray. All around it ran outgoing canyons. It was like the hub of a great wheel.

JANE: You paint such a vivid picture, Bern.

VENTERS: It's unforgettable. And then, Jane, only a few minutes later, as we made our way across the undergrowth, I ran across a broad cattle trail – and the tracks were fresh. What really surprised me was that they were wet.

JANE   Wet? Had it rained?

VENTERS: No, it hadn't. So it was obvious. The cattle – and I took it they were your cattle, Jane – had been driven through water.

                        (FADE IN)

ZANE: (*as narrator*) It was at that point that Venters heard Ring growling low. He looked out over all the greenery. A band of straggling horsemen were riding across the oval. He counted eight. He crouched down, holding the bristling dog, till they'd passed him by. Then he ventured to look. The rustlers were riding into one of the canyons, and he watched them disappear.

VENTERS: *(close)* That's Oldring's den. I've found it. But where has he driven the cattle?

ZANE: *(as narrator)* Then Whitie growled, his head turned away from where the rustlers had vanished. Venters wheeled. Two horsemen were within a hundred yards, coming straight at him. One, lagging behind the other, was Oldring's Masked Rider. The leading horse seemed to detect Venters's presence. It stopped short. The rider jerked a gun from its sheath and fired.

(RIFLE SHOT)

Like a flash the blue barrel of Venters's rifle gleamed level and he shot – twice

(TWO RiFLE SHOTS IN QUICK SUCCESSION)

The foremost rider toppled from his saddle, one foot caught in the stirrup. His horse snorted wildly and plunged away, dragging the rustler through the sage. The Masked Rider huddled over, slowly swaying from side to side, and then slipped out of the saddle.

VENTERS: I hurried over. The horseman lay in deep grass. I was filled with curiosity. This was Oldring's infamous unknown lieutenant – the rider whose face had never been seen. One thing that surprised me as I walked up was that the Masked Rider was unarmed. And there were no gun sheaths on the saddle. I bent down, and saw that rider was wounded, but still alive. Blood was seeping from where a bullet had penetrated the shoulder. I took hold of the mask and drew it off.

"Why," I thought, "it's only a boy."

Then I ripped open the blood-wet shirt.

(EXTERIOR)

VENTERS: A woman! I've killed a woman!

BESS: *(weak, in pain)* I ain't dead yet.

VENTERS: Thank the good Lord for that. But I reckon that bullet of mine got lodged in your shoulder. I'll have to get it out.

BESS: Not here. Get me away from here. When they find us gone, they'll come looking for us.

VENTERS: You don't want to go back to your gang – to Oldring?

BESS: I do not. It's a long story. I don't reckon I have the strength to tell it. Just get me away from here. Get me somewhere safe. Please.

(FADE OUT. FADE IN. EXTERIOR)

BESS: Where am I? What is this place?

VENTERS: It's somewhere you can rest up – somewhere no tracker on earth will find you. You passed out, so I set your horse free and went looking into some of those canyons down there. There's hundreds of them. Didn't like the look of most of them. But then I found one which led straight upward. I followed the trail for three hundred feet, right up into a whole mansion of caves carved out of the canyon walls. I settled on this one, and then I went back down and carried you up here – you don't weigh no more than a feather. Then I went down for my horse. That's him, over there. Wrangle's his name. Looks contented enough, don't he? Isn't this a cosy spot?

BESS: I reckon.

VENTERS: I better get working on that bullet.

BESS: You got medical gear? Bandages and the like?

VENTERS: Always carry supplies with me. I reckon we all learned a lot about treating bullet wounds during the Civil War. Got a regular first aid kit in this tin.

BESS: Oh, Lord.

VENTERS: You're not going to enjoy this, ... What's your name? I got to call you something.

BESS: Bess. My name's Bess.

VENTERS: Well, Bess, perhaps you better have a slug or two from my whiskey flask before I begin.

BESS: Perhaps I better. Well, hand it over then.

(FULL UP LOLLOPING COWBOY MELODY. DOWN FOR FOLLOWING AND LOSE BENEATH . EXTERIOR. OCCASIONAL SNORT FROM HORSE, BARKING FROM DOGS IN BACKGROUND)

VENTERS: There, now, Bess. The bullet's out. That wasn't too bad, was it?

BESS: Bad enough. The whiskey helped.

VENTERS: Well, you're nicely bound up, now. It'll heal in God's good time.

BESS: And I don't even know who shot me.

VENTERS: My name's Venters. Call me Bern. And it wasn't you I shot. I shot at a masked rider whose mate had just fired off at *me*. For all I knew, my next second could have been my last.

BESS: Fair enough. I forgive you.

VENTERS: But why are you riding along with Oldring's band of rustlers? Don't seem right somehow. And why masked? Come on, Bess.

BESS: It's a long story Bern. Why don't I save it till after we grub up tonight? You do have something for us to eat?

VENTERS: Plenty of chuck in my saddle bags. I didn't know how long I'd be away when I set out from

Cottonwood. Come sundown, we'll eat really well.

BESS: I reckon your dogs can forage for themselves. But what about your hoss? What about Wrangle?

VENTERS: Oh, I'll lead him back down to pasture after it's dark. Don't want to risk running into your band of brothers.

BESS: They're no brothers of mine. It'd suit me never to see one of them again. And that goes for Oldring, too.

(FADE OUT. FADE IN. INTERIOR)

JANE: So what do you think happened to my riders, Zeb? Why weren't they there when my herd was rustled?

ZEB: I – I'd rather not say, Miss Jane.

JANE: Tell me, Zeb. Whatever you say I'll keep to myself. But I'm beginning to worry. Bern Venters hinted at something more than straight rustling... Tell me, Zeb.

ZEB: Well, ma'am, I think like Venters. I think your riders were bribed to desert you.

JANE: Bribed? Who by?

ZEB: Well, Miss Jane, you know who's the big noise in Cottonwood now.

JANE:	No, Zeb, I can't believe it. Mr Tull wouldn't scheme against me. Not Mr Tull. Not the sheriff.
ZEB:	Afraid he did, Miss Jane. I didn't want to tell you, but I know what I'm talking about. He wants to rule this roost, and you're a mite too independent for his liking. He ain't too keen on Venters, neither, and he sure don't like the way you took him under your wing. He reckons on teaching you who's boss in these parts. To tell the truth, I think he's got his eye on the Withersteen ranch and everything on it. One way or another, he plans on getting hold of the lot.
JANE:	One way or another?
ZEB:	Either ruining you and chasing you away, or marrying you.
JANE:	I can't believe it. How do you know all this?
ZEB:	I wouldn't have told you, but you've asked. Last night I went to my mother's house. While there, someone knocked and asked for me. I went to the door. He was wearing a mask. Soon as he saw me he said: "This is a warning. You value your life, don't you ride no more for Jane Withersteen. She's on her way out." Then he ran off.
JANE:	Did you know who he was? Did you recognise him?
ZEB:	I sure did, ma'am.

JANE: Well I won't ask his name. I'd rather not know.

ZEB: But don't you fear, Miss Jane. I'll never quit riding for you till you let me go.

JANE: Zeb, what can I say? Thank you. If I don't lose everything, one day I'll make sure your loyalty is rewarded.

(FADE OUT. FADE IN. EXTERIOR)

BESS: That was great. But what we going to eat tomorrow?

VENTERS: Oh, **I** got enough for another three days - four, if we eke out the rations. Reckon we might be able to get away from here by then. But only if you know what Oldring's done with Jane Withersteen's herd. Otherwise I'll have to go scouting.

BESS: No need, Bern. I know exactly what he does with them cattle he rustles. I could lead you to them.

VENTERS: Not right now, Bess. If we get safely back to Cottonwood, I'll head a posse and we'll go after Oldring and those cows. But that's not what I want to talk about. I want to know how someone like you comes to be riding all masked up with a gang of outlaws. Tell me your story Bess.

BESS: Well, I was raised over in Rio Virgin county – it used to belong to Utah State, afore it was taken over by Nevada. I had a lovely upbringing. My Ma - I called her Ma, though later I found out she wasn't - was MaryLou. MaryLou Oldring.

VENTERS: Oldring's wife?

BESS: Such a sweet, lovely woman. She married Oldring when she was only 17, but after a while she saw precious little of him. He was building himself up with a great posse of men, all intent on cattle rustling. He'd come back to the house from time to time. I remember him around once or twice as I was growing up.

VENTERS: Were there no other children?

BESS: Not a one. Just me. Then, when I was sixteen, MaryLou began to sicken. It wasn't long before the doctors told her there was nothing they could do. When she was clearly on her death bed, she called me into the bedroom one day and told me that I wasn't her daughter.

VENTERS: That must have come as a shock.

BESS: Terrible. I was devastated. Then, after a bit, I asked her who my real parents were.

(FADE OUT. FADE IN)

MARYLOU: *(sweet, low and close – but every word must be clear)* Darling Bess – I haven't the least idea.

BESS: You don't know?

MARYLOU: Let me explain. We'd been married five years, Oldring and me, and there was no sign of a baby. I guess by then I'd resigned myself to a childless marriage. Then one day, he arrived at the house with a three-year-old girl. You. He told me that he'd been visiting Cottonwood, when he heard about a young girl who'd just lost both parents. A man named Dyer had the child, but he wasn't married himself and couldn't care for her. So Oldring instantly said he'd take the girl and that we'd bring her up as our own daughter. That's the truth, Bess my darling. When I'm gone, I reckon you'd best stick by Oldring. He does love you. He won't let any harm come to you.

BESS: (*sobbing*) Oh, Ma. Ma.

(FADE OUT. FADE IN)

VENTERS: Well, ain't that the oddest thing. So that's why you ride with Oldring and his crew.

BESS: Ride with him, yes. But I got no time for his thieving ways, even though he looks out for me in his own way. I keep myself to myself wherever we camp. I mask up for obvious reasons, and I never carry a weapon. Never. But I've had enough of this life. Bern. It's been going on for four long years. I have to break free.

VENTERS: Of course you do, Bess. And you can count on me to help you. But I think I can help you in another way, as well.

BESS: What do you mean?

VENTERS: I've a darn good idea who your real mother was.

(FADE OUT. FULL UP. DOOR OPENS – SHUTS UNDER FOLLOWING)

JANE: Oh, thank heavens. It's you, Lassiter. I'm so pleased you're back.

LASSITER: Why, what's up?

JANE: Zeb's been here. He reckons my riders were bribed to stay away while Oldring rustled my herd. And he reckons Sheriff Tull is behind it.

LASSITER: He may well be right. And there may be more where that's coming from. I don't reckon Tull is going to stop till he's laid his hands on all you own, one way or another.

JANE: If he thinks I'm going to marry him, he's very much mistaken.

LASSITER: Then you must prepare yourself for more dirty tricks. Let me protect you, Jane.

JANE: By protect, you mean going out there with all guns blazing. Hasn't there been enough killing in these parts?

LASSITER: I agree with you. But with law and order in the hands of lawless thugs like Tull and that sidekick of his - Dyer, that's his name ain't it? – well, someone's got to take a stand.

JANE: Take a stand? You're right on that. I'll even go along with being prepared for a shoot-out, if it comes to it, though I'd far prefer to settle disputes in a peaceful way. But I'll never agree to killing just for the sake of it.

LASSITER: You have my word, Jane. That I've never done, nor ever will. But there ain't no saying what I'd do if I ever found the man who wronged your friend Milly Erne, nor the one who stole her little girl from her. I seem to recollect Venters telling me that some dude came calling on her, but she wasn't having any of it. Is that right?

JANE: That's so, Lassiter. Milly wouldn't give him the time of day. I don't know what passed between them, but last time I saw him he was stomping away from the House in a raging fury.

LASSITER: Who is he, Miss? Is he still around?

JANE: Sorry, Lassiter, but I'm just not about to tell you. I'm not having a man's death on my head for the rest of my days.

LASSITER: Well, I reckon I'll have to stick around these parts till you decide to let me know who he is.

JANE:	That suits me. Far better than have you go out hunting him down, with a Colt six-shooter in either hand.
LASSITER:	Well, since I seem to be staying, why don't I ride for you, and keep the rest of your cattle from being stolen in the night? I can use Zeb.
JANE:	Zeb may be all the help you get. He tells me the rest of my men may have been bought off by Tull. And Bern Venters is away, trailing that rustled herd.
LASSITER:	Don't worry. I'll go into town and see if I can't persuade a few boys to join me. Now I want you to tell me who the man was who came calling on my sister.
JANE:	Your sister? What do you mean, your sister?
LASSITER:	There, I've let it slip. Yes, I'm Milly's brother, and I loved her dearly.
JANE:	As did I, Lassiter. As did I. So Milly Erne was your sister?
LASSITER:	The only reason I came here was to find out who tore her and her little girl away from her husband. For years that's been my only aim in life. I back-trailed myself from women long ago. I was a ranger till – till Milly vanished, and then I became something else. I became Lassiter. For years I've been a lonely man set on one thing.

(CREEP UNDER FOLLOWING LOVE THEME FROM TCHAIKOVSKY'S "ROMEO AND JULIET" BALLET MUSIC)

Then I came here and I met you. And now I'm not the man I was. Now you're never out of my thoughts. I have no thoughts but thoughts of you. I live and breathe for you.

JANE: No Lassiter, no. No. You don't love me that way.

LASSITER: If that's what love is, then I do. I love you with all my heart.

JANE: Oh, I've been blind. Blind about you, and blind about myself. I haven't let myself see what was happening - to you, and to me.

LASSITER: To you? Then…?

JANE: Yes, Lassiter. Yes.

LASSITER: (*close*) Jane. (*kiss*)

JANE: (*close*) I don't know what your given name is, and I don't want to know. To me you're Lassiter – and always will be.

LASSITER: (*close*) Lassiter suits me fine.

(UP MUSIC. HOLD A LITLE. FADE OUT. FULL UP. EXT – OPEN AIR)

VENTERS: We'll have to go back into Cottonwood, Bess – to Withersteen House. I need to get a posse together to rescue Jane's herd.

BESS: There'll be a shoot-out.

VENTERS: I daresay there will. But we'll start odds on.

BESS: What do you mean?

VENTERS: We'll have Lassiter on our side.

BESS: Lassiter? You don't mean…

VENTERS: I do. He showed up at the Withersteen place couple of weeks ago. Saved me from Tull and his gang. Sheriff Tull! Some sheriff. That man's out to ruin me. Jane Withersteen as well, if she won't marry him - and that's the last thing on earth she'll do, to my way of thinking.

BESS: Heard a lot about Lassiter. I'd like to meet him.

VENTERS: You will, Bess. But before we go back, I need to know exactly where Oldring is hiding those cattle. The trail showed they'd been driven through water.

BESS: They sure have - and that's why no-one's ever come close to finding any of his rustled herds. Down there in the valley, if you know the right cave entrance, you come to a great waterfall. The water comes cascading down the cliffside in a great flood. Looks dangerous. People keep away. But Oldring drives those cattle right through the middle. Beyond it are acres of open ground.

VENTERS: Can you show me the way?

BESS: I sure can.

VENTERS: Then tonight we go there together. Once I've seen those cattle with my own eyes, we'll make our way back to Cottonwood. Wrangler can carry the two of us easily. You don't weigh much more than the food I brought with me...

BESS: *(laughingly)* And that's all gone.

VENTERS: } *(both burst out laughing)*
BESS: }

(FADE OUT. FADE IN. INT)

JANE: Well, here I am Mr Tull. I'm a law-abiding citizen. If the Sheriff asks to see me, I make haste to obey him.

TULL: Very praiseworthy, ma'am. What do you say, Dyer? Er … Judge Dyer.

DYER: Nothing less than I'd expect, Sheriff. Let's hope Miss Withersteen obeys your next instruction as readily.

JANE: You want me to do something, Mr Tull?

TULL: I sure do, ma'am. Miss Withersteen, I want you to marry me.

JANE: I'll do no such thing. I'm perfectly well aware that a husband gains complete control of his wife's assets, and I'm darned if I'm about to hand over my father's hard-earned fortune to someone like you.

DYER: Then who will you hand it to? That no-good Venters?

JANE: I'm not minded to hand it over to anyone just yet. But Bern Venters is nothing more than someone I gave a shelter to when he was down and out. Now he's a friend.

DYER: What's the matter with these women, Tull? This is exactly the sort of response I got when I came calling on that Milly Erne. Too independent by half.

TULL: Independent minded women need a lesson. I hear some of your cattle seem to have strayed, Miss Jane.

JANE: Twenty-five hundred head of steer. My minders paid off, and the cattle rustled,

TULL: Dear, dear. I wonder who could have took them. Any ideas, your Honour?

DYER: Not a one. But never mind, ma'am, you still have five thousand left.

TULL: Unless the same bandit takes a fancy to them as well.

JANE: Are you threatening me, Mr Tull?

TULL: I sure am, ma'am – threatening and warning. I aim to gain control of the Withersteen estate one way or another. Either you marry me, or I take everything you own and chase you out of Cottonwood.

DYER: There's one other possibility. You could end up like your dear friend Milly Erne - dead. And buried in some nameless grave.

TULL: Take your pick.

(FADE OUT. FADE IN. EXT. HORSE CLATTERING IN ON STONE OR GRAVEL. UNDER THE FOLLOWING, HORSE COMES TO HALT. MOVEMENT OF DISMOUNTING ETC)

VENTERS: *(remote, advancing, calling)* Hulloo! Hi, there! I'm back!

JANE: *(remote, advancing, calling)* Bern Venters, by all that's wonderful. Welcome back, Bern. Welcome indeed. Lassiter, see who's come back to us.

LASSITER: Good to see you, Venters. Did you find what you were after? Did you find Jane's cattle?

VENTERS: I sure did, Lassiter.

JANE: And who's this, Bern?

VENTERS: Jane, this is Bess. She's been forced to live alongside Oldring and his gang for years. I've rescued her and brought her to you.

JANE: You're very welcome, my dear.

BESS: Hullo, Miss Springsteen. Bern has told me so much about you.

JANE: Come along, both of you. You must be exhausted. Come into the house, and freshen up. We can hear all about everything over our evening meal. Come along, now. Come along.

(FADE OUT. FADE IN. CROCKERY CUTLERY)

LASSITER: Now, before anything else. You located the rustled steers?

VENTERS: Saw the whole herd with my own eyes not eight hours since.

LASSITER: Then I'll form a posse tomorrow, and we'll go out and bring them back.

JANE: No killing for killing's sake, Lassiter.

LASSITER: You have my word. Though I doubt Oldring and his crew will give them up without a fight. And there'd be little point in seeking the help of the law – not with Sheriff Tull and Judge Dyer in charge.

JANE: You know, I went to see them earlier today.

LASSITER: Both of them?

JANE: Well, Judge Dyer was present. It was Sheriff Tull who sent a message. He wanted to see me. So I went into town.

VENTERS: What did he want?

JANE: He gave me a choice. Either marry him, or he'd do to me what he did to you, Bern. Rob me of every head of cattle I own and ruin me. I wouldn't put it past him to burn down Withersteen House. Then Dyer pitched in. He threatened me with poor Milly Erne's fate – death and an obscure grave. I'd better tell you now, Lassiter. Dyer was the man who came calling on Milly.

LASSITER: Then my guess is it was Dyer who snatched her baby girl. Some sort of sick revenge for being rejected

VENTERS: And that's what I've been keeping up my sleeve, Jane. I'll wager my hat that Bess here is that little girl.

JANE: What?

VENTERS: You just hear her story. She was raised by Oldring's wife, MaryLou, who she called Ma all her life. That is, until MaryLou was on her deathbed, when she told Bess the truth. The

Oldrings, they had no children of their own, and a little girl had been handed to them years before to bring up. Bess here must have been snatched from Milly and whisked away to the Rio Virgin where Oldring was operating at the time.

LASSITER: But there's something you don't know, Venters. I let it slip a few days ago, talking to Jane.

VENTERS: Yes. What?

LASSITER: Milly Erne was my sister. I spent years looking for her, till I finally tracked her down to this neck of the woods.

BESS: But Lassiter, if this is all true, then you and me - we're family.

LASSITER: We sure are, Bess. You're my niece. I'm your uncle.

VENTERS: Well dang me.

JANE: Bess, my dear. Milly was my dearest, dearest friend. The last time I saw you, you were just a tot. Many and many's the time I've held you in my arms.

BESS: Oh, Jane. Jane.

JANE: Welcome home, my darling. Welcome back to Withersteen House.

(FADE OUT. FULL UP)

ZANE: (*as narrator*): Well, folks, that proved to be but a brief moment of happiness in the drama that was encompassing poor Janes Withersteen and her friends. Next morning, as Lassiter and Venters were out in Cottonwood town, trying to recruit a posse to rescue Jane's stolen herd, Sheriff Tull came alongside with three deputies, and arrested Bern Venters. True to his word to Jane, Lassiter refrained from drawing to protect his friend, who was carted off to the jailhouse.

(EXTERIOR. HORSES STAMPING, SNORTING)

LASSITER: (*calling*) What's he charged with, Tull?

TULL: (*calling, retreating*) You'll learn soon enough, Lassiter. Trial's set for tomorrow, ten sharp. Don't be late.

(HORSES GALLOP OFF. CROSSFADE TO GAVEL BEING BANGED ON WOOD. CROWD CHATTING. GROWS SILENT. INT)

DYER: Marshal, read out the charges.

MARSHAL: Bernard Venters, you are charged with kidnap, in that you did unlawfully seize the daughter of William Oldring and carry her away. How do you plead?

VENTERS: Not guilty.

DYER: Mr Blake?

BLAKE: Your Honour, I'm prosecuting this here case on behalf of the County.

DYER: And I understand the prisoner is defending himself.

VENTERS: That's right, Mr Dyer.

DYER: That's right, your Honour.

VENTERS: That's right, your Honour.

DYER: Gentlemen of the jury, that's his own decision. He was offered a lawyer.

VENTERS: Being defended by one of your lawyers, I might just as well have pleaded guilty at once.

DYER: Well, let's get on with it. Mr Blake?

BLAKE: Your Honour, having looked into the circumstances of this case, the County has decided to prosecute two people for this crime. We reckon they can stand trial together. Sheriff Tull has arrested the second person, and they're waiting outside the courtroom at this moment.

DYER: Marshal, fetch Sheriff Tull and his prisoner.

MARSHAL: Yes, sir, your Honour.

(FOOTSTEPS ON WOOD)

(*remote, calling*) Sheriff Tull and prisoner.

(GASPS FROM CROWD)

DYER: Miss Jane Withersteen, I do declare. What are you charging this woman with, Sheriff?

TULL: Being a co-conspirator in kidnap. I visited Withersteen House earlier this morning, and I found Mr Oldring's daughter on the premises.

DYER: Do you deny the charge, Miss Withersteen?

JANE: No, it's perfectly true, Mr Dyer ... er, your Honour

DYER: In that case. you will stand trial alongside Mr Venters, there. Now Mr Blake get on with it.

BLAKE: The facts are quite simple. The Oldrings were living up north in Rio Virgin when, some three years ago, Mrs MaryLou Oldring died. Their only daughter, Elizabeth, known as Bess, was sixteen. Oldring decided to come down here to Cottonwood, and of course he brought his daughter with him. He cared for her and made sure no trouble came to her. Last week, Bess was out riding with one of Oldring's men, when the prisoner Venters drew a gun, shot at both of them. Bess's companion, as he made his getaway, saw her slump in her saddle and the prisoner Venters riding towards her. When she failed to appear, Oldring had his men search the whole area for days. After a while he decided to come back to Cottonwood. It was here he learned that Venters had been seen riding into town, with Bess pinioned in front of him on the same horse.

DYER: Facts seem pretty clear. Do you deny them. Venters?

VENTERS: Some of them, your Honour.

DYER: Which ones, in particular?

VENTERS: That Bess is Oldring's daughter, to start with.

DYER: Nonsense. What proof have you got that she isn't?

VENTERS: I call Elizabth Erne to the stand.

DYER: Who's Elizabeth Erne?

BESS: *(remote, advancing)* That's me, your Honour. I'm the girl who's supposed to have been kidnapped.

DYER: Well, what have you to say for yourself?

MARSHAL: Just a minute, your Honour. Will the witness take hold of this book, and raise her right hand. Do you swear to tell the truth, the whole truth and nothing but the truth?

BESS: I do.

MARSHAL: You may proceed.

BESS: I grew up in the Oldring household, all right. But when she was on her deathbed, MaryLou told me that I wasn't her blood child. She told me that when I was very little I'd been left with her, and since the Oldrings were childless, she'd gladly taken me in and brought me up.

DYER: Do you have any proof of this story?

VENTERS: Not at the moment, your Honour. But perhaps we'll have it by the time this trial is over.

DYER: Hope on, Venters. Anything else?

VENTERS: Yes, your Honour. The simple fact is that I didn't kidnap Miss Bess here. She asked me to rescue her from Oldring and his crew. She came away with me willingly and at her own wish. And as she's 19 and well past the age of majority, she's at perfect liberty to do so.

BLAKE: Do you so testify, Miss Bess?

BESS: I do.

BLAKE: Then, your Honour, there is no case to answer. The County withdraws its charges.

TULL: *(shouts)* The County does no such thing. There's not an atom of proof that all this rigmarole is true. That girl could be 16, for all we know. Does she have a birth certificate?

JANE: Yes she does, Mr Tull. I have it here. My dear friend Milly Erne entrusted it to me before she passed on. Many people in this courtroom know why she wasted away, and sickened and died. She was pining for her baby daughter, snatched from her and never discovered. Bess Erne is 19.

DYER: Enough of all this. It's got no bearing on this case.

LASSITER: *(remote, calling)* There I disagree, Mr Dyer.

DYER: Silence. Silence in court. One more interruption like that, and I'll clear the public out.

VENTERS: Bess, you are excused. You can go. I call Mr Lassiter to the stand.

TULL: *(furious)* No, no, no. That man will not take the stand.

DYER: I can't prevent it, Sheriff. Venters is defending himself. He has a right to call witnesses.

TULL: *(close, whisper)* You lily-livered son of a bitch. Who put you up there? Me. You'll do as I say. Find these two guilty and lock them up.

DYER: *(close, whisper)* I'll do no such thing. This is a court of law. And you talk to me like that again, I'll have you escorted out. *(loud)* Mr Lassiter, take the stand.

MARSHAL: Take the book in your right hand. Do you swear to tell the truth, the whole truth and nothing but the truth?

LASSITER: I do.

VENTERS: Are you able to verify what Miss Bess Erne has told this court?

LASSITER: I am. Bess Erne is my niece.

(CROWD SHOCK)

Milly Erne was my sister. The family was living in Dakota when she met this Erne character and fell for him. They got married just a month or two after. It was a disaster. He was a drunk, and after a while he took to beating her. He did that even when she got pregnant. After her daughter was born, she was fearful of what he might do to the child. So one day she just upped and left with her baby. No one knew where she'd gone. I spent years trying to track her. In the end I ran her down to this neck of the woods, only to find that she'd died years since.

VENTERS: And the baby girl who'd disappeared?

LASSITER: As soon as I knew about her, I hoped to trace her. But you did it for me – and there she is.

VENTERS: What about the man who snatched the child from its mother?

DYER: That's quite enough. We've strayed a long way from the original charge. I instruct the jury to find the two prisoners not guilty. Case dismissed.

(GAVEL ON WOOD)

LASSITER: Then, Judge Dyer, I suppose you want us all to say that justice has been done.

DYER: Well, at least no injustice has been done.

LASSITER: That I grant you. But I had just one or two more things to say. How's about I say them?

DYER: I won't stop you.

LASSITER: Miss Jane Withersteen told me that before her friend Milly's baby was snatched, a man had been pestering her, and that she rejected that man time and time again. I begged her to tell me that man's name, but she refused. She was fearful that I'd live up to my reputation and gun him down. Ain't that so, Jane?

JANE: It is.

DYER: Well, then.

LASSITER: But once Bess here arrived at Withersteen House, all that changed. Even Jane saw that the man who was rejected by Milly took his revenge in a shoddy. wicked and inhuman way. So she told me who it was. Judge Dyer, you are that man. Judge Dyer, I accuse you of kidnapping little Bessie Erne, aged three, and handing her over to your co-conspirator, Bill Oldring, and his wife.

(CROWD SHOCK)

DYER: That's a mighty big accusation, even for you Lassiter. Can you prove one word of it?

LASSITER: Well, Dyer, take a look down there in the public benches. Do you see – next to where I was sitting – do you see that woman? Would you like me to call her up here to say what she knows.

DYER: I don't know that woman. Never seen her before in my life.

LASSITER: Oh, but you have, Dyer. Just once. Many years ago. That woman is Jenny Barnes. Sixteen years ago she was a maid-of-all-work in the Oldring house in Rio Virgin. She was present when you turned up with a baby girl one afternoon. She is willing to swear that you are the man who handed that child over to MaryLou Oldring.

DYER: Sixteen years ago, and she saw the man once. You call that proof? That wouldn't stand up for a second in court.

LASSITER: Maybe not, Dyer. But she's convinced me. And as God's my witness, if you don't tell the truth about this, I'm coming after you with six-shooters in both fists, whatever I've pledged to Jane here.

DYER: All right, all right. It was a long time ago. I was young and raw. That Milly Erne – she turned her nose up at me. I wasn't good enough for her. Nothing I said or did made any difference. She never had a kind word for me. I got sore. It rankled. It turned round and round in my head. I couldn't think of anything else. So I thought I'd teach her a lesson - a lesson she'd never forget. It was a terrible thing I did. I know that now. But once it was done, it couldn't be undone. We've all had to live with the consequences.

JANE: Milly died because of them.

DYER: That's true, Miss Withersteen – and mighty guilty I feel about it. I don't know how to make amends.

LASSITER: I do. You can tell us how it came that Miss Withersteen's two thousand five hundred steer were rustled.

TULL: (calls) That's enough. Clear this courtroom. This farce of a trial is over. Get out of here – all of you. Leave.

(CROWD. MOVEMENT. FADE OUT. FULL UP)

ZANE: Now hear this, folks. A thousand years ago the two great ruling bodies in England were the king and the Church. They were always in conflict, and King Henry the Second grew sick of having his authority constantly challenged – so he dreamed up a clever way of winning the struggle. He appointed a close friend of his, a man called Thomas Becket, to be the archbishop of Canterbury - that is, head of the Church in England. Then a strange thing happened. As soon as Becket was installed, he began to realize how important his new position was, and the vital part the Church played in the lives of ordinary people. So he began to challenge the king, just as his predecessor had done. In the end, on purpose or by accident, King Henry authorized Becket's assassination, and he was slaughtered on the very steps of the altar inside Canterbury cathedral.

I tell you this sad little tale, because precisely the same thing happened to his Honour, Judge Dyer. Once hand in glove with Sheriff Tull in organizing all kinds of villainy, as soon as Dyer took office he began to realize the value of law and order, and the sanctity of justice He could no longer play along with Tull's corruption. I 'm sorry to tell you that he paid the same price as Becket. A few weeks after Dyer called a halt to the trial against Venters and Jane Withersteen, he was gunned down outside the courthouse by a couple of masked riders who nobody could identify.

But the scene in that courtroom had weakened Tull's grip on the town. At the next election for Sheriff, a newcomer called Lassiter was overwhelmingly voted into office.

(FULL UP INT CHURCH – SLIGHT ECHO. CROWD IN BACKGROUND. CLOSING CHORDS ON AN ORGAN)

PREACHER: Dearly beloved. This is far from a normal ceremony. In fact, folks, it's the first time I've every presided over such an occasion. But we have come together in the presence of God to witness and bless the joining together in Holy Matrimony of this man and this woman – and of *this* man and *this* woman. To avoid any possibility of confusion, I will name the two couples. This here is Amos Lassiter (he offered up his given name, only after much persuasion). Standing by his side is Jane Withersteen. And here, to my left, are Bernard Venters and Elizabeth Erne, known as Bess.

Now, if any of you can show just cause why these two couples may not lawfully be married, speak now; or else for ever hold your peace.

(CREEP MUSIC IN UNDER FOLLOWING. INCREASE VOLUME. WE MUST NOT LOSE JANE'S "I WILL" BEFORE THE MUSIC SWELLS UP)

Jane Sarah Withersteen, will you have this man to be your husband, to live together in the covenant of marriage? Will you have and hold from this day forth, for better for worse, for richer for poorer, in sickness and in health, to love, cherish, and obey, and, forsaking all others, be faithful to him till death do you part?

JANE: I will.

           (UP MUSIC. HOLD A LITTLE. DOWN FOR CLOSING ANNOUNCEMENT)

NEVILLE TELLER'S FIRST VOLUME

AUDIO DRAMA: 10 PLAYS FOR RADIO AND PODCAST

CONTAINS THE FOLLOWING AUDIO DRAMA SCRIPTS

"ALADDIN AND THE WONDERFUL LAMP"
(NEVILLE TELLER)

"THE LOOKING GLASS"
(EDITH WHARTON)

"THE MAN THAT CORRUPTED HADLEYBURG"
(MARK TWAIN)

"OZMA OF OZ"
(FRANK BAUM)

"THE PROBLEM OF CELL 13"
(JACQUES FUTRELLE)

"BOX AND COX"
(J M MORTON)

"THE TURN OF THE SCREW"
(HENRY JAMES)

"THE GHOST SHIP"
(NEVILLE TELLER BASED ON A STORY BY ARTHUR CONAN DOYLE)

"THE FOUR JUST MEN"
(EDGAR WALLACE)

"THE DAMNED THING"
(AMBROSE BIERCE)

CPSIA information can be obtained
at www.ICGtesting.com
Printed in the USA
BVHW052110070223
658071BV00011B/241